COLLINS

CLANS &
TARTANS

George Way of Plean
& **Romilly Squire**

HarperCollins Publishers
Westerhill Rd, Bishopbriggs Glasgow G64 2QT

www.fireandwater.com

First published 1995
This edition 2000

Reprint 10 9 8 7 6 5 4 3 2 1 0

© George Way of Plean and Romilly Squire (all text), 1995, 2000 except for
© HarperCollins Publishers, 1995, 2000 (text on pp.5–39)

ISBN 0 00 472501 8

A catalogue record for this book is available from the British Library

Illustration acknowledgements

All clan crests by Romilly Squire
Map on p.4 and illustration on p.23 by Iain Robinson
Illustration on p.25 by Roy Boyd
All other illustrations by HarperCollins
All tartans were kindly supplied by Peter MacArthur & Co. Ltd, Hamilton
and the Scottish Tartan Society, Pitlochry

Printed in Italy by Amadeus S.p.A., Rome

CONTENTS

Major Battle with Date ✖

Scale

0 10 20 30 40 50 miles

MORRISON
MACLEOD
OF
LEWIS
MACAULEY
MACLEOD
OF
HARRIS
MACNEIL
MACDONALD
MACQUEEN
MACNICOL
MACKINNON
MACLEOD OF HARRIS
MACRAE
MACDONALD
MACDONALD OF
CLANRANALD
MACDONALD OF
GLENGARRY
MACDONALD OF
CLANRANALD
MACIAN
MACLEAN
MACLEAN
MACINNES
MACQUARRIE
MACLEAN
MACDOUGALL
MACLEAN
MACFIE
MACLEAN
MACBETH
MACDONALD

SINCLAIR
MACKAY   GUNN
MACLEOD   SUTHERLAND
MACNICOL

Invercarron
1650
ROSS

MACDONNELL
MACLEOD
OF
LEWIS
MUNRO   DUNBAR   MACDUFF
MACBAIN   INNES   CUMMING   BAIRD
DAVIDSON   ROSE   BRODIE
URQUHART   CUMMIN   BARCLAY   KEITH
MACKENZIE   MACKINTOSH
CHISHOLM   Culloden 1746   ANDERSON   HAY
FRASER   MACGILLIVRAY   Cromdale Braes   Harlaw
MATHESON   MACGILLIVRAY   1690   Glenlivet   LESLIE   1411
MACLENNAN   GRANT   1594
Glenshiel   GRANT   SHAW   FORBES
1719   MACPHERSON   FARQUHARSON   SKENE
MACDONELL OF   CLAN CHATTAN   BURNETT
KEPPOCH   Blar-na-Leine 1544   GORDON
Inverlochy   MACDONNELL OF
1645   KEPPOCH
CAMERON   Killiecrankie   ARBUTHNOT
Glencoe   MENZIES   STEWART   1689   LINDSAY
1692   ROBERTSON   MURRAY   GRAHAM
Pass of   GOW   Dunkeld   Nectansmere
Brander   RUTHVEN   1689   OGILVIE   685
1308   CAMPBELL   Luncarty   RATTRAY
MACINTYRE   977
MACALPINE   MACGREGOR   CARNEGIE
MACNAB   Methven
MACARTHUR   Perth
MACLAREN   Murray 1306 1396
MACNAGHTEN   Tippermuir 1644
MACEARLANE   MACLEAN   LINDSAY
DRUMMOND   Dupplin
GRAHAM   1332   ROLLO
BUCHANAN   Sheriffmuir
Glenfruin 1488   1715
1602   Sauchieburn   ERSKINE
LAMONT   Bannockburn   1488   Inverkeithing
COLQUHOUN   1314   Stirling Bridge   1651
STEWART   LIVINGSTONE   1297   DALZEIL
Largs   Falkirk   BRUCE   NAPIER   Prestonpans   Dunbar
1263   1298 & 1746   MELVILLE   1745   1296 & 1650
BOYD   OLIPHANT   Pinkie   SETON
MONTGOMERIE   Bothwell Bridge   RAMSAY   1547
HAMILTON   1679   HAMILTON   DUNDAS   MAITLAND   Halidon Hill
CUNNINGHAM   Langside   COCKBURN   1333
1568   CRANSTOUN
MACBETH   Drumclog   CAMPBELL   HOME
1679   DOUGLAS   HAY   Carham
WALLACE   SCOTT   HAIG   1018
CRAWFORD   KERR
FERGUSSON   DOUGLAS   Philiphaugh   TURNBULL   Flodden
KENNEDY   1645   ELLIOT   1513
JOHNSTONE
Dunaverty
1647
HUNTER
HAMILTON
STEWART   MAXWELL   ARMSTRONG
Solway Moss
1542

A History of Clanship

Alan Macinnes

Burnett-Fletcher Professor of History, University of Aberdeen

The most distinctive feature of Scotland's history, nationally and internationally, is probably that of clanship and the predominantly Highland clans. Too often, however, writings on the clans give precedence to literary romanticism over historical realism. In order to see the clans in their true historical perspective, the examination of five key themes is essential – the origins of the clans, the structure of clanship, clanship and disorder, the clans and the royal house of Stewart and the aftermath of Culloden.

ORIGINS OF THE CLANS

Mythological founders have often been claimed by clans, reinforcing both their status and a romantic and glorified notion of their origins. Most powerful clans appropriated for themselves fabulous origins based on Celtic mythology. Thus the political rivalry between Clan Donald, who claimed to be descended from either Conn, a 2nd-century king of Ulster, or Cuchulainn, the legendary hero of Ulster, and the Campbells, who claimed Diarmaid the Boar as their progenitor, was rooted in the Fenian or Fingalian cycle. On the other hand, others such as the McKinnons and the McGregors were content to claim common ancestry from the Alpin family who united the Scottish kingdom in 843. Only one confederation of clans, that of the Macsweens, Lamonts, Macleys, Maclachlans and Macneills, who emerged to prominence in Knapdale and Cowal in the 12th century, can trace one line of their ancestry back to the fifth century – to Niall of the Nine Hostages, High King of Ireland. In reality, the progenitors of the clans can rarely be authenticated further back than the 11th century and a continuity of lineage in most cannot be detected until the 13th and 14th centuries.

The emergence of the clans has less to do with ethnicity than with political turmoil and social opportunity. The Scottish Crown's reconquest of Argyll and the Western Isles from the Norse in the thirteenth century, following on from the pacification of Moray and the northern rebellions in the 12th and early 13th centuries, created opportunities for lay and even ecclesiastical warlords with the assistance of their immediate kindred, to impose their dominance over diverse localities whose indigenous families accepted their protection, either willingly or by force. Although these warrior chiefs can be primarily categorised as Celtic, their origins range from Gaelic to Norse-Gaelic to British. Moreover, the political instability and dislocation which resulted from the Wars of Independence fought against the English Crown had, by the outset of the 14th century, created further scope for Celtic territorial expansion. It also allowed an influx of Anglo kindreds such as Camerons, Frasers, Chisholms, Menzies and Grants, whose ethnic origins ranged from Anglo-Norman to Anglian to Flemish, to move into the Highlands.

Another significant milestone in the emergence of clanship also arose during the Wars of Independence with the introduction of feudal tenures to regulate landholding, as Robert the Bruce sought to harness and control the martial prowess of the clans through the award of charters. Comprehensive grants of lands and the right to dispense justice in the name of the Crown were given to chiefs and leading gentry of the clans prepared to support the national cause against the English kings. Thus, the Macdonalds were elevated over the Macdougalls, with whom they shared common descent from Somerled, the great Norse-Gaelic warlord of the 12th century. The subsequent political and cultural aggrandisement of the MacDonalds as Lords of the Isles, over the next two centuries, has tended to obscure the fact that they, like their acquisitive rivals, the Campbells, owed their position not only to their strong ties of kinship and local association, but also to the acceptance and promotion of their territorial influence by the Scottish Crown. Clanship was thereby essentially defined as a product of local association, kinship and feudalism. It is this feudal component, grounded and reinforced by Scots law, which separates clanship from tribalism, and which historically differentiates Scottish clans from aboriginal groups in Australasia, Africa and the Americas.

In the Highlands as in the Lowlands, shared local affinities and assumptions were reflected in the dominance of lordship based on family affiliations until the 17th century. In the Highlands, however, clanship had an added cultural association with the Gaelic language. Hence, the territory settled by the indigenous clans was designated Scottish Gaeldom.

THE STRUCTURE OF CLANSHIP

The authority of the clan

Clanship contained two complementary but distinct concepts of heritage. The collective heritage of the clan, their 'duthchas', was their prescriptive right to settle the territories over which the chiefs and leading gentry of the clan customarily provided protection. This concept meant that the personal authority of the chiefs and leading gentry as trustees for their clan was recognised by all clansmen; thus justification for and recognition of the chief's authority came from below and from within the clan itself. However, the wider acceptance of the granting of charters by the Crown, and by other powerful landowners to the clan chiefs, chieftains and lairds defined the estates settled by their clan as their 'oighreachd', and gave a different emphasis to the basis of the clan chief's authority. This concept was one of individual heritage, warranted from above, and it institutionalised the authority of chiefs and leading gentry as landed proprietors – owners of the land in their own right, rather than as trustees for the clan's collective good. The absence of this land concept differentiates the clanship of the Irish from Scottish Gaels. Of course, the two concepts could co-exist, and from the outset of clanship in Scotland, the 'fine' – the clan warrior elite – strove to be landowners as well as territorial warlords.

Clans and the law

Whereas in the middle ages the concept of duthchas held precedence, the balance was tilting in favour of the concept of oighreachd in the early modern period. This shifting balance reflected the continuing importance of Scots Law in shaping the structure of clanship. In addition to the award of charters to the fine, continuity of heritable succession was secured by the acceptance of primogeniture. The 'tainistear', the heir to the chief, was usually the direct male heir and although attention has tended to focus on those clans where the direct heir was set aside in favour of a more politically accomplished or belligerent relative, disputes over succession were not characteristic of the Highlands beyond the 16th century; indeed, by the 17th century, not only was the setting aside of primogeniture a rarity, but male succession over several generations was increasingly governed and restricted by the law of entail which prevented the division of landed estates among female heirs and thus the loss and alienation of clan territories.

The legal process primarily used to settle criminal and civil disputes within clans was that of arbitration. Within the clan, the offending and aggrieved parties put their respective case to an arbitration panel drawn from their leading gentry and over which their chief presided. In disputes between clans, the chiefs served as the procurators (legal agents) for the offending or aggrieved parties before an arbitration panel drawn from equal numbers of leading gentry from each clan and presided over by a neighbouring chief or landlord. The decision of the arbitration panel, from which there was no appeal, was recorded in the most convenient royal or burgh court. Arbitration was based on reparations, known as assythment, rather than retribution. The compensation awarded to the aggrieved party took account of such variables as the age, status and family responsibilities of the victim, as well as the nature of the crime. On payment of reparation the offending party was indemnified against any further action for redress. The process depended ultimately on the willingness of clans to make prompt reparation, a situation made more likely by the regular contracting of bands of friendship between clans which made standing provision for arbitration. Again, these bands had the force of law and were recorded in the most convenient royal or burgh court.

Clans and social ties

The most important forms of social bonding in the clans, in addition to legal bands, were fosterage and manrent. The marriage alliance, which reinforced links with neighbouring clans as well as kinship within territorially diverse families, was also a commercial contract involving the exchange of livestock, money and land through payments which in the case of the bride was known as the 'tocher' and for the groom, the 'dowry'. The gentry of the clan were expected to underwrite the contracts made by their chiefs or leading lairds, a legal obligation which grew in importance as increasing numbers of marriage contracts were made outwith Gaeldom in the course of the 17th century. Marriage ties, even when forms of trial marriage such as handfasting had been repressed in the wake of the Reformation, were the least durable aspect of social bonding. Conversely, fosterage, the bringing up of the chief's children by favoured members of the leading clan gentry and in turn, their children by other favoured members of the clan, cemented ties of such intensity that it was not regarded as exceptional for foster-brothers to sacrifice themselves in protecting their chiefs. The commercial facet of this relationship reinforced feelings of clan cohesion in making particular provision, usually in the form of livestock, for foster-children on their reaching adulthood or on the death of their foster-parents.

The third form of social tie was manrent. This was a bond contracted by the heads of satellite families who did not live on the estates of the clan elite, but to whom they affiliated to ensure territorial protection. Bonds of manrent were reinforced by calps, the payment of death duties. On the death of these satellite heads, their families usually paid their best cow or horse to the chief in recognition of his protection and as a mark of personal allegiance. Although calps were banned as oppressive by Parliament in 1617, the need for protection could not be proscribed by legislation and manrent continued covertly. While manrenting was apparently less frequent, bands were made less to create new ties of dependency then to renew protection after a lapse of a generation, and notably after the political divisions occasioned by civil wars in 1644–47 and 1689–90.

The management of the clan

All members of the clan living on the estates of the chief and leading gentry paid rents and calp; those outwith the estates paid calp only. Such payments, which could be in money, in kind and in labour, were channelled through the tacksmen, the lesser gentry who served as the lynch-pins of clanship and the clan system and who gave tangible force to protection, hospitality and the productive use of clan resources. Until the advent of written leasing in the sixteenth century, the tacksman's holdings were held from the clan chief or his lairds according to oral tradition. Their role was essentially that of managers who aimed to attain a comfortable sufficiency for the farmers, crofters and cotters as well as the clan nobility. As the environment of Scottish Gaeldom was not particularly conducive to farming, the objective required the adaptation of customary rents and services owed by clansmen to the fine through the balanced management of landed resources, commercial demands and man-power.

The basic unit of management for every tacksman was the baile or township, which supported anything from four to over sixteen families, who were each assigned individual holdings but worked the land communally. Within this context, the tacksmen adapted customary estate management: they oversaw the reallocation of strips of land in open fields held as run-rig by the individual families within each township; arranging for crop manuring and herding; and organising the movement to summer pasture on upland and island shielings. They collected rents (from which they apportioned a share), and were responsible for controlling the amount of crops sown, work-services to be performed and numbers of livestock to be grazed. Incoming and newly inheriting tenants were given loans of seed-corn, livestock and tools – which were known as steel-bow – their needs having been assessed by the tacksman. The tacksman also played a key role in the rounding up and marketing of cattle by droving to the Lowlands.

Their managerial role, however, has tended to be subsumed by their military role as mobilisers of the clan host. Notwithstanding the martial exhortations of bards and other Gaelic poets, and the impressive numbers of clansmen that could be mobilised expeditiously on the passing round of the fiery cross, the calling out of the host was as much social and recreational as military. The host was mobilised particularly during the summer downturn in the agrarian cycle to provide gainful employment for clansmen who might otherwise drift into banditry. Thus, the month of August was traditionally assigned for the hunts, where the chiefs and their noble kinsmen and guests were attended by their followers to act as beaters and to engage in a variety of virile sports which have come down to posterity as Highland games. A large turn-out of followers was also expected for weddings and funerals. A chief who failed to secure a large turn out of his clansmen was deemed to have detracted from his own personal standing. The substantial mobilisation of the host to perambulate and control the estates of the clan elite served as a discouragement to the territorial ambitions of other chiefs or landlords. However, the calling out of the host for social and recreational reasons was not without a large measure of military ambivalence as these occasions – which were especially noted for copious consumption of strong drink – could degenerate into disorder often caused by disputes relating to individual rank and precedence fanned by a highly developed sense of personal honour.

CLANSHIP AND DISORDER

The association of the clans with disorder was partly the product of their turbulent origins and was particularly marked by the disputes surrounding the break-up, forfeiture and abortive attempts at restoration of the Lordship of the Isles in the late 15th and early 16th centuries. Public perceptions of unruly elements within Gaeldom tended to make the blanket association of clanship with feuding and banditry commonplace, a perception that was not discouraged at the Scottish Court or by central government after the Union of the Crowns in 1603.

Territorial dispute

Feuding was essentially an issue of territorial hegemony – the outcome of the failure of the estates comprising the oighreachd of the clan elite to match up to the territories claimed as the collective duthchas of their clan. On the one hand, the clan gentry were frustrated that some of their clansmen were obliged to pay rents to other landlords; on the other, acquisitive clans, most notably the Campbells and the Mackenzies, were prepared to play off territorial disputes within and among clans to expand their own landed influence. Feuding on the western seaboard, which was conducted with such an intensity that the Macleods and Macdonalds on Skye were reputedly reduced to eating dogs and cats in the 1590s, was further compounded by the involvement of the indigenous clans in the wars of the Irish Gaels against the English Tudor monarchy in the sixteenth century. Indeed, within these clans there had evolved a military caste, the 'buannachan', who were regarded as members of the lesser gentry, even although they were purely warriors and not managers, and who migrated seasonally to Ireland to fight as mercenaries. When not contracted by the Irish Gaels, they lived parasitically off their own clan. The plantation of Ulster by James VI drove a wedge between the Gaels which eventually resulted in the redundancy of the buannachan within a generation. Their redundancy was an integral aspect of a Crown-inspired programme, which commenced with the Statutes of Iona of 1609, to assimilate the chiefs, their chieftains and gentry into Scottish landed society.

Despite the opportunities created for perpetuating feuding in the civil wars between Covenanter and Royalist during the 1640s, chiefs and leading clan gentry, like their landed counterparts in the Lowlands, preferred increasingly to settle landed disputes by recourse to law. Following the restoration of the monarchy in 1660, the incidents of feuding between clans declined markedly. The last clan feud which led to a battle actually occurred at Mulroy on 4 August 1688, when the Macdonalds of Keppoch successfully resisted the government backed efforts of the Mackintosh chief of the Clan Chattan to take over their territory in the Braes of Lochaber.

Reiving

The decline of militarism among the clans was further evident in the phasing out of the 'creach', a ritualistic rite of passage whereby the young men of the clan demonstrated their virility by removing livestock from neighbouring clan territory. By the 17th century the most prevalent form of reiving or plundering was the 'spreidh', essentially a freelance operation involving rarely more than ten associates which usually preyed on the Lowland peripheries of Gaeldom. Livestock 'lifted' by these raiders could usually be recovered through the payment of 'tascal' – information money – and the guarantee of an indemnity from criminal prosecution. Conversely, certain clans, such as the Macfarlanes in the southern and the Farquharsons in the eastern Highlands offered their services as a professional watch for their Lowland neighbours, although their rates for protection could not be dissociated from accusations of 'blackmail'. Continuance of such reiving can be linked geographically to the Macgregors in the southern and eastern Highlands and to the clans of the Lochaber region – clans in which the chiefs and nobles had little or no title to the territories settled by their clansmen. Yet even here, the acquisition of comprehensive landed titles by the Cameron chiefs in the course of the 17th century resulted in a marked decline in freelance reiving by the Lochaber clansmen.

From the later 16th century, central government, in the shape of
the Scottish Privy Council, had demanded generally that clan leaders
provide bands of surety promising the orderly conduct of themselves
and their clansmen, who were defined not only as the tenants on
their estates but all followers who owed territorial allegiance, including anyone resident within their bounds more than 12 hours.
Although these bands carried considerable financial penalties including the forfeiture of land and title for persistent non-compliance,
their issue was also recognition that Gaeldom could not be governed
without the co-operation of the chiefs. Moreover, as the bands
required the regular attendance of the clan leadership in Edinburgh,
their sojourns to the Lowlands became increasingly prolonged.
Absenteeism, in turn, led to the accumulation of debts which could
only partially be recouped through raising rents. 'Wadsets', or mortgages, were increasingly used by the fine to raise money, particularly
after the civil wars of the 1640s confirmed their commitment to
Scottish as against Gaelic politics. With the expansion of droving in
the later 17th century, tacksmen had sufficient funds to finance these
mortgages which led to an acquisition of landed status themselves as
the debts were secured against the revenues of the chief's estates.
When the debts could not be discharged, the tacksmen acquired the
land itself. The consequent expansion of land ownership amongst
the tacksmen and lesser clan gentry meant that they, in turn, became
liable for bands of surety. By the 1680s, this expansion of land ownership meant that for the first time the estates of the clan elite, held
individually as their oighreachd, largely coincided with the territories settled collectively as the duthchas of their clan. The acceptance
of responsibility by the expanded elite for the conduct of clansmen
settled on their townships as tenants can directly be related to the
decline of banditry as well as feuding.

Despite the growth of social responsibility amongst the landed proprietors, freelance reiving persisted. This can be attributed primarily
to the proliferation of 'cateran' bands, groups of up to 50 bandits,
who had thrown over the social constraint of clanship and were usu-

ally led by a renegade member of the clan gentry. These bands were also for hire, mainly on the peripheries of Gaeldom, where their principal employment was as thugs, settling or exacerbating landed disputes between Lowland lords and lairds. Within the Highlands, they remained a parasitic influence on clanship, their numbers being readily augmented in the social dislocation resulting from the civil wars of the 1640s and the Jacobite rebellions of 1689, 1715 and 1745.

Successive Scottish governments, intent on taking punitive military action against the clans – including the forcible exaction of taxes – deliberately confused clanship with banditry. This defamatory and crude association was continued with less intelligence and growing virulence by successive British governments in the aftermath of the Treaty of Union of 1707 and the abolition of the Scottish Privy Council the following year. Official smearing with a charge of banditry was an integral, if blatant, aspect of anti-Jacobite propaganda because of the overwhelming identification of the clans, politically and militarily, with the royal house of Stewart.

THE CLANS AND THE ROYAL HOUSE OF STEWART

Notwithstanding the forfeiture of the Lord of the Isles in 1493, the Scottish Crown under the house of Stewart from the mid 14th to the outset of the 17th century had no coherent policy towards Gaeldom other than occasional military expeditions to daunt refractory clans. After the Union of the Crowns in 1603, James VI did not abandon the military option. Indeed, he rigorously expropriated three clans – the Macdonalds of Kintyre and Islay, the Macleods of Lewis and the Macdonalds of Ardnamurchan – and proscribed another, the Macgregors. However, he was also resolved that chiefs and their leading gentry should be bound over as de facto agents for local government, a policy followed less systematically by his son, Charles I, whose political power in Scotland was eclipsed by the emergence of the Covenanting movement in 1638.

The civil wars

Clan support for the house of Stewart as hereditary rulers of
Scotland was based primarily on the projection of traditional values
of clanship onto the national political stage. As the chiefs were the
protectors of the clan duthchas, so were the Stewarts trustees for
Scotland. At the same time, clan support for Charles I during the
civil wars of the 1640s was essentially reactionary. The clans who
declared unequivocally for the Royalist cause were fighting less in
favour of that absentee monarch than against the Covenanting
movement which was making unprecedented demands on the Scots
for ideological, financial and military commitment. More especially,
the clans were reacting against powerful noble houses, pre-emi-
nently those of Argyll and Sutherland, whose public espousal of the
Covenanting cause masked their private pursuit of territorial ambitions. Conversely, aversion to the hitherto pervasive influence of the
powerful pro-Royalist house of Huntly persuaded some clans in the
central Highlands to side with the Covenanters and others to
remain neutral. Civil wars divided the clans no less than the rest of
Scotland, although religious affiliation was not such a divisive issue
among them even although the Campbells and other Covenanting
clans were in broad sympathy with Presbyterianism.

However, religion was a principal factor influencing clans to come
out for the Jacobite rising in 1689. The sporadic efforts of Catholic
missions in the Highlands had served to solidify the opposition of
former Royalist clans to the deposition of James VII. However, the
spread of Episcopalianism during the Restoration era was more significant in attracting support from hitherto neutral clans and in persuading former Covenanting clans to adopt a neutral standpoint.
Episcopalianism not only provided a religious complement to the
hierarchical nature of clanship, but inculcated a spirit of obedience
and submission to royal authority throughout Gaeldom. Accordingly,
the replacement of James VII by William of Orange was interpreted
as a breach of patriarchal duty by Gaelic poets for whom the sunder-
ing of genealogical continuity imperiled the lawful exercise of gov-

ernment which, in turn, subverted the maintenance of a just political order. Far from being tyrannical or oppressive, James VII had won favour among the clans when, as Duke of York during his brother's reign, he instituted the commission for pacifying the Highlands in 1682 which had sought the willing co-operation of chiefs and leading clan gentry in maintaining order. Moreover, James had proved notably responsible in redressing the acquisitiveness of the house of Argyll in particular and all Campbells in general.

The clans and Jacobitism

Following the death of James in 1701, clan support for his son James, 'the Old Pretender', and his grandson Charles Edward, 'the Young Pretender', was boosted by widespread public antipathy in Scotland to the passage of the Treaty of Union in 1707. However, as the Union had underwritten the establishment of Presbyterianism and had opened up English and imperial markets, it had won some support and the subsequent Risings of 1715, 1719 and, above all, 1745, again took on the character of civil wars in Scotland. Rebellions were marked by militant divergence of opinion among Highland clans as well as Lowland families. Such were the divisions in the clans caused by the Forty-Five, that clansmen in Skye and Wester Ross blatantly defied their more cautious chiefs to support 'the Young Pretender'. More audaciously, the Mackintosh chief of Clan Chattan raised a company for the British government, of whom all but nine deserted to join the 600 clansmen raised by his wife for Prince Charles Edward. Militarily, the attraction of the Highlands for the launching of risings was the ready mobilisation of the clan hosts. Moreover, social occasions such as the hunts, involving Lowland landlords as well as the clan elite, provided convenient cover to plot rebellion, as was demonstrated by the Earl of Mar, the Jacobite commander in 1715; he used the excuse of a hunt on his Braemar estates to assemble his forces in order to raise the Jacobite standard and launch the Fifteen. The British government in London found it difficult to take prompt military action against Highland insurgency because of communication difficulties, both with the predominantly Gaelic-speaking people and also across unfriendly terrain. Yet, as manifest by the fluctuating nature of clan support in all Jacobite risings, the further away the campaigns progressed from the Highlands, the more the appeal of the cause diminished as the clans' traditional territories remained unprotected. However, the greatest political and strategic contradiction lay in the attempt of the Jacobite claimants to reconcile their main goal – the English throne – with their military support, which was almost exclusively Scottish and predominantly clannish; a contradiction that ultimately proved to be the fatal flaw in the two campaigns which came tantalisingly close to success in 1715 and 1745.

Each Jacobite failure was marked by government reprisals of varying degrees of barbarity against the clans. Frustrated by the continuance of the Jacobite clans in arms for two years after the outbreak of rebellion in 1689, the government of William of Orange contrived the massacre of the MacDonalds of Glencoe in February 1692. Forfeiture of land among certain clans followed the risings of 1715 and 1719, but the government's attempted pacification of the Highlands by Disarming Acts in 1716 and 1725 mainly gained compliance from clans favourably disposed to the British establishment. The greatest severity followed the Jacobite defeat at Culloden in April 1746. Captured Jacobites, if they survived imprisonment and show trials in Carlisle, York and London, were usually shipped off to the plantations of the American South or the Caribbean. As a sop to English public opinion, the now anachronistic obligation to give military service to chiefs and nobles in return for landholding was abolished, along with the right to dispense justice enshrined in the feudal heritable jurisdictions; the government seemed unaware that these latter rights were in fact predominantly the preserve of the Lowland landed classes and were not in fact the bedrock of Highland society at all. Further repressive legislation rigorously enforced disarmament and banned such cultural trappings as the wearing of tartan. Speaking Gaelic was proscribed.

THE AFTERMATH OF CULLODEN

Clanship, as the working basis of Highland society, was destroyed after the Forty-five. The most critical external contribution was that of the Duke of Cumberland, son of George II and commander of the government forces. Having contemplated the wholescale transportation of the Jacobite clans, Cumberland settled instead for a draconian purge of Scottish Gaeldom by authorising the wanton butchery perpetrated by the government troops. The policy, which might now be called ethnic cleansing, was a disgrace, and one of the major troughs for British imperialism.

A more insidious contribution to the demise of clanship, however, was that made by the clan leaders themselves in their commercial determination to place greater emphasis on their individual rights as landowners (oighreachd) at the expense of their customary role as trustees for their clans (duthchas). The episodic establishment of Independent Companies – an early form of the later Highland regiments – from the Restoration era had to undermine their traditional role as protectors of their clan territories. The abolition of the Scottish Privy Council in 1708 was also the end of central government's attempts to govern the Highlands in co-operation with the traditional hierarchy of the clans.

The threat of renewed forfeiture persuaded some chiefs, including the Mackenzies and the Macdonalds of Sleat to abstain from the Forty-Five. Other chiefs, including Clanranald and Glengarry, thought the campaign so ill-advised that although they permitted contingents of their clansmen to fight for the Jacobite cause, they personally stayed at home; the latter chief dissociated himself from his Jacobite clansmen. The distinctly pro-government chief of the Mackays of Strathnaver actually advised Cumberland that it was easier to conquer than to civilise the Highlanders.

For almost two decades prior to the Forty-Five, clansmen were leaving the Highlands for the Americas, either being led from Argyll, the central Highlands and Sutherland by clan gentry seeking to re-establish a traditional lifestyle in Jamaica, Georgia, New York and the Carolinas or as victims of land raids in the Hebrides designed to secure cheap labour for the colonial plantations. The clan elite's desire for higher rents from the profits of the thriving droving trade, at the expense of the tacksman, led to acquiescence in the emigration of the first group; to the second they turned a blind eye. Culloden and the ultimate failure of Jacobitism in Scotland provided the psychological escape clause for those chiefs and other members of the clan hierarchy intent on throwing over traditional obligations of clanship. They were generally marked by a preference for absenteeism allied to the agricultural improvement of their estates; oighreachd now replaced rather than complemented duthchas. The ground was prepared for the Highland Clearances and the emasculation of the working system of clanship.

Tartan and the Highland Dress

Alastair Campbell of Airds

*Unicorn Pursuivant & Chairman, Advisory Committee
on Tartans to the Lord Lyon*

There is no clearer symbol of Scottish identity than tartan, particularly when worn in the form of a kilt. Tartan's popularity guarantees its use in a variety of situations but, attractive as it is, it is its underlying significance as a means of clan or family allegiance that gives tartan and the Highland garb its real appeal. While perhaps not unique, this identification is given by few other forms of dress, and certainly not in such a versatile form – the Highland dress can be used for every occasion from the most formal appearance in front of the monarch to attendance at an international football match, and from the smartest of ballrooms to walking the hill. Its symbolism is powerful and Neil Armstrong, the first man to walk on the moon, took a piece of his clan tartan with him on his historic journey.

The kilt is now worn by all Scots, Lowlanders and Highlanders alike, although not very long ago the former recoiled in disgust from what they regarded as a primitive form of dress worn only by those dismissed as 'redshanks' whose naked nether limbs were pinched and red from exposure to the cold weather.

Part of its appeal doubtless lies in its warlike associations, summed up in the quote that 'a man in a kilt is a man and a half'. Sir Colin Campbell sent out the Highland Brigade at Lucknow during the Indian mutiny of 1857 with the order 'Bring furrit (forward) the tartan'; German intelligence during the First World War rated the kilted 51st Highland Division – elsewhere, the Highland troops had been described as 'The Ladies from Hell' – as the most formidable of all the Allied formations encountered by their army. The Cameron

Highlanders were the last to wear the kilt in action, during the Second World War in France in 1940.

The whole subject has such a romantic appeal that the rather more prosaic facts concerning its origins and development tend to be over-laid by myth and fantasy. As a result it causes controversy which is all too often fuelled by emotion and wishful thinking rather than objective historical research and knowledge.

The exact derivation of the word 'tartan' is uncertain, but originally it referred to a type of material rather than to its pattern as is the case today. This pattern is created by the interweaving at right angles of the same sequence and proportions of coloured thread. In the majority of tartans this sequence is one which can be repeated back or forward in either direction between two pivot points which can then be reproduced by multiplying each number to achieve the scale required. In practice, when the scale is a small one, some lines are given an inflated value to avoid their becoming invisible.

But this type of weaving is not exclusively Scottish, and similar forms can be found elsewhere. Its use is certainly very ancient and it was early to be found in the Highlands, its use spreading across Scotland in the 18th century, some time before the idea of using tar-tan as a means of identification of clan or family took root.

THE HISTORY OF THE KILT

The use of a simple length of material as a garment is, of course, one of the earliest forms of attire; perhaps one of the earliest instances of it on record in northern Europe is in its adoption at the end of the 11th century by the Norse King Magnus Barefoot, who is said to have been given his nickname as a result.

The war dress of the medieval Scot was essentially the 'leine croich', a long, pleated coat which came down below the knees, its heavy pleats combining some form of protection with freedom of movement. It was worn with a pointed metal helmet, with the neck and shoulders protected by chain mail. Weapons were the spear and the double-handed claymore, a long double-handed sword with a

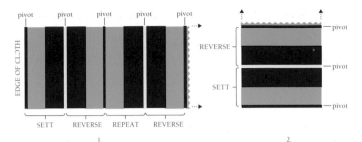

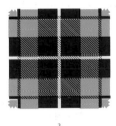

The construction of a tartan. Although apparently complex, the design of tartan is often quite straightforward. A number of coloured stripes of varying width are woven from the edge of the cloth, running its full length. The basic sequence of stripes (the sett) is then reversed around a number of pivot points so that the stripes continually repeat and reverse across the width of the cloth, reminiscent of a medal ribbon. This woven sequence is known as the warp (1). The same sequence of stripes, the weft (2) is then interwoven at right angles to the warp to create the finished tartan (3).

cross hilt (nothing to do with the modern basket-hilted broadsword which is often erroneously given the name). Representations of medieval warriors so clad are to be found on many tombstones in Argyll and the Isles, from which it would appear that the dress was being worn right up to the early 1600s.

It was around this date that it appears the belted plaid, forerunner of today's kilt, became common wear. It has been suggested that this form of dress in fact was that of the Picts (the tribes who inhabited Scotland north of the borderlands) which was later adopted by the incoming Scots (who came from Ireland). Known as the 'feileadh breacan' or 'feileadh mor' – the big kilt – it consisted of a width of tartan several yards in length. To dress, the wearer first set his belt on the ground and laid the plaid lengthwise over it with material below the belt approximating to the distance from his waist to the upper part of his knee. He would then kneel down and gather the cloth in pleats until only enough remained unpleated at either end to cover the front of his body.

Lying down on top of the pleated material, he would then fold the unpleated ends across his front and, grasping the ends of the belt, buckle it around his middle. On standing up, something like today's kilt would result below the waist; after he had donned coat and waistcoat the surplus material hanging down would then be gathered up and secured under the belt and around the shoulders in a number of possible variations which would vary according to the demands of weather, temperature, or the freedom of movement required. At the close of the day, unbuckling the belt would once again convert the garment into a warm covering for the night.

There is much argument over the question of how and when the kilt as we know it today – the 'feileadh beg' or little kilt – developed. It is effectively the lower part of the big kilt separated from the upper half which now evolved into the later form of plaid. (It may be noted that the word 'plaid' in Gaelic means a blanket – nothing to do with the modern American usage of the word to denote tartan.)

Certainly the feileadh mor did restrict movement somewhat as evidenced during the clan conflict of Blar-na-Leine, 'The Field of Shirts', in 1544 between the Clan Donald and the Frasers, so called because both sides threw off their outer covering and fought to the death in their shirts. At some stage around the middle of the 18th century, the small kilt emerged and became increasingly popular;

Dressing in the feileadh mor. To dress, the wearer first set his belt on the ground and laid the pleated plaid lengthwise over it, with material below the belt approximating to the distance from his waist to the upper part of his knee. Lying down on top of the pleated material, he would then fold the unpleated ends across his front and, grasping the ends of the belt, buckle it around his middle (1). On standing up, something like today's kilt would result below the waist (2); after he had donned coat and waistcoat the surplus material hanging down would then be gathered up and secured under the belt and around the shoulders (3) in a number of possible variations which would vary according to the demands of weather, temperature, or the freedom of movement required (4).

25

time could be saved by sewing in the pleats and a neater appearance resulted. Intense indignation is caused by the claim that the inventor of what is the kilt of today was in fact an Englishman named Rawlinson, who was in charge of a Lochaber iron-smelting works. The truth of the matter, however, will never be known.

TARTAN IN THE 17TH AND 18TH CENTURIES

A major subject of dispute is the antiquity of the practice of using tartan as a means of clan or family identification. Examples of ancient usage are very few in number but they do exist in two or three known instances. Apologists for the theory claim that the various thread-counts were recorded in the form of sticks around which were bound the correct number and sequence of coloured threads. However, no example of these pattern sticks has survived; hardly any setts, or patterns, among those in use today can be traced to early times, and there is no indication that they then had any sort of clan identity attached to them. Indeed, the evidence is very much the other way, as instanced by the patterns of such old plaids and scraps of tartan that have come down to us from before the closing years of the 18th century; these are very different from today's clan patterns, as are the tartans shown in those portraits of chiefs and lairds which have survived from the late 17th and 18th centuries. Indeed, few were painted in tartan, as their best clothes were seldom of this material, but of those that show the tartan it is evident that a number of different setts was often worn at the same time by the picture's subject and that none of them equate to the respective clan patterns of today.

This is borne out by the famous painting, 'Episode from the Scotch Rebellion', by David Morier, of the Battle of Culloden in 1746, in which Barrell's Regiment is shown receiving the Jacobite charge. The Highlanders are shown clad in a whole variety of tartans, and each man is clothed in more than one sett, none of which can be identified as any of today's clan tartans. The models for the painting are said to have been Jacobite prisoners held at Carlisle Castle. Counter claims that the diversity of patterns shown might be due to their having borrowed garments from their neighbours to be painted in, or that the artist was inaccurate, do not stand up against the number of portraits painted at this period and later, which show conclusively that no organised system of clan or family identification through tartan existed at the time.

In fact, armies of this period (and subsequently) commonly used some form of badge in the head-dress as identification, such as the leaves of a plant or a scrap of paper or coloured ribbon. At Culloden, the Jacobites wore a bunch of white ribbon in their bonnets – the famous White Cockade – while the government forces were distinguished by a black cockade or a cross of red ribbon. (The contemporary story is told of a fugitive who was on the point of being cut down, abjuring his attacker, 'Hold hard, I'm a Campbell', to which the response was 'Where's your bonnet?' – this obviously being the vital clue to its wearer's identity, rather than his tartan.)

It has also been claimed that, rather than clan tartans, those setts classed as district tartans represent an ancient general system of identification. The theory rests heavily on the statement by Martin Martin in 1703 that it was possible to tell a man's residence by the pattern of his tartan. His claim is not corroborated by other contemporary writers and may mean no more than that certain patterns had gained popularity in certain areas – which is entirely possible. A recent work on the subject lists just under a hundred tartans with a geographical name. Leaving aside those with English and overseas titles which are of modern origin, there remain 56 whose names are Scottish. Of these, 14 are post-1945 in origin and 22 are to be found on record prior to 1820. Of these 22, the vast majority appear to be 'trade' names, found in Wilson's Pattern Book alongside such fanciful titles as 'Robin Hood', 'Rob Roy', 'Durham', 'Flora MacDonald' and 'Wellington'. Others include such doubtful examples as 'Lennox' from a portrait which is thought to be that of the Countess of Lennox; 'Strathspey' from a waistcoat worn by an officer thought to have served in the Grant or Strathspey Fencibles in the 1790s; while 'Dunblane', it appears, derives from a portrait of the English Duke of Leeds, whose secondary title was 'Viscount Osborne of Dunblane'. A mere handful show any sign of having possibly been used as true district tartans and the evidence for any general system as such remains unimpressive.

It was the army which was almost certainly responsible for the general acceptance of tartan as a means of identification. The early Highland Independent Companies, raised from shortly after the Restoration of 1660 onwards 'to Keep Watch upon the Braes', seem to have worn their own tartan, with no regulation. The first Highland regiments raised at the close of the 17th century wore the standard uniform of the line. But, from the raising of the final six Highland Independent Companies in 1725, an effort seems to have been made to standardise the tartans worn; this was certainly the case when these same companies were regimented in 1739 into what is now the Black Watch. The basic military tartan as worn by the

The Government, 42nd, or Black Watch tartan.

original regiment is still worn by the Black Watch today – the familiar blue, green and black sett, whose sombre hues are said to have given the regiment its title. Frequently used by other regiments, it is also known as 'Government' or '42nd' as well as 'Black Watch'. It is worn as a clan tartan by Clan Campbell (usually today in lighter tones) and by such clans as the Grants, the Munros and the Sutherlands. The argument has been put forward for its having originated as the Clan Campbell tartan, as its use by the regiment, it is argued, was due to the large number of that clan serving in its ranks. In fact the reverse is almost certainly the case: the regimental tartan was adopted by the Campbells as theirs because so many of them were already used to wearing it when the whole idea of clan tartans became general. This would, of course, account for its use by the other clans mentioned, all of whom were involved in the Black Watch alongside the Campbells.

Many later Highland regiments also used the same sett, either in its original form or with a slight differentiation, usually in the form of the addition of coloured over-stripes. For example, a yellow stripe was added by the 92nd Regiment, red and white stripes were added by the Mackenzie Lord Macleod's 73rd Regiment, and the same red and white, but in a different sequence, were added by the later Loyal Clan Donnachie Volunteers. The use of these modified setts by the regiments led to their adoption as clan tartans by, respectively, the Gordons, the Mackenzies and the Robertsons, the last as a hunting tartan. Other examples also exist.

As far back as 1700 there is evidence of the Royal Company of Archers – founded in 1672 and now The Queen's Bodyguard for Scotland – wearing a uniform made of tartan akin to that given the name of Ogilvy today.

As the origins of the use of tartan as a means of identification lie with the army, so too in a large measure does the actual survival of tartan and of Highland dress after the Forty-Five rebellion. Part of the Government's punishment of the Highlands and its determination to quash any further threat of a Jacobite insurrection, was a proscription of the wearing of Highland dress and of tartan in any form by civilians. For the next 37 years, it was only in the Highland regiments of the army that the Highland dress could legally be worn. It was not until 1782 that the Marquess of Graham, acting as the

A Highland soldier, c. 1744 showing an early representation of a Government tartan feileadh mor. Note how the plaid is being used to protect the lock of the musket from the elements.

spokesman of a campaign organised by the Highland Society of London, succeeded in a measure to overturn the ban. Paradoxically, it was at this time that there began the romanticisation of the Celt, a phenomenon which developed in the 19th century and which had an enormous influence on later images of Scottishness.

This romanticisation of, and subsequent lessening of suspicion towards the Highlanders, was manifest in a number of ways. The Romantic Movement in Europe in the late 18th century sought new forms of art and literature to counteract the Classical, and the publication by James Macpherson of the supposed works of the mythical Irish poet Ossian helped bring about a change in attitude to Gaels. MacPherson's work attained a popularity that spread right across Europe. Indeed, the bedside reading of the Emperor Napoleon in his campaigns was an Italian translation of Macpherson's book. The renown of the Highland regiments also had been steadily growing and they quickly attained an outstanding and glamourous reputation. By the end of the 18th century, the events of over fifty years previously began to appear less threatening, and 'Bonnie Prince Charlie' (who died in 1788) began to emerge as a figure of veneration. This change in attitude was also fostered by the writings of Sir Walter Scott, who, along with General Stewart of Garth, masterminded George IV's State Visit to Edinburgh in 1822 – the first to Scotland by the monarch for over 200 years and the occasion of a quite extraordinary charade which, not unjustly, has been dubbed 'a Tartan Extravaganza'. Finally in the later 19th century, came Queen Victoria's love affair with the Highlands. Within a century the character, the image and the perception of Highlandness and Scottishness had been changed enormously. It was against this background that the modern system of clan tartans was to evolve.

THE DEVELOPMENT OF THE MODERN TARTAN

One factor which has been decisive throughout the history of the development of the modern system has been the influence of the tartan manufacturers. At the close of the 18th century, the opportuni-

ties offered by tartan weaving on a large scale had become obvious
to Border weavers and henceforth it was the large firms that they set
up that became the main suppliers of tartan to the army and to private individuals alike.

The largest and most successful of these firms was that of Wilson's
of Bannockburn, whose early order books give a most illumi-nating
insight into the early naming of tartans. As with any marketing
organisation it was important to maintain a steady flow of 'new
products', and every year new patterns were introduced. Originally
they were often identified only by a number but were subsequently
made more attractive by being given a glamourous name – possibly
that of some famous figure in history, real or fictional, or sometimes
that of a well-known town or district.

The idea of individual tartans providing a clan or family identity
was a most attractive one, which was adopted enthusiastically by
both wearer and seller alike. A whole new market opened up, one
that is still growing today. Chief and clansmen were all asking for
'their' tartan, a demand which the manufacturers were only too
happy to meet. So it was, for instance, that Wilson's pattern known
originally as 'no. 250', became known as 'Argyle' and, finally,
'Campbell of Cawdor'. And the manufacturers were eager to increase
the number of customers by actively promoting the identification of
more and more 'clan septs'.

With this sudden demand for clan tartans confusion was
inevitable, as may be discerned today by the number of clans who
claim the same tartan; ingenious solutions to the confusion were
found: the Forbes and Lamont tartans which, derived from the basic
military tartan with a white over-stripe, are claimed to differ from
each other by the said overstripe being outlined, in the case of the
Forbes tartan, by a thin black 'guard-line' – a distinction which it is
quite impossible to pick up at a range of more than a few feet.

It was soon accepted that the authority for stating what was the
correct tartan for a clan must be its chief. In 1815, the Highland
Society of London began its collection of tartans with a limited num-

ber signed and sealed as correct by the chiefs of the clans concerned. Even at this stage, the idea that such setts must have been used in this fashion from the dawn of history was being encouraged. Some chiefs and chieftains, such as Robertson of Struan and the Marquess of Douglas, were considerably embarrassed, since – hardly surprisingly – they had no idea of what pattern was 'theirs'.

The first book on clan tartans appeared in 1831. *The Scottish Gael* was written by John Logan, one-time secretary of the Highland Society of London. It was followed in 1842 by *Vestiarum Scoticum* by two remarkable brothers who, after several changes of surname, eventually settled on that of Sobieski Stuart, claiming to be grandsons of Prince Charles Edward Stuart. Managing to convince many people, they claimed to possess an old manuscript, long held at the Scots College at Douai and dating from the 16th century, which gave details of some seventy five early clan tartans which, although only described in supposedly archaic language, enabled them to include illustrations of the setts concerned in their text. The original document somehow was never available for inspection. It was clearly a figment of the brothers' fertile imagination but a surprising number of today's clan tartans derive from it.

The Sobieski Stuarts' books, however, were merely among the earliest of a whole string of works on clan tartans which have appeared at regular intervals from then on right up to the present day. Often produced at the instigation of the cloth manufacturers, they usually include a potted history of each clan. Few of these works show any originality and most are merely rewrites of previous efforts on the subject and of dubious historical accuracy. There have been honourable exceptions, however, and for work on tartan itself, full credit should be given to, among others, the work of John Telfer Dunbar, Christina, Lady Hesketh, James Scarlett and, in particular, D. C. Stewart.

But identifiable tartans have grown from a trickle into a flood. Many clans have more than one tartan; there are a host of names who are distinguished by a tartan of their own although they have never constituted a clan; and against a list of around one hundred recognised clan chiefs today, records of some two thousand named tartans exist, of which a number represent public bodies or commemorate specific events.

VARIETIES OF TARTAN

In addition to the normal clan tartan, in some cases a clan may also have 'Hunting' or 'Dress' setts. The former is in less violent colours to act as better camouflage while out on the hill, the latter designed specifically for show, often in a pattern which contains a lot of white. This fancy, which is popular alike with tourists, manufacturers and professional Highland dancers, would appear to originate in the women's arisaid, or cloak, which was largely of undyed and therefore less expensive wool.

Confusion can be caused by the use of the descriptions of tartan as 'Ancient', 'Modern', 'Reproduction', 'Weathered' and 'Muted'. Strictly speaking, the first three have nothing to do with the antiquity of the pattern, but with the dyes employed. Early dyes were not particularly lightfast and rapidly faded or changed colour; to overcome this problem, in the mid 19th century 'Modern' aniline dyes were introduced. These produced much stronger, lasting colours, although they tend to be rather heavy and dark in tone. In the 1920s, the old vegetable dye colours were revived using modern methods, and these have become widely popular under the title of 'Ancient'.

'Weathered' and 'Muted' are used for tartans either dyed in colours which seek to reproduce the effect of ageing, sometimes by the interposing of a brown or drab thread between each coloured one.

There is no strict law which lays down the shade of colour to be employed, unless a sett specifically contains a lighter and darker form of the same colour. Campbell of Cawdor, for instance, contains both a light and a dark blue but one manufacturer's 'light blue' may in fact be darker than another's 'dark blue'. Red is red and green is green, whatever kind of red or green it is and many variations may be found; for this reason, the modern practice found in some cases

1.

2.

3.

Ancient (1), Modern (2) and Reproduction (3) versions of the Macdonald tartan illustrating the considerable colour variations that can be achieved by varying the dyes used for the fabric.

of specifying such niceties as 'plum' or 'cerise' is to be deplored; there are too many possibilities of interpretation for such specifics to be clear and the Lord Lyon will dissuade would-be users of such terms when they are put before him.

Another entirely modern conceit for which there is no historical foundation is the claim for symbolism in the colours employed – gold for the cornfields, green for the pinewoods, blue for the shining rivers, and so on. In some cases this has been carried as far as using threads of various colours in numbers which reflect a date or some other significant number, a fantasy which is unlikely to lead to good design.

As far as tartans are concerned, there is no overall system of control. As already stated, chiefs are considered the authority as to what tartans their clan should wear. Any tartan specified in a Grant of Arms by the Lord Lyon is registered by him, and clan chiefs recognised as such may have their tartans recorded in Lyon Court Books. Otherwise the rules are not strict. Any individual or organisation may have a tartan woven and claim it as theirs; whether it has any commercial success is, of course, another matter. Such tartans have become increasingly popular among commercial organisations or as a means to commemorate a particular event. The Scottish Tartans Society will, for a fee, research any such new sett and, if it does not clash with any previously recorded, include such a tartan in their records. The work they undertake is of great value but it has no official standing as such.

Similarly, there is no real restriction on the wearing of a specific tartan, apart from good taste. The typical statement 'my great-grandmother was a Macpherson therefore I have the right to wear the clan tartan' has no basis in fact. No such 'right' exists. Also, a man takes his father's identity only, and any claims made through the female line are not, strictly speaking, valid. In fact, there is nothing to stop anyone wearing whatever pattern of tartan takes their fancy but they should not, it is suggested, make invalid claims as to any reason they may have for doing so.

There are, however, shibboleths which exist over the wearing of different tartans at the same time: wearing two different tartans of your clan may be defensible, but wearing tartans of more than one clan is almost certainly not. Another concerns the 'correct' fashion in which a lady should wear her tartan sash over her evening dress. Lyon Office has issued a code of practice suggesting that the sash is worn over the right shoulder and tied in a bow over the left hip. It is doubtful whether such niceties have any historical base; in one area of the Highlands, certainly, it appears to have been the case that the sash was worn over the opposite shoulder from normal to indicate that the lady concerned was in 'an interesting condition' and therefore needed extra consideration on the dance-floor.

THE WEARING OF HIGHLAND DRESS

As already stated, the evolution of Highland dress as we know it today owes much to the military. Initially, the army very much followed the civilian dress of the day and adapted it to military purposes, but after the proscription, the opposite became the case and civilian dress followed that of the military. Such characteristic features as the shoulder straps on today's jackets and the buttons on the sleeve are of military origin, the latter patterns once being found throughout the British Army as a means of discouraging the soldiery from wiping their noses on their cuffs.

The cuts of various forms of evening jacket can also be traced back to the late 1700s. The plaid became a separate garment and survives in military uniform today in two forms, the fly plaid, a vestigial piece of tartan draped from the left shoulder, usually worn by drummers, and the full shoulder plaid worn by pipers and bandsmen. The plaid is still carried as a length of tartan over the shoulder in civilian dress. Correctly used, it is a good form of protection against the weather.

The great kilt gave way to today's little kilt towards the end of the 18th century. Early kilts tended to consist of less material than today's for reasons of economy; they were worn much higher up the leg than is now fashionable and the sett of the tartan seems to have been of a smaller scale. Recently, the hem of the kilt is being worn lower and lower – frequently to ridiculous lengths.

Sporrans started out as an entirely utilitarian leather pouch hung round the waist, drawn together by draw-strings and usually with a brass top or cantle; towards the second half of the 18th century the 'sporan molach', or hair sporran, made its appearance, and from then on the sporran became too decorative and heavy to be used in the field.

Waistcoats have become less common, although they may make a return. At present they have been replaced by the waistbelt – by day, this is normally a plain brass buckle on a broad leather belt, but increasingly, a silver-plate buckle with or without heraldic device is now often worn both by day and night.

Hose were originally made of cloth, usually a red and white dicing called 'cath dath' or 'war pattern'. They got hideously out of shape and even the ornate garters employed had difficulty in keeping them up. They were in due course replaced by knitted woollen hose which did not have the same problem. Today's white hose are of modern origin, originating in the 1960s as a poor substitute for diced or tartan hose for evening wear.

Dirks, originally worn as personal weapons, became part of the uniform of military officers and musicians only; in civilian attire their use was as an ornament for evening wear. They appear today only on the fullest of full-dress occasions. The 'sgian dubh', worn in the hosetop, became general wear only in the 19th century.

The round knitted bonnet, originally worn flat, towards the end of the 18th century was cocked up vertically and then decorated by an increasing number of ostrich plumes which eventually resulted in the military feather bonnet in which the original bonnet is virtually obscured. By creasing the unadorned bonnet front-to-rear, the Glengarry bonnet was created, worn as undress head-dress by the whole British Army in late Victorian times and once very popular as an article of civilian wear, although less so now. Bonnets as part of

Highland dress are also worn less frequently. One observance of bonnet-wearing which is military in origin is that Lowlanders allow the ribbons behind their bonnets to fall, while Highlanders tie them in a knot.

Although the story by which the tartan kilt has become the national dress of Scotland is tortuous and myth-laden, and the way in which it is worn can vary from the sublime to the ridiculous, Highland dress is a powerful symbol of the wearer's pride in a Scottish ancestry and in Scotland itself. There are few, if any, other forms of national dress which can claim to make such a clear and unequivocal statement, and to be so instantly and widely recognisable.

Agnew

The origin of this name is disputed, although it has generally been asserted to be Norman, from the Barony d'Agneaux. It first appeared in England, but then in Liddesdale in Scotland at the end of the 12th century. A separate Celtic origin has also been suggested through the native Ulster sept of O'Gnimh, hereditary poets or bards to the great O'Neils of Clan Aodha Bhuidhe in Antrim who acquired the anglicised name of Agnew. The name was first written in English as O'Gnive, which later became O'Gnyw, and, latterly, O'Gnew. This would give the Agnews a common descent with other great names such as Macdonald and Macdougall through Somerled, the 12th-century King of the Isles.

The fortunes of the family in Scotland were established when Andrew Agnew of Lochnaw was granted the lands and constableship of Lochnaw Castle in 1426. He was appointed hereditary Sheriff of Wigtown in 1451, an office still held by his direct descendants to this day. Andrew Agnew of Lochnaw was killed at the Battle of Pinkie in 1547. Sir Patrick Agnew was MP for Wigtownshire from 1628 to 1633, and again from 1643 to 1647. He was created a Baronet of Nova Scotia in 1629.

The 4th Baronet married Lady Mary Montgomery, sister of the Earl of Eglinton. One of his grandchildren, Mary Agnew, married Robert McQueen who was to become notorious as the 'hanging judge', Lord Braxfield. Sir Andrew, the 5th Baronet, married his kinswoman, Eleanor Agnew of Lochryan, and produced no less than 21 children.

He was a distinguished soldier who commanded the 21st Foot, later the Scots Fusiliers, at the Battle of Dettingen in 1743, the last occasion when a British monarch, George II, commanded troops in person. Sir Andrew held Blair Castle, seat of the Duke of Atholl, against the forces of the 'Young Pretender' led by Lord George Murray in 1746. Murray, the Duke of Atholl's brother, had virtually starved out the garrison when he was ordered to lift the siege and return to Inverness to meet the advance of the Duke of Cumberland.

In 1792, Andrew Agnew, son of the 6th Baronet, renewed the family's links with Ireland when he married Martha de Courcy, daughter of the 26th Lord Kingsale. He died young and his son, the 7th Baronet, succeeded to the title and family estates when he was just 16-years-old. He devoted himself to the improvement of his estates and almost completely rebuilt the castle of Lochnaw.

Many of the the Irish Agnews were early emigrants to the new colonies in the Americas, and in particular to Pennsylvania. A thriving clan society now exists and a tartan has been designed by the chief to further unite Agnews throughout the world.

Arbuthnott

CREST
A peacock's head couped at
the neck Proper.

MOTTO
Laus deo
(Praise God)

This is a name of territorial origin, from the ancient lands of the same name in Kincardineshire. In early documents it is referred to as 'Aberbothenoth', and this has sometimes been translated as the 'mouth of the stream below the noble house'. Hugh, who may have been of the noble family of Swinton, is believed to have acquired the lands of Arbuthnott by marriage to the daughter of Osbert Olifard, known as 'The Crusader', some time during the reign of William the Lion. Another Hugh, 'Le Blond', named presumably for his fair hair, was Laird of Arbuthnott around 1282. He appears in a charter of that year, bestowing lands upon the monastery of Arbroath for 'the safety of his soul'.

Philip de Arbuthnott is the first of the name to be described in a charter as 'dominus ejusdem', or 'of that Ilk', in 1355. His son, Hugh Arbuthnott of that Ilk, was implicated in the murder of John Melville of Glenbervie, the highly unpopular Sheriff of the Mearns, around 1420. The Lairds of Mathers, Arbuthnott, Pitarrow and Halkerton invited Melville to a hunting party in the Forest of Garvock. The unsuspecting sheriff was lured to a prearranged spot where he was killed by being thrown into a cauldron of boiling water. It was claimed that the conspirators then sealed their murderous pact by each drinking from the fatal 'brew'. The laird of Arbuthnott was ultimately pardoned for his participation in the affair and he died peacefully in 1446. His direct descendant, Sir Robert Arbuthnott of that Ilk, was an adherent to the cause of

Charles I, and was elevated to the peerage in 1641 as Viscount of Arbuthnott and Baron Inverbervie.

Alexander Arbuthnott, who was descended from a younger branch of the chiefly house, was a distinguished cleric and staunch supporter of the Reformation in Scotland. He was Moderator of the General Assembly of the Church of Scotland which met at Edinburgh in April 1577.

Dr John Arbuthnott, the distinguished 18th-century physician and political humorist, also claimed near kinship to the chiefly family. He was educated at the University of Aberdeen but ultimately went to London to seek his fortune. In 1705, he was in Epsom when Prince George, husband of Queen Anne, was suddenly taken ill, and he was summoned to the royal sickbed. The prince recovered, no doubt to the doctor's great relief, and Arbuthnott was appointed one of the royal physicians. He died in September 1779.

The family seat is still at Arbuthnott House.

Armstrong

CREST
An arm from the shoulder,
armed Proper

MOTTO
Invictus maneo
(I remain unvanquished)

The legends and traditions of this powerful Borders family hold that the first of the name was Siward Beorn ('sword warrior'), also known as Siward Digry ('sword strong arm'), who was the last Anglo–Danish Earl of Northumberland and a nephew of King Canute, the Danish king of England who reigned until 1035. The family is said to have been related by marriage both to Duncan, King of Scots and William the Conqueror, Duke of Normandy and King of England. The name was common over the whole of Northumbria and the Borders, and the Armstrongs became a powerful and warlike clan in Liddesdale and the much-contested border land.

Black lists Adam Armstrong as being pardoned at Carlisle in 1235 for causing the death of another man and Gilbert Armstrong, steward of the household of David II, as ambassador to England in 1363. The Armstrongs continued to expand their influence into the valleys of the Esk and Ewes, and in about 1425 John, brother of Armstrong of Mangerton, in Liddesdale, built a strong tower. The Armstrongs were said to be able to raise 3000 horsemen and at one point were in virtual control of the contested border lands. In 1528 the English warden of the marches, Lord Dacre, attacked and raised the Armstrong tower; the family's response was to burn Netherby.

The Armstrongs' power was seen as a threat by James V to his own authority and, according to tradition, the king tricked John Armstrong of Gilnockie to a meeting near Hawick, where the king duly hanged the laird without further ado. The historian Pitscottie

attributes to Armstrong the brave retort that 'King Harry would downweigh my best horse with gold to know I were condemned to die this day'. King James was to rue his treatment of the Armstrongs when they failed to support his invasion of England which ended in the dismal rout of Solway Moss in 1542. The Union of the Crowns in 1603 brought an official end to the Anglo–Scottish border wars and a ruthless campaign then followed as the Crown attempted to pacify the Borders. The last of the Armstrong lairds was hanged in Edinburgh in 1610 for leading a reiving raid on Penrith and the families were scattered. Many sought new homes in Ulster, particularly in Fermanagh.

There have been many distinguished Armstrongs, including Sir Alexander Armstrong, the Arctic explorer and, in keeping with the Armstrong spirit of adventure, the most far-travelled must be Neil Armstrong, the first man to walk upon the moon.

There has been no Armstrong chief since the dispersal of the clan in the 17th century, but a powerful and active clan association is in existence and the Clan Armstrong Trust was established in 1978.

Baird

The coat of arms of this family proclaim the legend of its origin which, like so many, involves a feat of strength which saves the life of a king. This version states that the first Baird saved William the Lion from a wild boar. The name appears to be territorial, from lands held by the family in Lanarkshire near the village of Biggar. Henry Debard witnessed a deed by Thomas De Hay between 1202 and 1228. Richard Baird received land at Meikle and Little Kyp in Lanarkshire, during the reign of Alexander III. Anderson states that Fergus Debard, John Bard and Robert Bard, who swore submission to Edward I of England at the end of the 13th century, are supposed to be of the family of Baird of Kyp. The principal family of the name came to be that holding the lands of Auchmedden in Aberdeenshire, whose influence in that county was strengthened by marriage into the powerful Keith family, Earls Marischal of Scotland. James Baird, a younger son of the house of Auchmedden, became an advocate in Edinburgh and his son, John, was created a baronet and then a High Court judge under the title of Lord Newbyth; his splendid house of Newbyth in East Lothian still stands.

The estate of Auchmedden passed into the hands of the Earls of Aberdeen and, according to local tradition, a pair of eagles which had regularly nested on the nearby crags left the area, fulfilling an ancient prophecy by Thomas the Rhymer, that 'there shall be an eagle in the craig while there is a Baird in Auchmedden'. Lord Haddow, eldest son of the Earl of Aberdeen, married a younger

daughter of William Baird of Newbyth, and the eagles returned. However, they reputedly fled once more when the estate passed to another branch of the Gordon family. Sir David Baird, who succeeded his second cousin in the baronetcy of Newbyth, was one of the leading soldiers of his day and saw action in India and throughout the Napoleonic Wars.

The name gained prominence again in the 20th century through John Logie Baird, the pioneer of television. In 1926 he demonstrated the first television transmission, and he remained heavily involved in its development until his death in 1946.

Barclay

CREST
(On a chapeau Azure doubled Ermine)
a hand holding a dagger Proper

MOTTO
Aut agere aut mori
(Either to do or die)

The Barclays came to Britain with the Norman Conquest. The first spelling of their name was 'de Berchelai', believed to be the Anglo–Saxon version of 'beau', meaning 'beautiful', and 'lee' a 'meadow' or 'field'. The early settlers in Gloucestershire bore the Norman fore-names of Roger and Ralph and the Domesday Book lists them as owning 20 hamlets between the Rivers Wye and Usk.

Lord Roger de Berchelai, who is mentioned in Domesday, and, by tradition, his son, John, came to Scotland in the retinue of Margaret, sister of the Saxon Edgar the Aetheling, in 1067. She married Malcolm III, who bestowed various lands on her followers, includ-ing the lands of Towie to John de Berchelai.

The Barclays soon established themselves in strong positions in lands, offices and alliances. Sir Walter de Berkeley was Chamberlain of Scotland in 1165, in close attendance upon his royal master, William the Lion. Sir David Barclay was one of the chief associates of Robert the Bruce.

In the 17th century, the 1st Laird of Urie, Colonel David Barclay, was a professional soldier who served in the armies of Gustavus Adolphus, king of Sweden. When civil war broke out in his own country, he returned home and became a colonel of a regiment of horse fighting for the king. During a period of imprisonment he was converted to the Society of Friends (Quakers) by the Laird of Swinton who was confined in the same prison. His son, Robert Barclay, second of Urie, was also a Quaker, and published *An Apology for the true Christian Divinity as the same is held forth and*

48

preached by the people called in scorn Quakers in 1675. He moved with his family to London, and corresponded with Princess Elizabeth, the niece of Charles I. In 1679 Charles II granted him a charter under the Great Seal, erecting his lands of Urie into a free barony. David Barclay of Cheapside, the apologist's second son, founded Barclay's Bank.

In 1621 Sir Patrick Barclay, Baron of Towie, the 17th Laird, signed a letter of safe conduct in favour of John and Peter Barclay who were merchants in the town of Banff and who wished to settle in Rostock in Livonia, on the shores of the Baltic. The brothers became silk merchants and burghers. From Peter, in five generations, was descended Field Marshal Michael Andreas Barclay de Tolly, born in 1761. He was made the Russian Minister of War in 1810 and two years later was given command of the Russian armies fighting against Napoleon. The appointment of a Scottish commander-in-chief was much resented by the Russian nobility, but, nevertheless, his capabilities were respected. Barclay de Tolly was created a prince by the Tsar, and his memory is still honoured in Russia, where his portrait hangs in the Hermitage in St Petersburg.

Borthwick

This name is of territorial origin, and it seems likely to have been assumed from lands on Borthwick Water in Roxburghshire. The family is one of the most ancient in Scotland and some recent research suggests that they may have opposed Caesar's legions. It is traditionally asserted that the progenitor of this noble house was Andreas, who accompanied the Saxon Edgar the Aetheling and his sister, Margaret, later queen and saint, to Scotland in 1067. The family soon became prominent in Scottish affairs. Sir William Borthwick possessed substantial lands in Midlothian and the Borders, and he obtained a charter confirming his lands of Borthwick around 1410. During the 15th century, the Borthwicks acquired immense influence and became Lords of Parliament.

The 1st Lord Borthwick erected what remains one of the most impressive fortified dwellings in Scotland on a strong position near Middleton in Midlothian. He died some time before 1458 and is commemorated by a splendid tomb in the old church of Borthwick.

The Borthwicks fought alongside James IV at the ill-fated Battle of Flodden in 1513. William, Lord Borthwick, succeeded his father who fell at Flodden, and was given command of the strategic Stirling Castle and charged with the safety of the infant James V. His son, William, was a staunch friend and confidant of Queen Mary, who was a frequent visitor to Borthwick castle. She took refuge there with her husband, Bothwell, but they were forced to flee before a substantial force under Lords Murray and Morton. The queen is said to have escaped disguised as a pageboy.

David Borthwick of Lochhill was a prominent lawyer who became the King's Advocate, or principal legal adviser, in 1573. He may have been the first to bear the title, 'Lord Advocate', still in use today for the Government's chief law officer in Scotland.

The Borthwicks adhered to the royalist cause during the civil war, and their castle was besieged after the Battle of Dunbar in 1650. The splendid fortress was spared from inevitable destruction when Oliver Cromwell offered Lord Borthwick honourable terms of surrender, which he accepted. Various branches of the family disputed the right of succession in the 18th and 19th centuries, but in June 1986, Major John Borthwick of Crookston was recognised by the Lord Lyon, King of Arms, as The Lord Borthwick of that Ilk and chief of the name and arms of Borthwick.

Boyd

This is said to be a descriptive name, deriving from the Gaelic, 'buidhe', meaning 'fair' or 'yellow'. The original fair-haired man is said to have been Robert, nephew of Walter, the first High Steward of Scotland. However, this derivation is challenged by some scholars, who point out that the High Stewards were from Brittany, and would be unlikely to use a Celtic nickname for one of their close family. Sir Robert Boyd was a staunch supporter of Bruce and was one of the commanders at the Battle of Bannockburn in 1314. His gallantry on the field of battle was rewarded by lands, including Kilmarnock and other substantial holdings in Ayrshire.

The fortunes of the family continued to advance and they were raised to the peerage by James II. Lord Boyd was a trusted royal officer, and was appointed one of the regents to the young James III, while his younger brother was appointed military tutor to the young king. The influence of the Boyd brothers on their young charge was considerable. Lord Boyd was appointed Great Chamberlain, and his son, Thomas, was married to Princess Mary, the king's sister, with the title of Earl of Arran.

As the family had risen so high, it is not surprising that they made many powerful enemies. Those opposed to the Boyds began to conspire against them, and eventually persuaded the king that the ambition of this family was a threat to the throne itself. In 1469, Lord Boyd, his son, the Earl of Arran, and his brother, Alexander Boyd, were summoned to appear before the king and Parliament to answer charges brought against them. Lord Boyd made his escape to

England but Sir Alexander, already a sick man, was brought before Parliament, and in spite of a spirited defence, was executed for treason. The Earl of Arran had been abroad on state business, and on learning of the total reversal of his family's fortunes, he accepted his exile, and was well received at royal courts throughout Europe.

The family were restored to royal favour when Robert, a descendant of the younger son of the 1st Lord Boyd, received confirmation from Mary, Queen of Scots, of all the estates, honours and dignities of the family. After the queen's escape from Loch Leven castle, Lord Boyd was one of the first to join her at Hamilton, and fought at the Battle of Langside in 1568. William, Lord Boyd, was created Earl of Kilmarnock in 1661. The 4th Earl was a Jacobite who fought at the Battle of Culloden where he was captured. He was conveyed to the Tower of London and was beheaded on Tower Hill on 18 August 1746. All the Boyd titles were declared forfeit, but his eldest son succeeded through his mother to the earldom of Erroll in 1758, and assumed the name of Hay. The brother of the 22nd Earl resumed the name of Boyd, the title Lord Kilmarnock, and the chiefship of the clan.

Brodie

CREST
A right hand holding a
bunch of arrows all Proper

MOTTO
Unite

This ancient family takes its name from the lands of Brodie near Forres in Morayshire. Michael Brodie of Brodie received a charter of confirmation of his lands of Brodie from Robert the Bruce. The charter declares that Brodie held the thanage of Brodie by ancient right of succession from his paternal ancestors. It has been suggested that the family may even have Pictish origins, being descended from the royal family who carried the name, 'Brude'. There is certainly evidence of Pictish settlement around Brodie.

The Brodies were certainly prominent among the local nobility, and the name appears throughout the 15th and 16th centuries in charters of the diocese of Moray. Alexander Brodie of Brodie was summoned before the Lords of Council in Edinburgh in 1484 to give account of one of his verdicts as a local judge.

Alexander Brodie of Brodie (1617–79) was a vigorous supporter of the reformed religion, and in 1640 he attacked Elgin Cathedral and destroyed its carvings and paintings, which he considered idolatrous. He represented Elgin in Parliament, and in 1649 was one of the commissioners sent to negotiate with the exiled Charles II for his return to Scotland. He was an able politician, and after the defeat of the royalist forces at the Battle of Worcester in 1651 he was summoned to London by Oliver Cromwell to consider a union between Scotland and England. He resisted attempts to appoint him to judicial office under the Protectorate, although he finally accepted after Cromwell's death in 1658. This brought him royal disfavour after the Restoration, when he was fined for his actions.

In 1727 Alexander Brodie of Brodie was appointed Lord Lyon, King of Arms and a splendid portrait in his official robes still hangs in Brodie Castle. He was Lyon during the Jacobite rebellion of 1745 and attended on the Duke of Cumberland throughout his Scottish campaign. His son, Alexander, died in 1759, and the chiefship passed to a cousin, James Brodie of Spynie. He married Lady Margaret Duff, youngest daughter of William, 1st Earl of Fife. His eldest son died as a result of a drowning accident and the estate passed to his grandson, William Brodie, who was Lord Lieutenant of Nairn from 1824 to 1873.

In 1979 the chief placed Brodie Castle in the care of the National Trust for Scotland.

Bruce

CREST
A lion statant Azure armed
and langued Gules

MOTTO
Fuimus
(We have been)

PLANT BADGE
Rosemary

It is believed that Adam de Brus built the castle at Brix between Cherbourg and Valognes in Normandy in the 11th century. Robert de Brus followed William the Conqueror, Duke of Normandy, to England in 1066 and, although he is thought to have died soon after, his sons acquired great possessions in Surrey and Dorset. Another Robert de Brus became a companion-in-arms to Prince David, afterwards David I of Scotland, and followed him when he went north to regain his kingdom in 1124. When David led a force into England, de Brus could not support his king, and resigned his holdings in Annandale to his second son, Robert, to join the English forces gathering to resist the Scottish invasion. At the Battle of the Standard in 1138, the Scottish forces were defeated and de Brus took prisoner his own son, now Lord of Annandale. He was ultimately returned to Scotland.

Robert, 4th Lord of Annandale, laid the foundation of the royal house of Bruce when he married Isobel, niece of William the Lion. The defeat of John Balliol by Edward I at the Battle of Dunbar in 1296 left the leadership of Scotland in the hands either of the powerful Comyn family or of the Bruces. Robert the Bruce met with John Comyn in February 1306 in the church of the Minorite Friars at Dumfries in the hope of negotiating a compromise. However, a quarrel quickly erupted which ended with Bruce murdering his rival. Within weeks, Robert was crowned king at Scone and began a long, hard campaign to make his title a reality, culminating in the Battle of Bannockburn in 1314. In 1370 the first Stewart monarch

succeeded to the throne by right of descent from Marjory, Bruce's daughter.

Sir Edward Bruce was made commendator of Kinloss Abbey and appointed a judge in 1597. In 1601 he was appointed a Lord of Parliament with the title of Lord Kinloss. He accompanied James VI to claim his English throne in 1603 and was subsequently appointed to English judicial office as Master of the Rolls. In May 1608 he was granted a barony as Lord Bruce of Kinloss. His son, Thomas, was created 1st Earl of Elgin in 1633. The 4th Earl died without a male heir and the title passed to a descendant of Sir George Bruce of Carnock, This branch of the family had already been created Earls of Kincardine in 1647, and thus two titles were united.

The 7th Earl of Elgin was the famous diplomat who spent much of his fortune rescuing the marbles of the Parthenon (commonly known as the Elgin Marbles) which were at that time falling into utter ruin. His son was an eminent diplomat and Governor General of Canada. He led two important missions to the emperor of China. He was Viceroy of India, a post also held by the 9th Earl of Elgin from 1894 to 1899.

Buchanan

CREST
A dexter hand holding up a ducal cap
(Proper), tufted on the top with a
rose Gules, within two laurel
branches in orle (also Proper)

MOTTO
Clarior hinc honos
(Hence the brighter honour)

'Buth chanain' is Gaelic for 'house of the canon', and the first of this name may have been a clergyman or from one of those families dedicated to the service of the ancient Celtic Church. In 1282 Morris of Buchanan received a charter confirming him in his lands with baronial rights. He also held the small island of Clarinch, the name of which was afterwards to become the battle-cry of the clan.

The Buchanans supported the cause of Bruce during the War of Independence and the fortunes of the family were thus assured. Sir Alexander Buchanan travelled with other Scottish nobles to fight for the French against Henry V of England, and fought at the Battle of Beauge in Normandy in March 1421. Buchanan's exploits during this battle are given as one explanation for the heraldry of this family: it is said that Sir Alexander killed the Duke of Clarence and bore off his coronet as a trophy, hence the ducal cap held aloft in the crest. The shield, which is virtually the Royal Arms of Scotland, is differenced only by changing the lion and the double tressure of fleurs de lis from red to black. This is said to allude to the marriage of Sir Walter Buchanan to the only daughter of Murdoch, Duke of Albany and Regent of Scotland. The regent was ultimately beheaded by his cousin, James I, in 1425, when his vast estates were confiscated. Albany's son had died childless and the Buchanans were the nearest relatives to this disinherited branch of the royal family. The arms are said to mourn the family's loss of status.

The ancient lands of Buchanan were to have been passed at the death of the last chief in 1682 to Buchanan of Arnprior, but instead

were sold to meet heavy debts. The mansion house of Buchanan is now in the possession of the Graham Dukes of Montrose. Perhaps the most famous Buchanan was the distinguished poet and Protestant reformer George, who was born at Killearn in Stirlingshire in 1506, the third son of Buchanan of Drumikill. He moved to Paris around 1520 to continue his education and travelled extensively on the Continent, embarking upon a literary career. He returned to Scotland around 1560 and in April 1562 he was appointed tutor in classics to the young Mary, Queen of Scots. He received a measure of royal favour but this did not prevent his launching vicious attacks upon the queen in his writings. He was appointed preceptor and tutor to the young James VI after the abdication of his mother, and he is generally credited with laying the foundations for that monarch's considerable academic prowess as well, unfortunately, as poisoning the child's mind against his mother.

James Buchanan was the 15th president of the United States of America. There has not been a recognised chief since the late 17th century.

Burnett

CREST
A cubit arm, the hand naked, vested
Vert doubled Argent pruning a vine-
tree with a pruning knife Proper

MOTTO
Virescit vulnere virtus
(Her virtue flourishes
by her wounds)

*T*his ancient family claims Norman descent, but it is possible that the name is also connected with the great Saxon family of Burnard who held estates in England before the Norman Conquest. The Saxon 'beornheard' means 'brave warrior'. It seems likely that the family, now calling themselves de Bernard, first came to Scotland on the return of David I from England, and they appear to have settled in Roxburghshire.

Alexander Burnett was a faithful adherent of Robert the Bruce, and on the defeat of the English he was rewarded by a grant of land in the royal Forest of Drum, together with the title of forester. In the main hall of the ancient seat of the Burnetts' Crathes Castle, pride of place is still given to an ancient and splendid ivory horn said to have been presented by Bruce as a symbol of the barony and title bestowed upon Burnett.

Sir Thomas Burnett, who had been created a Baronet of Nova Scotia in 1626, was a staunch supporter of the Covenant, but he was also related to the great Marquess of Montrose. Sir Thomas entertained Montrose at Crathes Castle and accompanied him on his march towards Aberdeen. His son, the 3rd Baronet, was commissioner for Kincardineshire in the last Scottish Parliament; he strenuously opposed the union of the Scottish and English parliaments which was ultimately effected in 1707. On the death of Sir Robert Burnett of Leyes without issue, the title passed to his cousin, Thomas Burnett of Criggie.

The 7th Baronet was an officer in the Royal Scots Fusiliers and

served throughout the American Wars, being taken prisoner after the surrender of General Burgoyne at Saratoga in 1777.

The family's great military traditions were carried on in more recent times by Major General Sir James Burnett of Leys, 13th Baronet, who commanded a brigade in the First World War and was colonel of the Gordon Highlanders. He was mentioned in dispatches 11 times and was awarded the Distinguished Service Order twice. He was appointed a companion of the Order of the Bath, and decorated by France with the Legion of Honour. His grandson is the present chief, and he still lives on the family lands although Crathes Castle, one of Scotland's greatest historic monuments, is now in the care of the National Trust for Scotland.

Cameron

CREST
A sheaf of five arrows points
upwards Proper tied with
a band Gules

MOTTO
Aonaibh ri chéile
(Unite)

There are several theories concerning the origin of this name: one states that they are descended from a younger son of Camchron, a king of Denmark, but the more likely explanation is that the first authentic chief of the clan, Donald Dubh, was descended either from the Macgillonios or from the mediaeval family of Cameron of Ballegarno in Fife. Donald Dubh married an heiress of the Macmartins of Letterfinlay, and by his prowess and leadership, united the confederation tribes which became known as the Clan Cameron. He is believed to have been born around 1400, and he and his successors were known as captains of Clan Cameron until the time of Ewan Macallan, in the early 16th century, when the lands of Lochiel were united by charter into the barony of Lochiel.

Ewan was one of the great Cameron chiefs, well favoured at court and successful in all he undertook. The untimely death of his eldest son, Donald, was a great blow to him and, resolved to give up the world, he went on pilgrimage to Rome. The pope ordained that he should build six chapels to expiate his sins – the church at Cilachoireil, Roy Bridge, is on the site of one of these chapels. The next great chief was Sir Ewen, who was born in 1629 and died in 1719. In 1682 he was knighted by the Duke of York in Edinburgh, and fought at the Battle of Killiecrankie in 1689. As a soldier, he was fearless and as a chief, he was loved, trusted and admired by his clansmen. His grandson, known as 'Gentle Lochiel', was an enlightened chief who tried to improve the lot of his clansmen. When Bonnie Prince Charlie landed in Scotland in August 1745, the chief,

as a staunch Jacobite, felt duty bound to meet him, and was eventually won over by the prince to support his cause with all his clan. The history of the Forty-five is well known, but if Lochiel had not come out with his clan, the rising might never have taken place, and the chief always felt guilty that he had allowed his better judgment to be thwarted by the prince's natural charm. He died in France in 1748, respected and mourned by friend and foe alike. In 1784 the estate was returned to Donald, grandson of the gentle Lochiel, subject to a large fine.

Donald, the 24th chief, who died in 1905, was the Member of Parliament for Inverness-shire for 17 years and a member of the Royal Commission enquiring into the grievances of the crofters in 1883. His son, Donald Walter, 25th chief, was a soldier, and at the outbreak of the First World War, he raised four new battalions of Cameron Highlanders. In 1934 Lochiel was created a Knight of the Thistle and subsequently appointed Lord Lieutenant of Inverness-shire.

Campbell

CREST
A boar's head fessways erased Or,
armed Argent, langued Gules

MOTTO
Ne obliviscaris
(Do not forget)

PLANT BADGE
Bog myrtle

The origin of this great clan probably lies among the ancient
Britons of Strathclyde, and the original seat was either Innischonnel
Castle on Loch Awe, or Caisteal na Nigheann Ruaidhe on Loch
Avich. The first Campbell in written records is one Gillespie in 1263
and the clan were at first dominated by the Macdougal Lords of
Lorne. However, this situation was reversed when Sir Neil Campbell,
staunch ally and friend of Robert the Bruce, was rewarded by his
king with extensive lands forfeited by the Macdougals and other
enemies in Argyll. The king also married his sister to Sir Neil and
from this royal union sprang John, who was created Earl of Atholl.
John was killed at the Battle of Halidon Hill in 1333 and the title
passed out of Campbell hands. In 1445, Sir Duncan Campbell of
Loch Awe became Lord Campbell and his grandson and heir, Colin,
created Earl of Argyll 12 years later. Argyll's uncle, another Colin,
founded a line which rivalled Loch Awe in splendour – the Earls of
Breadalbane. The Campbells were also to become Earls of Cawdor
and Loudoun. Internal rivalry for the chiefship between these great
houses led to a feud in the 16th century which threatened to split
the clan. Campbell of Cawdor, guardian of the 7th Earl of Argyll,
was murdered in 1592 as part of a plot which threatened the life of
his young ward. The earl, in fact, survived a further suspected
poison attempt to become an able soldier and to unite the clan.

Campbell support for central government brought rich rewards,
but not without some peril. Archibald, the 8th Earl, the great oppo-
nent of Montrose during the civil war of Charles I, was executed for

treason by Charles II, whose throne Argyll had helped to restore. His son, the 9th Earl, met a similar fate for supporting the Protestant rebellion of the Duke of Monmouth in 1685. The exile of the Stuarts shortly after restored the family fortunes and in 1703 William of Orange created the 10th Earl, Duke of Argyll and Marquess of Lorne and Kintyre, with a string of lesser titles. The 2nd Duke, one of the first British field marshals, was a renowned soldier, whose prowess rivalled Marlborough. He was succeeded by his brother, the most influential man in Scotland, and one of the architects of the union with England.

The clan remained a potent military force which, at the time of the Forty-five, was reckoned to have a strength of some 5000 men, and no less than 16 British regiments were raised at one time or another by Campbells.

Although the aftermath of Culloden saw the end of clanship as a working social system, much of the ancestral lands are still in family hands, including the castles of Dunstaffnage, Cawdor and the chief's seat, Inveraray.

Carmichael

The Carmichaels have been settled on the lands in the upper ward of Lanarkshire from which they derive their name, for almost eight hundred years. Records show that Sir John de Carmichael received a charter of the lands of Carmichael from William, Earl of Douglas around 1374.

The traditional hero of the Carmichael family is Sir John de Carmichael of Meadowflat, later of Carmichael, who fought in France with the Scottish army sent to the aid of the French in their resistance against English invasion in the early 15th century. In 1421, at the Battle of Beauge, Sir John rode in combat against the English commander, the Duke of Clarence, and unhorsed him, breaking his own spear in the action. Carmichael's victory so demoralised the English that they fled from the field. To commemorate this deed, Carmichaels bear the broken spear as their crest.

Sir John Carmichael, known as 'the most expert Borderer', was chief from 1585 until he was murdered in 1599. John was a favourite of James VI and was knighted at the coronation of James's queen, Anne, and was subsequently sent on a diplomatic mission to England. He was captain of the King's Guard, Master of the Stables, warden of the west marches and a Privy Councillor. He was later ambushed and shot after arresting some Armstrongs during a disturbance.

Sir James, 1st Lord of Carmichael, was created a Baronet of Nova Scotia in 1627 and raised to the peerage in 1647. In 1701, the 2nd Lord was created Earl of Hyndford, Viscount Inglisberry and

Nemphlar, and Lord Carmichael of Carmichael. The five succeeding
Earls of Hyndford all held high offices of state and often served in
the army. However, their loyalties shifted with the times. The 1st
Lord Carmichael was a staunch supporter of Charles I although two
of his sons took Parliament's side during the civil wars; two other
sons shared their father's royalist sentiments and at the Battle of
Dunbar in 1650, it is likely that the brothers took the field on
opposing sides.

The 3rd Earl, known in the family as 'the Great Earl', was a strong
adherent of the Hanoverians, and was an ambassador in the service
of George II. He was also noted as an agriculturalist, paying large
sums to plant trees and gardens and improve the soil. The 6th Earl
died unmarried in 1817, when the family titles and honours became
dormant and the great estates of Carmichael passed to Sir John
Anstruther of Anstruther, Baronet, who descended through a daughter of the 2nd Earl of Hyndford. On the death in 1980 of Sir
Windham Carmichael-Anstruther, Baronet, the lands and chiefship
passed to a branch of the family who resumed the name Carmichael
of Carmichael.

Carnegie

CREST
A thunderbolt Proper,
winged Or

MOTTO
Dred God

In 1358, a grant of the lands and barony of Carnegie, lying in the parish of Carmylie was made to John de Balinhard. The de Balinhards may have been related to the Ramsays, but there is no direct evidence of this. Duthac de Carnegie acquired part of the lands of Kinnaird in Forfarshire around 1401, which were confirmed by charter in 1409. Duthac was killed at the Battle of Harlaw in 1411, leaving an infant son, Walter. Walter Carnegie of Kinnaird fought at the Battle of Brechin in May 1452 under the standard of James II borne by the Earl of Huntly.

John Carnegie of Kinnaird fought and died at the Battle of Flodden in September 1513. His son, Sir Robert, was appointed one of the judges of the College of Justice in 1547 and sent to England the following year to negotiate the ransom of the Earl of Huntly, Chancellor of Scotland, who had been captured at the Battle of Pinkie in 1547.

Sir David Carnegie, born in 1575, was created Lord Carnegie of Kinnaird in 1616. He was advanced to the rank of Earl of Southesk in June 1633. James, 2nd Earl of Southesk, attended on the king-in-exile, Charles II, in Holland in 1650 and was one of the commissioners chosen for Scotland to sit in the English Parliament during the Protectorate. The Carnegies were Jacobites, and although the 4th Earl took no part in opposing the Revolution of 1688, he thereafter shunned the royal court. He had married Mary, daughter of the Earl of Lauderdale, by whom he had an only son, James, the 5th Earl. He followed the 'Old Pretender' in the Jacobite rising of 1715, and for

this he was attainted by Act of Parliament and his estates forfeited to the Crown. Sir James Carnegie, a distinguished soldier, was able to secure in 1855 an Act of Parliament reversing the attainder and restoring the titles of Earl of Southesk and Lord Carnegie of Kinnaird and Leuchars with their original precedence. The 9th Earl harkened back to his family's early ancestry when he chose the title 'Baron Balinhaird' when granted an additional peerage in 1869.

The Carnegies, in common with most Scottish noble families, sought to secure their fortunes by judicious and powerful alliances by marriage. No such alliance was more splendid than that of the 11th Earl who, as Lord Carnegie, married Her Highness Princess Maud, younger daughter of the Princess Royal and granddaughter of Edward VII. On her death, her son, as well as being heir to his father's earldom of Southesk and the chiefship of the Carnegies, inherited the dukedom of Fife, the title of his maternal grandfather. The 11th Earl died in 1992 and his son, the Duke of Fife, succeeded to the chiefship. He thereafter decreed that the subsidiary title of the dukedom, borne by the heir apparent, would be Earl of Southesk in honour of his Carnegie ancestors.

Chattan

CREST
A cat salient Proper

MOTTO
Touch not the catt but a glove

PLANT BADGE
Red whortleberry

There are many theories on the origin of this unique group of families which did not follow the ordinary pattern of other Scottish clans, but rather became a confederation, consisting of various descendants of the original ancestors. They were distinguished by the wildcat which figures prominently in their heraldry. One theory states that they came from the Catti, a tribe of Gauls driven out by the Romans; another says they took their name from Catav in Sutherland. The most widely accepted, however, says they descended from Gillichattan Mor, the great servant of St Cattan. Gillichattan was probably the co-arb, or baillie, of the abbey lands of Ardchattan. Around the time of Malcolm II they became possessed of lands at Glenloy and Loch Arkaig, where Torcastle became the chief's seat.

Little is certain until the clan became established around Lochaber at the close of the 13th century. In 1291, Eva, daughter of Gilpatric, or Dougal Dall, of Clan Chattan in Lochaber, married Angus Mackintosh, 6th of Mackintosh. After his marriage to Eva, Angus lived for some time at Torcastle in Glenloy, but due to the enmity of Angus Og of Islay, he withdrew to Rothiemurchus.

Prior to the 14th century, Clan Chattan appears to have been a conventional clan though little is known of it. Subsequently, however, it evolved into a confederation or alliance of clans made up of (a) the descendants of the original clan (Macphersons, Cattanachs, Macbeans, Macphails), (b) Mackintoshes and their cadet branches (Shaws, Farquharsons, Ritchies, McCombies, Macthomases), and (c) families not originally related by blood (Macgillivrays, Davidsons,

Macleans of Dochgarroch, Macqueens of Pollochaig, Macintyres of Badenoch, Macandrews). By the 18th century, the clans in and around Strathairn (Shaw, Macbean, Macphail, Macgillivray) looked to Mackintosh as their chief, having none of their own, but whether this was as Clan Chattan or Clan Mackintosh is unclear, the histories of both clans being inextricably entwined.

In the Jacobite risings of 1715 and 1745 Clan Chattan declared for the Stuarts, and suffered as a consequence. The Mackintosh chief was imprisoned until August 1716 and he died at Moy in 1731. Under Macgillivray of Dunmaglas, the Clan Chattan regiment fought at the Jacobite victory of Falkirk in 1746. The suppression of the Highlands after the Forty-five undermined the nature of the confederation, and its members largely sought independent destinies. The major families continued to dispute the vestiges of power, but no more violently than in heated debate before the Court of the Lord Lyon. The Mackintosh chiefs continued as captains of Clan Chattan until 1947, when Duncan Alexander Mackintosh of Torcastle was recognised by the Lord Lyon as chief of Clan Chattan in his own right

Chisholm

The Chisholm name was known in the Borders as early as the reign of Alexander III in the mid 13th century. One of the earliest recorded members of this family is John de Chesehelme, who was mentioned in a bull of Pope Alexander IV in 1254. Richard de Chesehelme of Roxburghshire rendered homage to Edward I of England and is listed in the Ragman Rolls of 1296. The seal he used shows a boar's head which remains this family's principal device to this day. This stems from the tradition that two Chisholm brothers saved the life of the king when he was attacked by a ferocious wild boar. By way of reward for this deed, the family were granted lands in Inverness-shire. They subsequently achieved prominence in the north when, in 1359, Robert de Chisholme was appointed constable of Urquhart Castle on the shores of Loch Ness in succession to his maternal grandfather. He had been knighted by David II and was taken prisoner at the Battle of Neville's Cross in 1346. His son, Alexander, married Margaret, heiress to the lands of Erchless, and Erchless Castle was to become the seat of the clan.

The family remained Catholic during the early Reformation, and Sir James Chisholm was denounced in 1592 for 'traffiking in sundry treasonable matters against the true Religion' and was excommunicated at St Andrews in September 1593. During the 17th century the clan chiefs became Protestant, but they remained tolerant of the Catholic faith. Roderic Maciain Chisholm was active in the 1715 Jacobite rising under the Earl of Mar. Chisholm of Crocfin, an aged veteran, led 200 men of the clan at the Battle of Sheriffmuir. The

family estates were forfeited to the Crown and sold, but a pardon was granted in 1727 and most of the lands were purchased back from Mackenzie of Allangrange. The Chisholms still adhered to the Jacobite cause, and when Bonnie Prince Charlie raised his father's standard in 1745, Roderick, a younger son of the chief, was appointed colonel of a battalion. Of the Chisholms who fought at Culloden, less than 50 survived, and Roderick was among the fallen. The Chisholms were, however, more wary than they had been in the 1715 rising, and as a clan, did not openly support the Stuart cause. The Chisholm lands were accordingly preserved.

In the mid 18th century, Ruairidh, the 22nd chief, tried to raise money by increasing his tenants' rents, precipitating mass emigration from the Chisholm lands to the New World overseas. Alexander, the 23rd chief, attempted to reverse this decline, but he died in 1793 leaving an only daughter, Mary, and the chiefship devolved upon his half-brother William. He made over most of the family land to sheep grazing and the emigrations continued. In 1887 the chiefship passed through an heiress to the present chiefly line.

Cochrane

CREST
A horse passant Argent

MOTTO
Virtute et labore
(By valour and exertion)

$\mathcal{T}$radition has it that the Cochrane ancestry goes back to a Viking invader who settled in Renfrewshire between the 8th and 10th centuries. The name of Cochrane may be the combination of two Gaelic words, meaning 'the roar of battle' or 'battle-cry'. The first certain record of the name appears to be Waldev de Coveran, who appears as witness to a charter in 1262.

William de Cochran of that Ilk obtained from Robert II a charter of the lands of Cochran, which had hitherto been held as vassals of the High Steward of Scotland. About 1350 Robert II built a castle at Dundonald in Ayrshire.

The Dundonald estate, with its castle, came into Cochrane hands around 1638, and it was from these lands that the 1st Earl of Dundonald, William Cochrane, took his title in 1669. The chiefship had almost been lost at the beginning of the 17th century, when William Cochrane of that Ilk was unable to produce a male heir. However, he made prudent provision in the marriage negotiations of his daughter, Elizabeth, requiring that her husband assume both the name and the coat of arms of Cochrane.

There then followed a most remarkable succession of chiefs who served their country with distinction, both on land and at sea; they have been called the fighting Cochranes, the most renowned of whom was undoubtedly Thomas, the 10th Earl. In 1807, before he inherited the earldom, he became a Member of Parliament although still a serving officer. A dedicated sailor and compassionate officer, he attacked the corruption and abuses which riddled the Admiralty

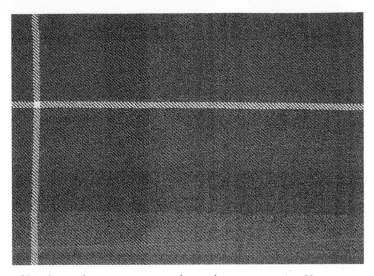

of his day, and as a consequence he made many enemies. He was ultimately prosecuted on a trumped-up charge of financial irregularity, was convicted and was struck off the Navy List. In 1817 he accepted an invitation from Chile to organise and command its navy. He helped to secure independence, not only for Chile but also Peru, Brazil and Greece. In 1832, a more liberal government restored him to all of his previous privileges, and he was promoted to rear admiral. He is buried in Westminster Abbey. The 14th Earl served with the Black Watch from 1938, and during the Second World War he was on the staff in North Africa, Sicily, Italy and Greece. After the war he served in Germany and with the War Office until retiring in 1953.

Colquhoun

CREST
A hart's head couped Gules,
attired Argent

MOTTO
Si je puis (If I can)

PLANT BADGE
Hazel saplings

The lands of the Colquhouns lie on the shores of Loch Lomond. Umphredus de Kilpatrick received from Malduin, Earl of Lennox, estates including Colquhoun during the reign of Alexander II in the early 13th century. The chief's early stronghold was Dunglas Castle, which perched on a rocky promontory above the River Clyde near the royal castle of Dumbarton. Later chiefs of Colquhoun were to be appointed governors and keepers of Dumbarton Castle. The barony of Luss, from which the chiefs now derive their territorial designation, came to the Colquhouns by marriage, when Sir Robert of Colquhoun married the heiress of the Lord of Luss around 1368. Sir John Colquhoun of Luss was appointed governor of Dumbarton Castle during the minority of James II, and was murdered in 1439 during a raid at Inchmurrin. The Colquhouns also controlled the castle of Camstradden, which had been obtained by a younger son of Luss in 1395. The 6th Colquhoun Laird of Camstradden was a renowned knight who fought at the Battle of Pinkie in 1547.

Sir John Colquhoun, the 11th Laird of Luss, was created a Baronet of Nova Scotia in 1625. He was accused in 1632 of absconding with his wife's sister, Lady Catherine Graham, daughter of the Earl of Montrose. It was alleged that he had used witchcraft and sorcery to accomplish his intrigue. He, perhaps wisely, did not return to answer the charges, and as a fugitive he was excommunicated and his estates forfeited. The estates were recovered, after much negotiation, by Sir John's eldest son in 1646. Sir Humphrey Colquhoun, 5th Baronet, represented Dunbartonshire in the last Scottish Parliament

in 1703, and strongly opposed the Treaty of Union. On 30 March 1704, having no male heir, he resigned his baronetcy to the Crown and obtained a new patent, allowing the title to pass on his death to the male issue of his daughter's husband, James Grant of Pluscardine. When Pluscardine's elder brother died, he succeeded to the substantial estates of his father and once more assumed the name of Grant. He was ancestor of the Earls of Seafield and the Barons Strathspey, on whom the baronetcy devolved. Sir James Grant Colquhoun, fourth son of James Grant and Ann Colquhoun, succeeded to the Colquhoun estates, and built the grand mansion of Rossdhu which is still the seat of the chiefs today. He was made a baronet in 1786.

Sir Ian Colquhoun, the 7th Baronet of the new creation, was mentioned in dispatches no less than five times in the First World War and was twice wounded. He was created a Knight of the Thistle and was Lord High Commissioner to the General Assembly of the Church of Scotland. A member of the Royal Commission on Ancient and Historical Monuments in Scotland, he was at the forefront of the movement to preserve Scotland's ancient heritage.

Cranstoun

The lands and barony of Cranstoun in Midlothian may have been derived from the Anglo–Saxon for 'place of the crane', the crest of this noble family. Another suggestion is the 'tun' or 'dwelling place' of Cran or Cren, which both appear as forenames in Saxon chronicles. Early appearances of the name include Elfrick de Cranstoun who was witness to a charter by William the Lion to the abbey of Holyrood; Hugh de Cranstoun appears on the Ragman Rolls of Scottish barons swearing fealty to Edward I of England in 1296; and Thomas de Cranston received a charter to his lands of Cranston from David II.

The Cranstons of that Ilk prospered until the late 16th century, when they became embroiled in the volatile contemporary political situation. Thomas and John Cranston, descendants of the house of Cranston of that Ilk, were among those accused of treason in 1592 for assisting the Earl of Bothwell in his attack on the Palace of Holyrood House. In 1600 Sir John Cranston of that Ilk was indicted for harbouring his kinsmen, forfeited traitor, and only obtained a stay of the proceedings against him on the intervention of the king. Also in 1600, another Thomas Cranston, the brother of Sir John Cranston, was executed at Perth for complicity in the Gowrie Conspiracy to kidnap James VI. Sir John Cranstoun of Morristoun, captain of the guard to James VI, was raised to the peerage with the title of Lord Cranstoun in 1609.

The 3rd Lord Cranston supported the royalist cause in the civil war and fought at the Battle of Worcester in 1651 where he was

taken prisoner. He languished in the Tower of London and his estates were sequestrated, save for a small portion which the Commonwealth allowed to his wife and children for their support. William, 5th Lord Cranstoun, sat in the last independent Scottish Parliament where he was a supporter of the Treaty of Union. James, 8th Lord Cranstoun, was a distinguished officer in the Royal Navy who commanded HMS *Bellerophon* in a squadron of only seven ships which was attacked on 17 June 1795 by a French fleet three times larger. After a running battle which lasted more than 12 hours, the French were completely defeated, and eight ships of the line were destroyed. Lord Cranston was later appointed Governor of Grenada, but before he could set foot upon the island, he died, reputedly of lead poisoning, in 1796. The peerage became extinct in 1813.

Lieutenant Colonel Alastair Cranstoun of that Ilk and Corehouse was recognised as chief in 1950. He was a distinguished soldier, holder of the Military Cross, and for a time, military attaché in Lisbon. He died in 1990 and was succeeded by the present chief who still lives at Corehouse in Lanarkshire.

Crawford

CREST
A stag's head erased Gules,
between the attires a cross
crosslet fitchée Sable

MOTTO
Tutum te robore reddam
(I will give you safety by strength)

The family name of the Crawfords, who are believed to be of Norman origin, is taken from the barony of the same name in Lanarkshire. In 1296, Sir Reginald Crawford was appointed sheriff of Ayr. His sister, Margaret, married Wallace of Elderslie, and was the mother of Sir William Wallace, the great Scottish patriot. The Crawfords rallied to their cousin in his struggle against English domination. The family of the sheriff of Ayr also produced the main branches of this family, who were styled 'of Auchinames' and 'of Craufurdland'. Sir William Crawfurd of Craufurdland was one of the bravest men of his time and was knighted by James I. He fought with the Scots forces in the service of King Charles VII of France and was wounded at the siege of Creyult in Burgundy in 1423. Craufurdland followed James IV to the sorry field of Flodden where he perished in the company of much of the Scottish nobility. The splendid Castle of Craufurdland was much extended by the 16th Laird in the 17th century. John Walkinshaw Craufurd, the 20th Laird, was a distinguished soldier who, after entering the army at an early age, rose to the rank of lieutenant colonel and was present at the victory of Dettingen in 1743, also distinguishing himself at Fontenoy two years later. Despite his faithful service to the house of Hanover, he was an intimate and faithful friend of the Jacobite Earl of Kilmarnock, and he attended his ill-fated friend on the scaffold as a last act of comradeship. He received the earl's severed head and attended to the solemnities of his funeral. This act of Christian charity resulted in his name being placed at the bottom of the Army List,

thus ensuring poor promotion prospects. However, he restored his fortunes and in 1761 he was appointed falconer to the king. Despite his devotion to his friends, he did not seem to share a similar affinity for his family. He died in 1793 and in his will left his entire estates to Sir Thomas Coutts, the eminent banker. The deed was, however, contested by Elizabeth Craufurd, who eventually won her case in the House of Lords in 1806, and the ancient estates passed back to the rightful heir. This branch of the family thereafter united the houses of Houison and Craufurd, and they still live at Craufurdland.

Cumming

CREST
A lion rampant Or, in his
dexter paw a dagger Proper

MOTTO
Courage

The Cumming family is Norman in origin, its name derived from Comines near Lisle in northern France. Robert de Comyn came to England with William the Conqueror in 1066 and was given lands in Northumberland. His grandson, William, came to Scotland in the reign of David I, who bestowed lands upon him in Roxburghshire. He eventually rose to become chancellor of Scotland. William's nephew, Richard, married a granddaughter of Donald Bane, later Donald III, second son of Duncan I. In the early 13th century as a result of good marriages, they were the holders of three earldoms: Monteith, Menteith, and Atholl and Buchan. When Alexander III was killed near Burntisland, two Comyns, both direct descendants of Duncan I, were appointed to the council of six guardians of Scotland. They were Alexander Comyn, Earl of Buchan, and 'Black John' Comyn, Lord of Badenoch. After the death in 1290 of the child queen Margaret, the 'Maid of Norway', and granddaughter of Alexander III, at least six claimants to the throne (including John Balliol, brother-in-law of the Black Comyn, Robert Bruce, grandfather of the future king, and the two Comyn guardians) invited Edward I of England to decide who should succeed to the Scottish throne. He agreed, providing the chosen successor recognised him as overlord of Scotland, a demand which the Scots were not in a position to resist at that time. Edward chose John Balliol, but open conflict soon erupted, with the claimants taking sides and switching allegiances in the struggles to win the throne and break free of English domination.

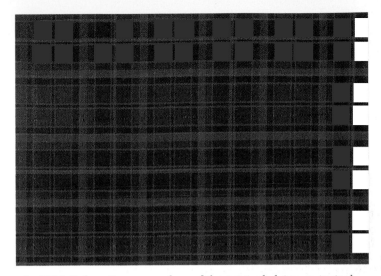

In 1306, Robert Bruce, grandson of the original claimant, invited the Red Comyn to a meeting in the church of the Greyfriars in Dumfries in the hope of negotiating a compromise. However, they soon quarrelled, daggers were drawn and Comyn was stabbed to death in the church, an act for which Bruce was subsequently excommunicated. In the conflict which followed as Bruce sought to establish his position as king, Comyn's son was defeated in a skirmish with Bruce and fled to join the English. He was killed at the Battle of Bannockburn in 1314.

The fall of the Badenoch Comyns removed the family from the centre of Scottish politics, but many branches had been established which continued to thrive. The name generally became spelt 'Cumming', and the Cummings of Altyre were recognised as the chiefly line. Sir Alexander Cumming of Altyre was created a baronet in 1804. Sir William Gordon-Cumming of Altyre, 4th Baronet, served with The Scots Guards in the Zulu War of 1879 and later in the Guards' Camel Regiment. The family acquired the estate of Gordounstoun which is now well known for the famous public school established there.

Cunningham

CREST
A unicorn's head couped Argent
armed Or

MOTTO
Over fork over

This is a territorial name found in Ayrshire. It is likely that it derives from 'cuinneag', meaning 'milk pail' and the Saxon 'ham', meaning 'village'. The first to take the name was Warnebald or perhaps his son, Robertus, who received a grant of the land of Cunningham, sometime between 1160 and 1180. One origin of the name states that Malcolm, son of Friskin, obtained the lands of Cunningham from Malcolm III by sheltering him in a barn and covering him with hay which in turn is said to give rise to the shakefork in the family arms and the motto, 'Over fork over'. This is a charming legend, but one authority states that the arms are in fact an allusion to the office of Master of the King's Stables.

It is certain that the Cunninghams were well settled in their lands and the parish of Kilmaurs by the end of the 13th century. Hervy de Cunningham, son of the Laird of Kilmaurs, fought for Alexander III against the Norse at the Battle of Largs in 1263. The family were supporters of the Bruces in their fight for Scottish independence, although in common with a great many of the Scottish nobility, their name appears on the Ragman Rolls, swearing fealty to Edward I of England in 1296. Sir William Cunningham was created Lord Kilmaurs in 1462 and later Earl of Glencairn. The 5th Earl was a Protestant reformer and a patron of John Knox, although he has been accused of being in the pay of the English, who saw the Reformation as an opportunity to discomfort the Scottish Crown. Whatever the case, Glencairn rose against Mary, Queen of Scots, and was one of the commanders at the Battle of Carbery Hill in 1657.

The 9th Earl was a royalist during the troubled politics of the 17th century and threw in his lot with Charles II in his bid to gain his father's throne. He raised a force in 1653 to oppose General Monck, who was governor of Scotland. In August he went to Lochearn in Perthshire where he met with some chiefs of the Highland clans, and with a body of fighting men, took possession of Elgin in 1654. The rising was a failure, but Glencairn escaped with his life and after the Restoration of Charles II in 1660, he was appointed Lord Chancellor of Scotland. The title is now extinct.

Other prominent Cunninghams include Alexander Cunningham, 18th-century historical writer and British envoy to Venice from 1715 to 1720, Charles Cunningham the artist, and the poet and writer, Alan Cunningham, whose work was widely held to have been surpassed only by that of Robert Burns.

Davidson

CREST
A stag's head erased Proper

MOTTO
Sapienter si sincere
(Wisely if sincerely)

This family had bonded with the Clan Chattan in the early part of the 14th century when Donald, the third son of Robert Comyn and grandson of the Comyn murdered by Robert the Bruce at Dumfries, married Slane Mackintosh, daughter of the 6th Mackintosh Chief. David, Slane's son, and his family and their followers were known as Clan Dhai, as the name of Comyn was prescribed around 1320. At Invernahaven in 1370 the Mackintoshes, along with their Clan Chattan supporters, the Davidsons and the Macphersons, gathered to oppose a strong force of Camerons who had marched into Badenoch intent on slaughter and plunder. A dispute arose between the Davidsons and the Macphersons concerning the right to command and when the Mackintoshes supported the Davidsons' claims the Macphersons, considering themselves insulted, left the field. The Camerons exploited their enemies' confusion, and in the ensuing battle the Davidsons seem virtually to have been destroyed. The Macphersons were goaded into joining the fray, and the Camerons were ultimately put to flight.

It has been said that after the 'Battle' of North Inch in 1396, the family of the chief of the Davidsons moved north and gave rise to the Davidsons of Cantray and Tulloch. There is little doubt that well before the end of the 14th century the name Davidson is recorded in the east and north east coastal towns of Perth, Dundee and Aberdeen. The best recorded is the alderman and customar of Aberdeen (the collector and distributor of the royal dues and taxes in the town), Sir Robert, named variously as Davisoun and David

Filius in civic records of the day. In 1411, he led a contingent from the burgh to fight at the Battle of Harlaw, where he was killed. He was a friend of the Earl of Mar, a son of the Wolf of Badenoch, and some evidence suggests the possibility that Robert could have been a son or grandson of the first Comyn, David. Alexander Davidson, known as Clerk Davidson, was the town clerk and a writer in Fortrose. Alexander had two sons: Henry, 1st Laird of Tulloch, who became a merchant in London and was succeeded by his brother, Duncan, who became a Member of Parliament. He was a great favourite of Queen Victoria, whom he used to visit during her stays at Balmoral and was her Lord Lieutenant of Ross-shire. Tulloch Castle was extensively restored in 1922 by the renowned architect Sir Robert Lorimer, but the castle and estates have since been sold.

The Clan Davidson Association, first formed in 1909, vigorously seeks to unite Davidsons throughout the world. A direct descendant of the Davidsons of Tulloch, now living in New Zealand, is seeking to matriculate arms in the Court of the Lord Lyon and claim the chiefship.

Douglas

CREST
On a chapeau Gules furred Ermine,
a salamander Vert encircled with
flames of fire Proper

MOTTO
Jamais arrière
(Never behind)

The Douglases were one of Scotland's most powerful families and it is therefore remarkable that their origins remain obscure. The first certain record of the name relates to a William de Dufglas who, between 1175 and 1199, witnessed a charter by the Bishop of Glasgow to the monks of Kelso.

William Douglas 'The Hardy' was governor of Berwick in 1296. He was taken prisoner when the town fell to the English in that year and was only released when he agreed to accept the claim of Edward I of England to be overlord of Scotland. He later joined Sir William Wallace in the struggle for Scottish independence but he was again captured and died in England in 1302. His son, 'Good Sir James', patriot and the founder of the Black Douglases, was killed in battle in Spain in 1330, carrying the heart of his life-long friend, Robert the Bruce, to the Holy land.

Marriage to a Stewart princess brought wealth and prestige to his great nephew, the 2nd Earl of Douglas, later to die in his moment of victory at Otterburn in 1388. Sir James' illegitimate son, Archibald 'The Grim', became the 3rd Earl and consolidated the family's position. By the early 15th century, the Douglases had become so powerful that they were seen as a threat to the nation's stability and the Crown felt compelled to take action against them In 1440 the young 6th Earl and his brother were invited by a rival to dine in Edinburgh Castle with the 10-year-old James II whereupon they were seized and subsequently beheaded. The 8th Earl suffered a similar fate at the hands of the king. Consequently, the 9th Earl prudently spent

much of his adult life in England. He had no issue and the line died with him in 1491.

George, 1st Earl of Angus, a great-nephew of Sir James, was the first of the Red Douglases. He too married a Stewart princess and the Red Douglases soon rose to as great a prominence as the family had held hitherto.

William, the 11th Earl of Angus and 1st Marquess of Douglas, was a Catholic and an ardent supporter of Charles I during the civil wars. He was created marquess in 1633 and lived in princely style at Douglas Castle. He joined Montrose after the Battle of Kilsyth in 1645 and was present when Royalist forces were surprised by Covenanter cavalry at Philiphaugh, barely escaping with his life.

William, brother of the 2nd Marquess became, through marriage, Duke of Hamilton in 1660. The titles of Marquess of Douglas, Earl of Angus and several others were ultimately all to devolve on the Dukes of Hamilton and the eldest son and heir of that house is always styled Marquess of Douglas and Clydesdale. Other branches of the family include the Earls of Morton, and the Marquesses of Queensberry, who gave their name to the famous rules of boxing.

Drummond

CREST
On a crest coronet Or, a goshawk,
wings displayed Proper, armed and
belled Or, jessed Gules

MOTTO
Virtutem coronat honos
(Honour crowns virtue)

On Compartment
Gang warily

This name is closely linked to the parish of Drymen which lies to the west of Stirling and appears to have derived its name from the Gaelic, 'dromainn', meaning a 'ridge' or 'high ground'. The traditional legend narrates that the first nobleman to settle at Drymen was Hungarian, having accompanied Edgar the Aetheling and his two sisters to Scotland in 1067 on their flight from William the Conqueror. The first chief appearing in written records was Malcolm Beg, Chamberlain of Lennox, who married Ada, the daughter of the Earl of Lennox and who died some time prior to 1260. The Drummonds firmly supported the cause of Bruce and Scottish Independence, and after the Battle of Bannockburn in 1314, the king bestowed upon them lands in Perthshire. Sir John Drummond rose to great power during the reigns of James III and IV. He was created a peer with the title of Lord Drummond in 1488, a title borne today by the present chiefs. James, the 4th Lord Drummond, was created Earl of Perth in 1605.

The family were staunch supporters of the Stuart kings, both during their quarrels with Parliament and after the exile of James VII in 1688. The 3rd Earl joined the Marquess of Montrose in August 1645 and was taken prisoner at Philiphaugh the following month. James, the 4th Earl, was appointed Lord High Chancellor of Scotland in June 1684. On the accession of James VII in 1685, he openly declared himself a Catholic. He was imprisoned for four years but was released to go into exile. He was summoned to France by his king, who raised him to the rank of Duke of Perth. His brother, the

Earl of Melfort, was with the king during his campaign in Ireland in 1690.

James Drummond, later the 2nd Duke, was one of the first to join in the Jacobite rising of 1715. He was responsible for a daring plan to seize Edinburgh Castle and commanded Jacobite horse at the Battle of Sheriffmuir. He escaped to France and his estates were forfeited. The 3rd Duke joined Bonnie Prince Charlie on his arrival at Perth in September 1745. He followed his prince into England and captured Carlisle. His brother, John, later arrived with troops sent to assist in the rising by the king of France. At the Battle of Culloden, the duke commanded the left flank, and after the defeat of the Jacobite forces he was forced to flee. His escape was a harrowing ordeal and he died on the passage to France in 1746. The estates and titles of the Drummonds were once again declared forfeit.

In 1853 George Drummond, Duc de Melfort, Comte de Lussan and Baron de Valrose in the peerage of France, was restored by Act of Parliament to the title of 'Earl of Perth', together with various subsidiary titles. The 16th Earl of Perth was the first secretary general of the League of Nations.

Dunbar

CREST
A horse's head Argent,
bridled and reined Gules

MOTTO
In promptu
(In readiness)

Gospatrick, Earl of Northumberland, received the lands of Dunbar and other parts of Lothian from Malcolm III. His son witnessed the foundation of the great Abbey of Holyrood House in 1128, and was accorded the rank of earl. Patrick 'Black Beard', Earl of Dunbar, was one of the competitors for the crown of Scotland at Berwick in 1291. The 9th Earl, another Patrick, sheltered Edward II of England at Dunbar after his flight from the field of Bannockburn in 1314.

The 10th Earl was one of the most powerful nobles in 14th century Scotland, with vast estates. In 1388 he accompanied the Earl of Douglas into England and fought at the Battle of Otterburn. He had arranged a marriage for his daughter with the Duke of Rothesay, son of Robert III, but through the influence of the Douglases the marriage did not take place. The earl was incensed by this slight to his family pride, and retired to his estates in England. He was eventually reconciled with the Douglases and returned to Scotland in 1409. George, the 11th Earl, succeeded to his father's title and vast estates in 1420, and was prominent in public affairs. His wealth, however, was to be his undoing: James I coveted the Dunbar estates and imprisoned the earl on trumped-up charges of treason, so the earldom and the estates were forfeited to the Crown. The last earl died in England in 1455.

The family had established a number of branches, including the Dunbars of Mochrum (to which house the present chief belongs), of Northfield, Hempriggs, Durn, and Both. It is a tribute to the distinction of this name that each of these five branches achieved the rank

of baronet. Gavin Dunbar, Archbishop of Glasgow and Lord High Chancellor of Scotland in the reign of James V, was a younger son of Sir John Dunbar of Mochrum. He distinguished himself at the University of Glasgow and in 1514 became Dean of Moray. In 1524 he was appointed Archbishop of Glasgow. He weathered the first storms of the Reformation and although deemed a good and learned man, was criticised for his participation in the persecution of Protestants instigated by Cardinal Beaton.

Sir James Dunbar of Mochrum was created a Baronet of Nova Scotia in March 1694 with a special royal honour of a grant of sup porters 'Imperially Crowned'. The 2nd Baronet served in the Duke of Marlborough's cavalry with great distinction and was recognised as chief on the death of Ludovic Dunbar in 1744. Sir William Dunbar, 9th Baronet, was Registrar General from 1902 to 1909.

The Baronets of Mochrum, chiefs of the Dunbars, now live in America.

Dundas

CREST
A lion's head affrontée looking
through a bush of oak Proper

MOTTO
Essayez
(Try)

The first reliable record of the family is found in the reign of
William the Lion in the late 12th century when Serle de Dundas
appears in deeds of that period. Sir Archibald Dundas was a
favourite of James III and was employed by him several times on
important missions to England. The king intended to bestow high
rank upon his ambassador, but died before he could do so. James IV
did, however, bestow lands upon the Dundas family, including the
island of Inchgarvie with the right to build a castle there.

George Dundas, the 18th Laird, was a staunch presbyterian who
fought in the wars of the Covenant. He was a member of the committee for the trial of the great Marquess of Montrose and was subsequently given command of Linlithgowshire and charged with its
defence against the forces of Oliver Cromwell. George Dundas, 23rd
Laird, was a captain in the East India Company and died in a shipwreck off the coast of Madagascar in 1792.

The principal branches of the family were Dundas of Blair Castle,
Arniston, Duddingston, and Fingask. William Dundas of Kincavel,
ancestor of the Dundases of Blair, was a Jacobite who was imprisoned for his part in the rising of 1715. Sir James Dundas, 1st of
Arniston, was governor of Berwick in the reign of James VI. His
eldest son, Sir James Dundas, was knighted by Charles I in
November 1641. He sat as member of the Scottish parliament representing Mid-Lothian, but violently disapproved of his king's interfer-
ence with the Church of Scotland. When the monarchy was restored
in 1660, he was offered a seat on the supreme court bench, in spite

of not being a professional lawyer, and he eventually accepted the post, taking his place with the title of Lord Arniston in May 1662. His eldest son, Robert Dundas of Arniston, was made a judge in 1689, 10 years after his father's death.

Henry Dundas, 1st Viscount Melville, was a distinguished politician. In 1775 he was appointed Lord Advocate and thereafter Treasurer of the Navy. In 1791 he became Secretary of State for the Home Department and in 1802 was raised to the peerage as Viscount Melville and Baron Dunira. His splendid town mansion in St Andrew Square in Edinburgh is now the headquarters of the Royal Bank of Scotland. He died in 1811, and his statue stands on a lofty column beside his former Edinburgh residence.

Sir David Dundas was born in Edinburgh in 1735. He was a distinguished soldier, rising ultimately to be commander-in-chief of the British army in 1809. Other branches of the family were also ennobled, including Sir Thomas Dundas of Kerse, who was created Lord Dundas of Skea in 1794, and whose descendants became first Earls, and then Marquesses of Zetland. The 2nd Marquess was Secretary of State for India from 1935 to 1937.

Eliott

CREST
A hand couped at the wrist
in armour holding a cutlass
in bend Proper

MOTTO
Fortiter et recte
(Boldly and rightly)

PLANT BADGE
White hawthorn

According to family tradition, the Ellots (as the name was then spelt) came from Angus at the foot of Glenshie, and moved to Teviotdale at the time of Robert the Bruce. It is true that to move from the north to the Borders, as suggested by the Eliott tradition, would be considered as exceptional. However, in 1320 William de Soulis, one of the most powerful nobles in Scotland, whose family had for nearly two hundred years held the Lordship of Liddesdale, was convicted of treason against Robert the Bruce and imprisoned for life. All his lands were forfeited. On the occasion of so sudden and dramatic change in the lordship, it would scarcely be remarkable for Bruce to ensure his hold on the strategically important frontier region by encouraging the settlement of a loyal and tested clan – such as the Ellots – in the district.

It is known from a Berwickshire pedigree that Ellot of Redheugh was living in the early 1400s. John Elwalde from Teviotdale is recorded in 1426. Robert Ellot of Redheugh appears as the 10th chief in 1476. Robert, 13th chief, was killed along with James IV and many of the Scottish nobility at Flodden in 1513.

The Union of the Crowns in 1603 marked the beginning of the end for the border reivers. There were many summary executions and, around this period, many Borderers accepted the offer of a new life in Ulster; this period has become known as 'the Plantation', when much of the province was colonised.

Sir Gilbert Eliott of Stobs became chief in 1673. He had been created a Baronet of Nova Scotia by Charles II in 1666 and the 3rd

Baronet remodelled the old Tower of Stobs into a mansion house around 1764, although it was subsequently rebuilt after a fire. His second son, Augustus, was a distinguished soldier who was rewarded for his spirited defence of Gibraltar in 1782 with a peerage. He was created Lord Heathfield, but this title became extinct within one generation.

Another branch of the chiefly family acquired the lands of Minto in 1703. Sir Gilbert Eliott of Minto was a diplomat who served first in Corsica, then in Vienna, before finally becoming Governor General of Bengal. He returned from India in 1813 to be created Earl of Minto and Viscount Melgund. Stobs passed from family hands at the turn of this century.

For a time the chiefs resided in America, but in 1932 the 10th Baronet reclaimed the ancient holding of Redheugh where he died in 1958. The baronetcy has, at least for the time being, passed from the chiefly house; on the death of Sir Arthur, the 11th Baronet, his daughter became chief and the baronetcy passed to a male kinsman.

Erskine

CRESTS
On a chapeau Gules furred Ermine,
a hand holding up a skene in pale
Argent, hilted and pommelled Or

MOTTO
Je pense plus
(I think more)

*T*his name was originally derived from the lands of Erskine on the south of the Clyde in Renfrew. The name itself may mean 'green rising ground'. Henry de Erskine held a barony as early as the reign of Alexander II. Sir John de Erskine had a son and three daughters, the eldest of whom married Thomas Bruce, brother of Robert I. A second daughter, Alice, married Walter, the High Steward of Scotland.

The Erskines were staunch in their support of the Bruce family and Sir Robert de Erskine became an illustrious and renowned figure in his time. David II appointed him constable and keeper of the strategic royal castle of Stirling. (The chiefs still hold this royal office.) In the mid 15th century the family claimed one of the great Celtic titles when Alexander, Earl of Mar, died in 1435. Sir Robert Erskine, who had been created Lord Erskine, now claimed the ancient earldom by right of his descent from Isabella, Countess of Mar. The king refused, insisting that the earldom now belonged to the Crown because the last male holder had been a Stewart. Despite this dispute with the king, the Erskines became guardians to young James IV and to five successive generations of royalty.

Alexander, 3rd Lord Erskine, constructed a massive tower in 1497 at Alloa, which was to be the seat of the chiefs for the next 300 years. The ill-fated Mary, Queen of Scots came to the Erskines when she was still a baby, and spent the first five years of her life around Alloa and Stirling Castle. She bestowed upon Lord Erskine a new title of Earl of Mar, although without the former precedence.

The ability to shift political allegiance according to the pragmatic

needs of survival or advancement was a skill not unknown to the Scottish nobility, and the 6th Earl of Mar, born in 1675, had the aptitude to such an extent that he has passed into history as 'Bobbing John'. Initially, he seemed reconciled to the Hanoverian succession, but when he attended court in London in 1714 he was not offered the post of Secretary of State for Scotland, and considered this to be a direct insult. He promptly returned to his ancestral lands and, raising the standard of the 'Old Pretender', James VIII, called out his own clansmen and all supporters of Stuarts. With an army of over 10,000 clansmen, the earl met an indifferent royal force under the Duke of Argyll at Sheriffmuir in November 1715. The battle was inconclusive and, although Mar's forces were probably victorious, they could not inflict any severe damage upon Argyll, who then claimed victory for himself. The rising was a failure and Mar fled to France, whereupon his title and lands were forfeited.

In 1824 the Erskine titles were restored and the earldom of Kellie, which had been bestowed in 1619 on a younger son of the chiefly line, passed to the chiefs in 1835, who are now the Earls of Mar and Kellie.

Farquharson

CREST
On a chapeau Gules furred Ermine,
a demi-lion Gules holding in
his dexter paw a sword Proper

MOTTO
Fide et fortitudine
(By fidelity and fortitude)

Farquharsons trace their origin back to Farquhar, fourth son of Alexander Cier (Shaw) of Rothiemurcus, who possessed the Braes of Mar near the source of the river Dee in Aberdeenshire. His descendants were called Farquharsons, and his son, Donald, married Isobel Stewart, heiress of Invercauld. Donald's son, Finla Mor, was the real progenitor of the clan. The Gaelic patronymic is MacFionlaigh Mor. He was royal standard bearer at the Battle of Pinkie, where he was killed in 1547. From his lifetime onwards the clan grew in stature, important branches being founded through the nine sons of his two marriages, in particular those of Craigniety, Monaltrie, Whitehouse, Finzean, Allanquoich, Inverey, Tullochcoy, Broughdearg, and Achriachan. The Farquharsons were not as numerous as some of their predatory neighbours, but formed part of the confederation known as Clan Chattan.

The clan's fierce reputation led to their being known as the fighting Farquharsons, and they were staunch supporters of the Stuarts. Donald Farquharson of Monaltrie fought with Montrose in 1644, and the family later supported Charles II. John Farquharson of Inverey, known as the Black Colonel, declared for James VII and followed Graham of Claverhouse, the famous 'Bonnie Dundee', in 1689. He burned Braemar Castle and was a thorn in the flesh of the government until his death in 1698. In the Jacobite rising of 1715, John Farquharson of Invercauld joined the Clan Chattan regiment of which he was colonel; he was taken prisoner at Preston, later being transferred to London and held in Marshalsea Prison for 10 months.

Undaunted, the Farquharsons supported Bonnie Prince Charlie and at Culloden in 1746 were led by Francis Farquharson of Monaltrie, the chief's nephew. He was taken prisoner and condemned to be executed at the Tower of London, only being reprieved along with two other Highland officers on the very morning of their execution. The chief died in 1750 and was succeeded by his son, James, who died in 1805. From his marriage to Amelia, daughter of Lord George Murray, the renowned Jacobite general, 11 children were born but sadly all but his youngest daughter, Catherine, predeceased him. In 1815 she was recognised by Lyon Court as chief of the name of Farquharson. She was succeeded by her son, James. On the death in 1936 of James's descendant, Alexander Haldane Farquharson of Invercauld, the arms were confirmed to his daughter, Myrtle Farquharson of Invercauld, but she was killed in an air raid in 1941. The succession then passed to her nephew, Captain Alwyne Compton Farquharson of Invercauld.

Fergusson

CREST
Upon a chapeau Gules furred
Ermine, a bee on a thistle Proper

MOTTO
Dulcius ex asperis
(Sweeter after difficulties)

PLANT BADGE
Poplar seedlings

The Gaelic patronymic, 'MacFhaerghuis', is translated alternatively as 'son of the angry' or 'son of the bold and proud'. Although tradition seeks to attribute a common ancestry to the various distinct families bearing this name, there is no real evidence to support this. The Argyllshire Fergussons claim descent from Fergus Mor mac Erc, a very early king of the Scots of Dalriada. There is evidence linking the Fergussons living in Ayrshire and Dumfries with Fergus, Prince of Galloway, an important figure in the reigns of David I and Malcolm IV. He restored the church at Whithorn, founded the abbey of Dundrennan and died at the Abbey of Holyrood in 1161.

The Fergussons held the lands of Kilkerran, probably from the 12th century, but the first certain record is John Fergusson of Kilkerran in 1464. He may have been descended from John, son of Fergus, one of the witnesses to a charter of Edward Bruce signed at Turnberry shortly after the Battle of Bannockburn in 1314. By 1600 there were Fergussons scattered over much of the southern part of Carrick, all of whom acknowledged Kilkerran as their chief.

The Ayrshire Fergussons adopted the Protestant faith during the Reformation. Sir John Fergusson of Kilkerran fought for the royalist cause in the civil war. His grandson was created a Baronet of Nova Scotia in 1703. General Sir Charles Fergusson of Kilkerran, 7th Baronet, served in the army for almost forty years. His early career took him in 1895 to Egypt and later to the Sudan. In 1914 he was the youngest major general on the Army List. He served throughout the First World War and was later a military governor of occupied

German territory. From 1924 to 1930 he was Governor General of New Zealand.

The Fergussons of Dunfallandy in Atholl may well have a quite separate descent, but their heraldry proclaims them as cadets of the principal house of which Kilkerran is the recognised head. They were ardent Jacobites who came out in both 1715 and 1745. Dunfallandy himself was captured after Culloden and was fortunate to escape execution at Carlisle in 1746. General Archibald Fergusson of Dunfallandy served in India under the East India Company for many years. He was wounded at the Battle of Seringapatam in 1799. In 1812 he rebuilt Dunfallandy House, where his descendants lived until very recently.

The Fergussons were not, however, without culture, and Robert Fergusson, who died in 1774, was the poet most admired by Robert Burns, who venerated his work and took it as his model.

Forbes

CREST
A stag's head attired with
ten tines Proper

MOTTO
Grace me guide

In that part of north-east Scotland which spreads itself from the mountain ranges of Aberdeenshire to the coast of Banff and Buchan, lie the lands of the Clan Forbes. Overlooking the Don today stands Castle Forbes, built in 1815 by James Ochoncar, 17th Lord Forbes, and still occupied by the direct descendants of Duncan Forbes upon whom the original lands were conferred in a charter dated 1271 by Alexander III.

The Forbes family grew in power in Aberdeenshire throughout the 14th century. Sir John Forbes of the Black Lip had four sons: William became the progenitor of the Pitsligo line; John was ancestor of the Forbes of Polquhoun; Alistair of Brux founded the lines of Skellater and Inverernan; while Alexander, his eldest son, fought in the victory at Harlaw in 1411 alongside the Earl of Mar against the invading hordes led by Donald of the Isles, and was elevated to the peerage some time between 1443 and July 1445, when he took his seat in Parliament. Since then the title has been handed down through successive generations, and on the union roll of 1701, Forbes was the premier lordship of Scotland, a precedence held to this day.

James, son of the 1st Lord Forbes, himself had three sons: William, the 3rd Lord Forbes; Duncan, who founded the family of Forbes of Corsindae and Monymusk; and Patrick of Corse, squire to James III, whose line later became Baronets of Craigievar.

In 1582, James VI confirmed his 'trusty and well beloved cousin', Lord Forbes, in the 'lands which have been in continuous possession

of his family in times past the memory of man'. However, constant feuds with the powerful Gordons had drawn the Forbeses deep into debt, making it necessary in later years for them to sell much of their land.

Through all these 'local' troubles, and indeed into this present century, members of the family have achieved great distinction in the service of their country. James Ochoncar, the 17th Lord Forbes, was an officer in the Coldstream Regiment of Footguards for 26 years, rising to the rank of general, having served as second-in-command of the British forces in Sicily in 1808 before commanding the Cork and Eastern districts in Ireland. It was during his time in Ireland that a castle was built near Alford on the site of the old family home of Putachie. Nigel, 22nd Lord Forbes, was Minister of State for Scotland in the Conservative government of Harold Macmillan in 1958–59.

Forsyth

CREST
A griffin segreant Azure, armed and
membered Sable, crowned Or

MOTTO
Instaurator ruinae
(A repairer of ruin)

PLANT BADGE
Forsythia flower

As with so many families whose history stretches back before the 12th century, the derivation of this family's surname is uncertain. If the name is Celtic in its origin, it may derive from the Gaelic personal name 'Fearsithe', meaning 'man of peace'. It may, however, allude to a place of peace, and refer to a particular place, or lands. One tradition provides a Norman descent from Forsach, one of the Norsemen who settled on lands on the River Dordogne in Aquitaine. The Viscomte de Fronsoc accompanied Eleanor de Provence to London to marry Henry III and lived at the English court from 1236 to 1246. It is believed that his family obtained lands in Northumberland, and thence to the Borders of Scotland.

Osbert, son of Robert de Forsyth, received a grant of lands at Sauchie in Stirlingshire from Robert the Bruce sometime after March 1306. He distinguished himself at the Battle of Bannockburn in 1314 and received confirmation under the Great Seal of the realm of his lands in 1320.

David Forsyth of Dykes in Lanarkshire acquired his lands some time prior to 1488. His seal bore heraldry similar to the arms of de Fronsoc, and he specifically claimed them as his ancestors.

William Forsyth, baillie of Edinburgh around 1365 had, with other issue, a son, William, who, in 1423, moved to St Andrews and subsequently acquired the barony of Nydie. Alexander, 4th Baron of Nydie, was Sheriff Depute of Fife, and the arms assigned to him are recorded in Balfour's Manuscript. Alexander died at Flodden in 1513. His grandson, James, married a substantial heiress, Elizabeth

Leslie, granddaughter of the Earl of Rothes and great-granddaughter of James III. The Forsyths of Nydie acquired lands around the royal Palace of Falkland, and in 1538 John Forsyth was appointed King's Macer and thereafter Falkland Pursuivant. It is from the Falkland Forsyth lairds that the present chiefly line descends.

The Reverend Alexander John Forsyth was a pioneer in the development of modern firearms and his work led to the invention of the percussion lock, which replaced the flint lock in the 18th century. William Forsyth, born at Old Meldrum in 1737, was a distinguished horticulturalist. In 1784, he was appointed Chief Superintendent of the Royal Gardens at Kensington and St James' Palace. In 1802 he published *A Treatise on the Culture and Management of Fruit Trees* which proved so popular that the first three editions were sold out. In honour of his name, there is now a genus of plants termed 'forsythia'.

Fraser

CRESTS
On a mount a flourish of
strawberries leaved and
fructed Proper

MOTTO
All my hope is in God

BADGE
A fraise Argent

The Frasers probably came originally from Anjou in France, and first appeared in Scotland around 1160, when Simon Fraser held lands at Keith in East Lothian. About five generations later Sir Simon Fraser was captured fighting for Robert the Bruce, and executed with great cruelty by Edward I in 1306. His cousin, Sir Alexander Fraser of Cowie, Bruce's chamberlain, was the elder brother of another Sir Simon Fraser, from whom the Frasers of Lovat descend. Simon's grandson, Sir Alexander Fraser of Cowie and Durris, acquired the castle now called Cairnbulg and the lands of Philorth by marriage with Joanna, younger daughter and co-heiress of the Earl of Ross in 1375. In 1592, Sir Alexander Fraser of Philorth received from James VI charters creating the fishing village of Faithlie, which he had transformed into a fine town, and a free port, called Fraserburgh.

The 9th Laird married the heiress of the Abernethy Lords Saltoun, and their son became the 10th Lord Saltoun. Saltoun was severely wounded at the Battle of Worcester in 1651, fighting for Charles II during the civil wars. Unlike their kinsmen, the Frasers of Lovat, the chiefs took no part in the Jacobite Risings. The Lovat branch were created 'Lords Lovat' around 1456 and established their influence around Beauly. Simon, 10th Lord Lovat, mustered his men for Prince Charles Edward Stuart in 1745 and they fought at Culloden. Lovat was captured and was beheaded on Tower Hill on 9 April 1747. In 1899, the 14th Lord Lovat raised the Lovat Scouts who fought in the Boer Wars and in the First and Second World Wars.

The 16th Lord Saltoun commanded the Light Companies of the First Guards in the orchard at Hougoumont on the morning of the Battle of Waterloo in 1815. It was he who, later in the day, first noticed the Imperial Guard emerge from the hollow where they had been hiding all day, and drew the Duke of Wellington's attention to them.

The 19th Lord Saltoun was a prisoner of war in Germany for most of the First World War. He subsequently became a member of the House of Lords from 1936 and devoted himself to numerous public works, and latterly to promoting the Royal National Lifeboat Institution (RNLI). He died in 1979 at the age of 93, when he was succeeded by his daughter, Flora Fraser, who became The Lady Saltoun in her own right. Lady Saltoun married Captain Alexander Ramsay of Mar, cousin of the Earl of Dalhousie and great grandson of Queen Victoria through his mother, HRH Princess Patricia of Connaught.

Gordon

CREST
Issuant from a crest coronet Or
a stag's head (affrontée) Proper
attired with ten tines Or

MOTTO
Bydand (Remaining)

PLANT BADGE
Rock ivy

The Gordons are one of the great families of the north-east of Scotland, and their surname has many suggested meanings. However, the family originally were almost certainly of Anglo–Norman descent. The first certain record of the name places the family in the Borders during the reigns of Malcolm IV and William the Lion in the second half of the 12th century. Richard de Gordon appears in numerous charters, and probably died around 1200. Sir Adam de Gordon became a staunch supporter of Robert the Bruce, and was one of the ambassadors sent to Rome to petition the pope to remove the excommunication which had been placed on Bruce after his murder of John Comyn in 1306.

In 1436 Sir Alexander Gordon was created Lord Gordon, and his son was raised to the title of Earl of Huntly. The family became embroiled in the deadly battle for power between the king and the Douglases during the 15th century. Huntly was for the king, but when he moved his forces south, the Earl of Moray, kinsman and ally of the Douglases, devastated the Gordon lands and burned Huntly Castle. The Gordons were recalled and soon defeated their enemies. A grand new castle at Huntly rose from the ruins of the old, and it soon rivalled any of the great houses of the realm.

George, 4th Earl of Huntly, became Chancellor of Scotland in 1547 and was a close confidant of the regent, Mary of Guise, the mother of Mary, Queen of Scots. The Gordons paid scant attention to the Reformation, remaining firmly Catholic. In 1599 the chief was created Marquess of Huntly. The 2nd Marquess was a fierce supporter of

the royalist cause in the civil war, but Huntly's pride was such that he found it impossible to co-operate with Montrose. Huntly was captured in Strathdon in December 1647 and was taken to Edinburgh, where in March 1649, he was beheaded. Lord Louis Gordon was restored to the family estates and titles in 1651, and was raised to the highest rank of the peerage as Duke of Gordon in 1684.

The Gordons fought on both sides during the Jacobite risings of 1715 and 1745. The 2nd Duke of Gordon followed the standard of the 'Old Pretender' at the Battle of Sheriffmuir in 1715. He later surrendered, but although he was imprisoned for a short period, no further proceedings were taken against him. The 3rd Duke remained loyal to the Hanoverians when Prince Charles Edward Stuart reasserted his father's claim in 1745, but his brother, Lord Louis Gordon, promptly raised a regiment of two battalions to fight for the Stuarts. After Culloden he escaped to France, where he died in 1754. George, 5th Duke of Gordon, was a general in the army and for a time governor of Edinburgh Castle. He died without issue, and the dukedom became extinct. The marquessate passed to a kinsman, from whom the present chief descends.

Graham

CREST
A falcon Proper, beaked and armed
Or, killing a stork Argent,
armed Gules

MOTTO
Ne oublie (Do not forget)

PLANT BADGE
Spurge laurel

The likely origin of this family is Anglo–Norman; when David I came to Scotland to claim his throne, the Grahams were probably among the knights who accompanied him. The family's acceptance in Celtic Scotland was assured when they married into the princely family of Strathearn, and from Malise of Strathearn they acquired the lands around Auchterarder which were to become their principal seat. Sir John de Graham was a companion-in-arms of Sir William Wallace, the great patriot. He fell at the Battle of Falkirk in 1298, and his gravestone and effigy can still be found in Falkirk Old Parish Church.

Patrick Graham of Kincardine was created a peer in 1451 with the title of Lord Graham. Two generations later they were created Earls of Montrose and in 1504 their hereditary lands of 'Auld Montross' were erected into a free barony and earldom of Montrose. The 1st Earl fell at the fateful field of Flodden in 1513.

James Graham, 5th Earl and 1st Marquess of Montrose, is perhaps the most glamorous figure in Scottish history. Although a signatory to the Covenant, Montrose refused to take up arms against his king during the civil wars, and was subsequently created captain general in Scotland. The Grahams rallied to their chief, and they were joined by a large force of Highlanders led by Alasdair Macdonald, 'Colkitto'. The campaign of 1644–45 is one of the most remarkable in Scottish military history. While the dominant force in Scotland, Montrose was surprised at Philiphaugh in the Borders by a substantial force of Covenant cavalry in September 1645. The royalist force was crushed

and although the captain general escaped, the king's cause in Scotland was fatally wounded.

Montrose thereafter travelled extensively on the Continent and was honoured at several royal courts. However, he believed that his duty and loyalty lay with his king and he was given commission by the newly proclaimed Charles II to recover Scotland. Montrose landed in Orkney in March 1650, but at Invercharron in Ross-shire, the tiny royal army was totally defeated and Montrose forced to flee. He was betrayed, captured and was executed in May 1650 in Edinburgh. After the Restoration, the Stuarts repaid their debt to the Grahams in some small measure by according the captain general's remains one of the grandest state funerals ever held in Scotland. In 1707, the 4th Marquess was created Duke of Montrose.

The 3rd Duke of Montrose was largely responsible for the Act of Parliament which in 1782 repealed the prohibition on the wearing of Highland dress which had been enforced after Culloden.

Grant

CREST
A burning hill Proper

MOTTO
Craig Elachie (The rock of alarm)

On Compartment
Stand Fast

PLANT BADGE
Seedling Scots pines fructed Proper

Some Grants claim the clan is part of the Siol Alpin, the Highland clans whose chiefs are said to descend from King Alpin, father of Kenneth Macalpin, king of the Scots. A Norman descent may also be asserted for the name, derived from the Norman French 'le grand' meaning 'great' or 'large'. The Grants first appear on record in the middle of the 13th century when they acquired lands in Stratherrick through the marriage of one of the family with Mary, daughter of Sir John Bisset. From this union there came at least two sons, one of whom, Sir Laurence le Grand, became sheriff of Inverness.

The Grants supported Bruce in the competition for the Scottish crown. John and Randolph de Grant were taken prisoner at the Battle of Dunbar in 1296. Bruce's victory confirmed the Grants in their holdings in Strathspey, and whatever their origins, they were now firmly established as Highland chiefs. In 1493 the lands were erected into the free barony of Freuchie, where in 1536 Sir James Grant built a castle, called at one time Castle Freuchie, but renamed at the end of the 17th century as Castle Grant.

When the Reformation came to Scotland, the Grants soon became staunch adherents of the new doctrine, and they declared for the National Covenant in 1638. After the Battle of Inverlochy in 1645 they joined the Marquess of Montrose, and thereafter remained faithful to the royal cause. After the Restoration of Charles II in 1660, the Laird of Grant was to have been rewarded with an earldom, but he died before the patent had been sealed. The Grants endeavoured to secure their territories by alliances with other clans,

and they were particularly associated with the Macgregors.

Ludovick Grant, the 8th Laird of Freuchie, was so rich and power-ful that he was popularly called 'the Highland king'. He abandoned his family's past loyalties, and supported the government of Mary and William. Although some individual members of the family were Jacobites, Clan Grant generally supported the house of Hanover dur-ing the risings of 1715 and 1745, so saving them from the relentless persecution inflicted on other Highland clans.

In 1811, Sir Lewis Grant of Grant inherited the Ogilvie earldoms of Seafield and Findlater, and the chiefs gained a seat in the House of Lords. But the 5th Earl of Seafield and 27th chief of Clan Grant fell into a serious dispute with his brothers, which resulted in the Grant estates being disentailed. The consequence of this was that when the Seafield earldom, which can descend in the female line, parted com-pany with the chiefs of Clan Grant, the lands were lost. The chiefs, however, retained the independent peerage which had been created in 1817 under the title of Baron Strathspey of Strathspey.

Castle Grant has fallen into neglect, but it is hoped a restoration scheme will save it from total ruin.

Gunn

CREST
A dexter hand weilding a sword
in bend Proper

MOTTO
Aut pax aut bellum
(Either peace or war)

This clan is of Norse origin. The Norse chieftan, Gunni, came to Caithness at the end of the 12th century when his wife, Ragnhild, inherited estates there from her brother, Harald, Jarl of Orkney. His wife was descended from St Ragnvald, founder of the great cathedral of St Magnus at Kirkwall. The first chief of Clan Gunn to appear definitively in records was George Gunn, who was crouner, or coroner, of Caithness in the 15th century. The proper Celtic patronymic of the Gunn chiefs was 'MacSheumais Chataich', but George was more widely known as 'Am Braisdeach Mor', the 'great brooch-wearer', so called for the insignia worn by him as coroner.

The Gunns' traditional enemies were the Keiths who, from their castle at Ackergill, challenged the Gunn chiefs for the political hegemony of the region. The Gunns repeatedly raided Keith territory but they suffered defeat in 1438 at the Battle of Tannach Moor and again in 1464 at Dirlot in Strathmore. Having suffered considerable loss of life, both families agreed to meet to settle their differences in what was intended to be a battle of champions. Each side were to bring 12 horse, but the devious Keiths arrived with two warriors on each horse and, outnumbering the Gunns, crushed them. The chief and four of his sons were killed and the great coroner's brooch stolen.

The Earls of Caithness and Sutherland entered into a pact to destroy Clan Gunn, probably sealed at Girnigoe Castle around 1586. There were a number of indecisive encounters and heavy casualties were inflicted on both sides. The Gunns strengthened their connection with the Mackays when Gunn of Killearnan married Mary, sister

of Lord Reay, the Mackay chief, and the next Gunn chief thereafter married Lord Reay's daughter. The Gunns of Braemore were the descendants of Robert, a younger son of 'Am Braisdeach Mor', and were generally known as the Robson Gunns. Although he was a Catholic, Sir William Gunn, brother of the Robson chieftain, served in the army of the Protestant king of Sweden. He fought for Charles I, who conferred a knighthood on him in 1639, but subsequently returned to the Continent, entering the service of the Holy Roman Empire. He married a German baroness, became an imperial general and was created a baron of the Holy Roman Empire in 1649.

The Gunns did not rally to the standard of the exiled Stuarts, and in the Jacobite rising of 1745 they fought on the government side. The 8th chief served as a regular Highland officer and was killed in action in India. The chiefship passed to a cousin in whose line it remained until the 19th century, when the 10th MacSheumais Chataich died without an heir. The clan is presently led by a commander, appointed under a commission from the Lord Lyon, King of Arms, although petitions have been presented to the Lord Lyon seeking to establish representation to the bloodline chiefs.

Haig

CREST
A rock Proper

MOTTO
Tyde what may

For 800 years Bemersyde has been continuously in the possession of the Haigs. Petrus de Haga, founder of the family, was witness to a charter of Richard de Morville, Constable of Scotland from 1162 to 1188, to the Monastery of Dryburgh. de Haga was one of the noblemen charged by Alexander II with the apprehension of John de Bisset for the murder of the Earl of Atholl at Haddington in 1242. The Haigs were staunch supporters of Scottish independence. They fought with Wallace at Stirling in 1297 and the 6th Laird followed the banner of Robert the Bruce to the Battle of Bannockburn, although he was only 17 years of age; he was subsequently killed at the Battle of Halidon Hill in 1333. Gilbert Haig was one of the commanders of the Scots host who defeated the Earl of Northumberland at Sark in 1449. His son, James, was an adherent of James III and when that monarch's reign came abruptly to an end with his murder in 1488, Haig was forced into hiding until he could make peace with the young James IV.

William Haig of Bemersyde fell at Flodden in 1513. Robert, 14th Laird, avenged his father's death when, at Ancrum Moor in 1544, he captured Lord Evers, the English commander, and carried him in a wounded condition to Bemersyde where he died a few days later. Haig buried him in Melrose Abbey.

In the 17th century, William Haig, the 19th Laird, held the office of king's solicitor for Scotland during the reigns of James VI and Charles I while Anthony, the 21st Laird was persecuted for his Quaker beliefs. Four sons of the chief were killed fighting in the service of the king of Bohemia between 1629 and 1630.

In the 19th century, the future of the Haigs lay in the hands of three unmarried daughters, Barbara, Mary and Sophia. Before their deaths, they executed a deed transferring the succession to their cousin, Colonel Arthur Balfour Haig, who was descended from the second son of the 17th Laird of Bemersyde. He accordingly became 28th Laird and chief.

The 1st Earl Haig was commander-in-chief of the British Expeditionary Forces in France from 1915 to 1919. On leaving Oxford University, George Haig entered the 7th Hussars in 1885. He served in the Nile expedition of 1898 and fought at the Battle of Khartoum. During the First World War, Haig was responsible for the policy of attrition employed by the British forces on the Western Front, a policy which made little real strategic impact until 1917 and has been the subject of great controversy ever since. He successfully halted the German offensive by July 1918 and launched the Allied counter attack which ended the war four months later. He was created Earl Haig, Viscount Dawick and Baron Haig of Bemersyde in September 1919.

Hamilton

CREST
In a ducal coronet an oak tree
fructed and penetrated transversely
in the main stem by a frame saw
Proper, the frame Or

MOTTO
Through

It is believed that this family descends from a Norman, Walter Fitz Gilbert of Hambledon, who appears in a charter to the monastery of Paisley around 1294. His lands appear to have been in Renfrewshire, but for his belated support of Robert the Bruce, the king rewarded him with lands in Lanarkshire and the Lothians. These included the lands of Cadzow, later to become the town of Hamilton.

James, 1st Lord Hamilton, married Princess Mary, daughter of James III, in 1474. Princess Mary's son was created Earl of Arran. The 2nd Earl of Arran was the heir to the throne of both James IV and Mary, Queen of Scots. He was appointed Regent of Scotland while the queen was still a child, and to secure his claim to the throne he proposed to marry his son to her. In the end, the match did not take place, and Mary married the heir to the French throne. When Mary's marriage to the Dauphin ended with his death, the Hamilton hopes of a royal match were again rekindled. However, Arran was sent into exile for five years in 1561 when he openly opposed Mary's marriage to Lord Darnley. However, on his return, he endeavoured to save the ill-fated queen, who stayed at Cadzow after her escape from Loch Leven in 1568.

The 4th Earl of Arran became chancellor of Scotland and keeper of both the strategic castles of Edinburgh and Stirling. In 1599 he was advanced to the rank of Marquess. His brother, Claud, was created Lord Paisley in 1587, and later Lord Abercorn. This branch of the family also prospered, Abercorn being translated into an earldom and ultimately a dukedom in 1868.

120

The 3rd Marquess was a staunch supporter of Charles I, who rewarded him in 1643 with a Scottish dukedom, making Hamilton the premier peer of Scotland. Captured after his defeat at Preston in 1648, he was beheaded at Whitehall in 1649 shortly before the king. His brother, the 2nd Duke, was killed at Worcester in 1651.

The title passed to Anne, the daughter of the 1st Duke. A woman of great intellect and determination, she inherited the title and estates heavily burdened by debts, but soon laid the foundations for Hamilton Palace, the greatest stately home in Scotland. The 5th and 6th Dukes extended the palace and built the splendid hunting lodge named Chatelherault, now part of a public park. Alexander, the 10th Duke, completed the enlargement of Hamilton Palace and adorned it with spectacular works of art collected from all over the world. He lived in regal style and crowned his royal ambitions by marrying his son, William, to Princess Marie of Baden, a cousin of Napoleon III.

The 14th Duke inherited his family's sense of adventure and in 1933 piloted the first aeroplane to fly over Everest. Hamilton Palace was demolished because of mining subsidence and the seat is now at Lennoxlove, near Haddington.

Hannay

CREST
A cross crosslet fitchée issuing
out of a crescent Sable

MOTTO
Per ardua ad alta
(Through difficulties to higher things)

PLANT BADGE
Periwinkle

The Hannays hail from the ancient princedom of Galloway. The original spelling of the name appears to have been 'Ahannay', and although its origin is uncertain, it may derive from the Gaelic 'O'Hannaidh' or 'Ap Shenaeigh'.

Gilbert de Hannethe appears on the Ragman Rolls among the Scottish Barons submitting to Edward I of England in 1296. This may be the same Gilbert who acquired the lands of Sorbie. The Hannays were suspicious of the ambitions of the Bruces, and supported the claim of John Balliol who, through his mother, Devorgilla, was descended from the Celtic Princes of Galloway. In the 15th and 16th centuries, they extended their influence over much of the surrounding countryside, building a tower on their lands at Sorbie around 1550. The tower was the seat of the chief family of this name until the 17th century, when it fell into disrepair after the family were outlawed.

There were many distinguished scions of the chiefly house, including Patrick Hannay, the distinguished soldier and poet whose literary output, once highly regarded, is now almost forgotten. Also from the house of Sorbie came James Hannay, the dean of St Giles' in Edinburgh, who has passed into legend as the minister who attempted to read the new liturgy in St Giles' in July 1637. It was at Dean Hannay's head that Jenny Geddes flung her stool crying, 'Thou false thief, dost thou say Mass at my lug?' A full scale riot ensued, which ultimately had to be suppressed by the town guard. In 1630, Sir Robert Hannay of Mochrum was created a Baronet of Nova Scotia.

At the beginning of the 17th century the Hannays of Sorbie became locked in a deadly feud with the Murrays of Broughton, which ended in the Hannays' being outlawed and ruined. The lands and tower of Sorbie were lost around 1640.

In 1582, Alexander Hannay, a younger son of Sorbie, had purchased the lands of Kirkdale in the Stewartry of Kirkcudbright. His son, John Hannay of Kirkdale, inherited the estate and established the line which is now recognised by the Lord Lyon as chief of the name. Sir Samuel Hannay, the elder son of Kirkdale, succeeded to the title and estates of his kinsman, Sir Robert Hannay of Mochrum, Baronet. The next baronet, another Sir Samuel, entered the service of the Hapsburg emperors, and prospered sufficiently to build for himself a grand mansion on his family lands. The house is said to have provided the inspiration for Sir Walter Scott's novel, *Guy Mannering*. Sir Samuel died in 1841 and the baronetcy became dormant. The estate of Kirkdale and the representation of the family passed to Sir Samuel's sister, Mary, and on her death in 1850 to her nephew, William Rainsford Hannay, from whom the present chiefly line descends.

Hay

CREST
Issuing out of a crest coronet
a falcon volant Proper, armed,
jessed and belled Or

MOTTO
Serva jugum (Keep the yoke)

PLANT BADGE
Mistletoe

This family descend from powerful Norman princes who followed William the Conqueror to England in 1066. The lands of Errol in Perthshire were confirmed to William de Haya by charter around 1172. The fortunes of the family were secured when Sir Gilbert Hay became one of the faithful comrades-in-arms of Robert the Bruce, sharing the hardships of the king's early campaigns to secure his crown. Gilbert was rewarded with the lands of Slains in Aberdeenshire, but more importantly with the office of Lord High Constable of Scotland. Hay was first created constable in 1309 and then, by charter dated 12 November 1314, the title was made hereditary. This dignity, which is still enjoyed by the present chief, gives the holder precedence in Scotland before every other hereditary honour, saving only the royal family itself.

Sir Thomas Hay, 7th Baron of Erroll, brought royal blood into the family when he married Elizabeth, daughter of Robert II. The family were also descended from Celtic kings, through the marriages of David de La Hay to Ethna, daughter of the Earl of Strathearn, and of Gilbert, 3rd Baron of Erroll, to Idoine, daughter of the Earl of Buchan. Another Sir Gilbert Hay fought for the cause of Joan of Arc and attended the coronation of Charles VII of France at Rheims. From this knight errant descend the Hays of Delgatie, whose castle near Turriff is now restored as the clan centre.

The Hays did not embrace the Reformation, and in consort with other Catholic nobles, including the Gordons and the Red Douglases, they negotiated with Philip II of Spain in the hope of

bringing about a Catholic alliance. As a result, Slains Castle was taken and destroyed under the personal supervision of the king, and it has remained a ruin ever since.

A brief period of exile convinced Erroll of the wisdom of converting to the reformed religion, and he returned to Scotland and to royal favour. The Hays remained loyal to the Stuarts, and came out in both Jacobite risings of 1715 and 1745. On the death of the 13th Earl's sister in 1758, the title passed to her great nephew, James Boyd, whose father, the Jacobite Earl of Kilmarnock, had been beheaded for treason in 1746. James, in addition to the earldom of Erroll, assumed the surname of Hay and the chiefship of the clan.

The 18th Earl was Lord High Constable during George IV's visit to Scotland in 1822, and he lavished a fortune on the affair, which nearly ruined him. The 19th Earl, William Hay, fought in the Crimea where he was wounded at the Battle of Alma in 1854. He was passionately concerned for the welfare of his clanspeople, and founded the fishing village of Port Erroll. In 1950 Diana, Countess of Erroll, founded the Clan Hay Society, which now has branches throughout the world. Her son succeeded as 24th Earl, and chief, in 1978.

Henderson

CREST
A cubit arm Proper the hand
holding an estoile Or surmounted
by a crescent Azure

MOTTO
Sola virtus nobilitat
(Virtue alone ennobles)

PLANT BADGE
Stem of cotton grass

There are three origins of this name from opposite ends of the kingdom. The Hendersons in the Borders seem simply to be the 'sons of Henry', and the name is often found in the variant of Henryson. The family spread from Dumfries-shire across into Liddesdale, but they do not appear in the list of border clans named by Parliament in 1594 in its attempts to suppress the border reivers.

From this line descended James Henderson, who became Lord Advocate around 1494 and was later appointed to the Bench. He acquired the lands of Fordell in Fife and there erected a fine fortified mansion. Fordell was to become the designation of the Lowland chiefs, and it is from this family that the present chief descends.

Perhaps the most prominent of the Hendersons of Fordell was Alexander Henderson, who was born around 1583. He was educated at the University of St Andrews where he became a professor of philosophy, sometime before 1611. He later became minister of the parish of Leuchars and was violently opposed to Charles I's attempts to reform the Church of Scotland, particularly with regard to the introduction of the new prayer book in 1637. Henderson, along with Johnston of Warriston, drafted the National Covenant which was first sworn and subscribed in Greyfriars Churchyard in Edinburgh in February 1638. He was in the forefront of church affairs and, therefore of politics, throughout the troubled reign of Charles I, and was also responsible for drafting the Solemn League and Covenant in 1643. When the king surrendered himself to the protection of the Scottish army in 1646, it was for Henderson that he sent to discuss a

reconciliation with his disaffected subjects. He is buried in Greyfriars Churchyard, the scene of his greatest triumph and site of a monument to his memory.

Hendersons also lived in Glencoe, and took the English version of their name from the Gaelic 'Maceanruig', claiming descent from a semi-legendary Pictish prince, Eanruig Mor Mac Righ Neachtain, or 'Big Henry, son of King Neachtain'. Their individual identity was lost when the last of their chiefs, Dugall Maceanruig, produced an heiress who, according to tradition, had a son, Ian Fraoch, by her lover, Angus Og of Islay. His son, called Iain Abrach, took as his patronymic Maciain, which was thereafter to designate the Macdonald chiefs of Glencoe. The Hendersons were not forgotten, however, and they traditionally formed the chief's bodyguard.

In the far north, the Henderson name arises again, but from a quite different source. Hendry, one of the younger sons of a 15th-century chief of Clan Gunn, hereditary crowners, or coroners, of Caithness, formed his own gilfine, or sept, which took his name. There is no obvious connection between the Caithness Hendersons or Mackendricks with either the Glencoe or Borders families.

Home

CREST
Qn a cap of maintenance Proper,
a lion's head erased Argent

MOTTO
A Home • A Home • A Home

A Borders family of immense power, the Homes are said to have been the descendants of the Saxon Princes of Northumberland through Cospatrick, Earl of Dunbar. William, kinsman of Waldegrave, the 4th Earl of Dunbar, married his cousin, Ada, around 1225 and she brought as part of her dowry the lands called 'Home'.

Sir Alexander Home of Dunglass was captured at the Battle of Homildon in 1402 and was killed in battle in France in 1424. He left three sons, from whom most of the principal branches of the family were to descend. His eldest grandson was created a Lord of Parliament, taking the title of Lord Home in 1473. He joined in the rebellion against James III, which ended in the murder of the king. Alexander, the 2nd Lord Home, led the vanguard of Scots knights, and although he personally escaped the slaughter, many of his family and supporters were not so fortunate. Home was appointed one of the counsellors to the Queen Regent. When the regency was transferred to the Duke of Albany, the fortunes of the Homes suffered. Lord Home was arrested for treason, and he and his brother were executed in October 1516. The title and estates were, however, restored to another brother, George Home.

The politics of the reign of Mary, Queen of Scots were complex, and the Homes, along with many others, shifted their allegiance more than once. Lord Home, supported the marriage of Mary to Bothwell, but later led his men against the queen at the Battle of Langside in 1568. Fortunes shifted again, and in 1573 he was arrested and later convicted of treason against the young James VI. He

was only released from Edinburgh Castle when his health had failed and he died a few days later. Despite his father's chequered political history, Alexander, the 6th Lord Home, was unswerving in his devotion to James VI, and was a royal favourite throughout his life. In March 1605 he was raised to the title of Earl of Home.

The 3rd Earl was a staunch supporter of Charles I although the Home allegiances were inconstant during the Jacobite risings. The 7th Earl was imprisoned in Edinburgh Castle in 1715, and his brother, James Home of Ayton, had his estates confiscated for his part in the rebellion. When the 'Young Pretender' asserted his father's claim in 1745, the 8th Earl joined the Government forces under Sir John Cope at Dunbar and later fought at the Battle of Preston.

The family came to public prominence in the 20th century, when the 14th Earl disclaimed for his own lifetime, his hereditary peerage to become Prime Minister of the United Kingdom as Sir Alec Douglas Home. The family seat is the splendid border estate of the Hirsel, from which the former Prime Minister named the life peerage bestowed upon him, as Lord Home of the Hirsel.

Hunter

CREST
A greyhound sejant Proper, gorged
with an antique crown Or

MOTTO
Cursum perficio
(I accomplish the hunt)

PLANT BADGE
Stem of thrift Proper

The Hunter family claims a long descent from both Norman origins, coming first to England in the retinue of William the Conqueror's wife, Matilda and thence to Scotland at the invitation of David I in the early 12th century. They were granted lands which eventually became known as Hunter's Toune. Preserved on a frail parchment at Hunterston in Ayrshire is a charter signed by Robert II in May 1374, confirming the grant of land 'for his faithful service rendered' to William Hunter, believed to be the 10th Hunter of Hunterston. By the 15th century, the family were hereditary keepers of the royal forests of Arran and Little Cumbrae.

John, the 14th Laird, died with his king at Flodden in 1513. His son, Robert, was 'trublit with sikness and infirmity', and in 1542 was excused from army service by James V. His son, Mungo was killed at the Battle of Pinkie in 1547. Robert, son of the 20th Laird, graduated from Glasgow University in 1643. He was minister of West Kilbride, where he bought land and so founded the Hunters of Kirkland. Robert, a grandson of the 20th Laird, served under Marlborough and became Governor of Virginia and then of New York.

The early 18th century brought financial problems for the family. These were resolved by Robert Hunter, a younger son of the 22nd Laird, who succeeded to the estate and managed it with vigour. He died at the age of 86 and was succeeded by his daughter, Eleanora. She married her cousin, Robert Caldwell, and together they began extensive improvements to the estate. They built the present Hunterston House, a fine example of late-18th-century architecture

and their son altered and extended the house in 1835. He had two daughters: Jane, who married Gould Weston, and Eleanor, who married Robert William Cochran-Patrick.

Jane Hunter Weston died in 1911 and was succeeded by her son, Lieutenant General Sir Aylmer Hunter-Weston, a distinguished soldier. In the First World War he took part in the Gallipoli landings, and later commanded the 8th Army on the Western Front. He was awarded many decorations and honours, including the Distinguished Service Order and a Knighthood of the Bath. He served as Member of Parliament for North Ayrshire and Bute for 27 years. He died in 1940 without issue, and on the death of his widow in 1954, the estate passed to the descendants of his mother's younger sister, Eleanora, granddaughter of Eleanora Hunter and Robert William Cochran-Patrick, and daughter of Sir Neil Kennedy Cochran-Patrick. In 1969 she passed the estate to her nephew, Neil, who was officially recognised by the Lord Lyon as 29th Laird and chief.

Innes

CREST
A boar's head erased Proper

MOTTO
Be traist

$\mathcal{T}$he barony of Innes lies in Morayshire. Berowald, a Flemish noble-man, was granted this barony in 1160 by Malcolm IV. In 1226, Alexander II granted a charter of confirmation to Berowald's grand-son, Walter, who assumed the surname of Innes. The 8th Laird, 'Good Sir Robert', who died around 1381, had three sons: Sir Alexander, who later succeeded as 9th Laird, and who married the heiress of Aberchirder; John, later Bishop of Moray, who restored Elgin Cathedral after it had been destroyed by the Wolf of Badenoch; and George, head of the Scottish Order of Trinitarian Friars. Sir Alexander's son, Sir Walter, was chief for 42 years until his death in 1454. His son, Sir Robert Innes, the 11th Laird, fought under the Earl of Huntly at the Battle of Brechin in 1452 and sought to expiate the sins of his life by founding the Greyfriars of Elgin. His eldest son, James, was armour-bearer to James III, and entertained James IV at the Castle of Innes in 1490. He and his son, Alexander, were noted patrons of the arts and architecture.

Alexander the Proud, the 16th chief, was executed by the Regent Morton for the murder of Walter Innes and was succeeded by his brother, John, who resigned his chiefship to his cousin, Alexander Innes of Crommey. He was murdered at Aberdeen in 1580 by his kinsman, Robert Innes of Innermarkie, during a family quarrel. His grandson, Sir Robert, the 20th chief, was a Privy Councillor who represented Moray in Parliament, and he was created a Baronet of Nova Scotia in 1625. Although a prominent Covenanter, he wel-comed the uncrowned Charles II at Garnoch in 1650, and raised a

regiment to fight for the royalist cause. He sold the Aberchirder estates but built Innes House.

The 3rd Baronet married Lady Margaret Ker through whom Sir James Innes, the 6th Baronet and 25th chief, succeeded to the dukedom of Roxburghe in 1805. His son was granted the additional title of Earl Innes in 1836. The present Duke of Roxburghe would be the chief of Clan Innes but is barred from the title as he bears a compound, or double-barrelled, surname.

Sir Thomas Innes of Learney, a descendant of the Lairds of Innermarkie, was Lord Lyon, King of Arms from 1945 to 1969 and was one of Scotland's greatest heraldic experts. He was also passionately interested in his family heritage and restored a number of castles with Innes connections. He passed on his love of the science of heraldry to his son, Malcolm, now Sir Malcolm Innes of Edingight, who became Lord Lyon in 1981.

Irvine

CREST
A sheaf of holly consisting of nine
leaves Vert slipped and banded Gules

MOTTO
Sub sole sub umbra virens
(Flourishing both in sunshine
and in shade)

The lands which first bore the name of Irvine appear to have been in Dumfries-shire and family tradition asserts that the origin of the chiefly branch is linked with the early Celtic monarchs of Scotland. Duncan Eryvine, whose eldest son settled at Bonshaw, was the brother of Crinan, who, through the lay Abbots of Dunkeld, claimed descent from the High Kings of Ireland. William de Irwin was a neighbour of the Bruces, whose seat was at Lochmaben near Bonshaw, and he became armour-bearer and, later, secretary to Robert the Bruce. As a reward for 20 years of faithful service, de Irwin was granted the royal forest of Drum in Aberdeenshire, which was thereafter to become the chief seat of the family.

The 3rd Laird of Drum, the first of 12 Irvines who successively bore the name Alexander, was a knight of almost legendary prowess who followed the Earl of Mar to the French wars. He later fought at the Battle of Harlaw in 1411, only 20 miles from Drum itself. The next laird figured prominently in the negotiations to ransom James I from the English. When the king's release was secured, he knighted de Irwyne. After the king's murder in Perth in 1437, Sir Alexander took control of the city of Aberdeen to try and restore order.

Alexander, the 10th Laird, was a staunch royalist and supporter of Charles I. He was sheriff of Aberdeen, and was offered the earldom of Aberdeen, but the king was executed before he could confirm the grant. Drum was ultimately attacked while the laird was absent. A strong force with artillery surrounded the castle, and after Lady Irvine's surrender, it was occupied and looted. The laird's sons also

fought in the civil war, and both were captured: Robert, the younger son, died in the dungeons of Edinburgh Castle, but his brother, Alexander, was set free after Montrose's victory at Kilsyth in 1645. Alexander survived the war to succeed his father as 11th Laird, and yet again the royal offer of a peerage was made. This time the laird refused it when he discovered that the king was unwilling to offer reparation for the destruction of the Drum estates.

The 14th Laird was a Jacobite and fought at the Battle of Sheriffmuir in 1715. He received a severe head wound in the battle from which he never fully recovered. After years of illness, he died leaving no direct heir. The estate passed to his uncle, John, and then to a kinsman, John Irvine of Crimond. The Irvines continued in their adherence to the Jacobite cause, and fought for Bonnie Prince Charlie at Culloden in 1746. The laird only escaped capture after the prince's defeat by hiding in a secret room at Drum.

More recently, the 22nd Laird fought with the Grenadier Guards in the First World War while an Irvine from another line, Sir Robert Irvine of Bonshaw was captain of the great Cunard liner, *Queen Mary*.

Jardine

A name derived from the French, 'jardin', meaning 'garden' or 'orchard'. The family of du Jardin came to England with William the Conqueror in 1066. The name is first encountered in Scotland prior to 1153, in charters to the abbeys of Kelso and Arbroath and one Humphrey de Jardin witnessed a charter by Robert Bruce to the abbey of Arbroath around 1178. The name is also met in the form 'de Gardinus'. Patrick de Gardinus was chaplain to the Bishop of Glasgow at the beginning of the 13th century.

The chiefly line appears to have established itself at Applegirth on the River Annan in Dumfriesshire by the 14th century. Their earliest stronghold was Spedlings Tower, which was abandoned in the late 17th century when the family moved across the River Annan to the more convenient Jardine Hall, according to legend, to escape the ghost of an unfortunate miller who had been left to starve to death in the tower's dungeon.

The Jardines, following the Johnstones, supported Mary, Queen of Scots until her marriage to Bothwell, when they declared allegiance to the infant King James VI. Sir Alexander Jardine, born in 1645, was created a Baronet of Nova Scotia in May 1672.

The 4th Baronet, born in 1712, embraced the Catholic faith and lived on the Continent. He became a Knight of the Sovereign Order of Malta, taking a vow of celibacy. He died in Brussels in December 1790 when he was succeeded by his brother, Sir William. A nephew of Sir William, Frank Jardine, married Princess Sana, the niece of Moliatoa, king of Samoa, in 1873. His royal connections helped him

to develop north-east Australia and the new state of Queensland.

Dr William Jardine went to the Far East as a surgeon for the East India Company. In 1827 he went into partnership with James Matheson. The house of Jardine Matheson prospered, particularly after the Opium Wars established a strong British merchant base in Hong Kong. The company grew to dominate trade in the Far East and is still a force today.

Another cadet of Applegirth was the Reverend John Jardine, born in 1716. An eminent clergyman and one of the intellectual and literary elite of Edinburgh in the mid 18th century, he helped to launch the critical journal, *The Edinburgh Review*. He was appointed dean of the Order of the Thistle and a royal chaplain. His son, Sir Henry Jardine was Deputy King's Remembrancer in Exchequer for Scotland and was one of those present when the Scottish Crown Regalia, the 'Honours of Scotland', were re-discovered in Edinburgh Castle in 1818; these valuable treasures had been 'missing' since 1707 when they were hidden to prevent them being removed to England following the Union of the Parliaments.

Johnstone

CREST
A winged spur Or

MOTTO
Nunquam non paratus
(Never unprepared)

The Johnstones, whose name is a simple patronymic, were at one time among the most powerful of the Borders clans. The first recorded of the family was John Johnstone, whose son, Gilbert, is named in records dated after 1194. Sir John Johnston, knight of the county of Dumfries, appears on the Ragman Rolls swearing fealty to Edward I of England in 1296. Adam Johnstone was Laird of Johnstone before 1413, and fought at the Battle of Sark in 1448. Adam's son took part on the royal side in the desperate struggle between James II and the Douglases, and was instrumental in the suppression of the rebellion of that great house by the Crown.

The Johnstones had a hereditary feud with the Maxwells. Lord Maxwell, the head of this great family, was the most powerful man in the south-west of Scotland in the 16th century. He was slain, with many of his men, at the Battle of Dryfe Sands near Lockerbie in 1593. In turn, at a meeting held in 1608 to reconcile their differences, Johnstone was treacherously killed by the 9th Lord Maxwell who eventually paid with his life for this act on the scaffold in 1614.

James Johnstone, the chief of the clan, was created Lord Johnstone of Lochwood by Charles I in 1633. Ten years later, he was made Earl of Hartfell, a title designated to him and his heirs male only. He joined Montrose after the Battle of Kilsyth in August 1645. He was captured at Philiphaugh later that year, but was spared through the intercession of Argyll. To recompense Lord Hartfell for the hardships he had suffered in the royal cause, Charles II created him Earl of Annandale and Hartfell, a charter in 1662 erecting the land into a

territorial earldom entailed to the heirs male of his body, and failing that to heirs female. Although James later had a son, William, this grant was to be of consequence two centuries later.

In 1701, William, 3rd Earl of Hartfell and 2nd Earl of Annandale and Hartfell, was raised to the rank of Marquess of Annandale. In 1747, George, 3rd and last Marquess, was declared to be incapable of managing his affairs, and a curator was appointed. On the Marquess's death in 1792 the family titles became dormant and the estates devolved upon his grand-nephew, James, 3rd Earl of Hopetoun.

Unsuccessful attempts were made in the 19th century to revive the Annandale titles. In 1971 it was decided to proceed upon the basis of the charter of 1662. In 1982, the Lord Lyon recognised Major Percy Johnstone of Annandale and of that Ilk as baron of the lands of the earldom of Annandale and Hartfell and of the lordship of Johnstone. From there the case was presented to the House of Lords in 1985, who found in favour of Major Percy's son, Patrick, Earl of Annandale and Hartfell and chief of the name and arms of Johnstone.

Other senior branches of the clan also flourished, particularly the house of Caskieben.

Keith

CREST
Out of a Crest Coronet Or, a
roebuck's head Proper, attired Or

MOTTO
Veritas vincit
(Truth conquers)

PLANT BADGE
White rose

A Norman adventurer, Hervey, married the native heiress of the line of Marbhachair, a warrior said to have slain the enemy general at the Battle of Barrie in 1010. Hervey received a charter for the lands of Keth from David I around 1150. Hervey's son was styled 'Marischal of the King of Scots' in a charter of 1176, an office the family held until the attainder of George, 10th Earl Marischal.

Robert the Bruce granted Halforest, the Aberdeenshire royal forest to his friend, Sir Robert de Keth, in 1308, and it was there that the marischal built his castle. By a charter of Robert in 1324, the office of marischal became hereditary in the family of Sir Robert de Keth, the cavalry commander at Bannockburn, conditional upon their bearing the ancient arms inherited from Marbhachair.

The 3rd Lord Keith was created Earl Marischal in 1458, the only peer to be styled by his great office of state. The 3rd Earl Marischal, with the Earl of Glencairn, invited the reformer John Knox to return to Scotland in 1559, while the 4th Earl founded Marischal College in Aberdeen.

After the coronation of Charles II in 1651 at Scone, William, the 7th Earl, was captured and imprisoned in the Tower of London, where he remained until the Restoration in 1660. The king, in recompense for the great sufferings the earl and his family had endured in the royal cause, made him a Privy Councillor and later Lord Privy Seal. The earl's brother, John, was created Earl of Kintore for his part in hiding the Scottish Crown jewels during Cromwell's occupation.

The Keith family supported the Jacobite cause in the Forty-five, for

which the 10th Earl and his brother, James, forfeited their lands, castles and titles. The Keith brothers thereafter played a prominent part in Continental affairs during the 18th century. The earl was one of the very few Jacobite Knights of the Garter. James continued his earlier career as a successful professional soldier. He served in the army of Tsar Peter the Great and received Russia's highest decoration, the Order of St Andrew. He went on to achieve the highly appropriate rank of marshal of the Prussian army under Frederick the Great.

Keith of Ravelston and Dunnottar was recognised as a representer of the Marischals by the Lord Lyon in 1801. His nephew was dubbed Knight Marishal for George IV's visit to Edinburgh in 1822. However, the flamboyant 9th Earl of Kintore, who was Governor General of South Australia from 1889 to 1895, decimated the Kintore estates.

The Earls of Kintore continue to reside on the Keith Hall estate in Aberdeenshire.

Kennedy

CREST
A dolphin naiant Proper

MOTTO
Avise la fin
(Consider the end)

Cunedda, a chieftain of the Votadini tribe of Lothian, was sent by the Saxon leader, Vortigern, to south west Scotland to establish settlements intended to resist Picto-Scottish sea raids. These settlements spread down the west coast as far as north Wales. In the Celtic language, Cunedda was rendered as Cinneidigh (meaning ugly- or grim-headed), and the name gradually became especially associated with the district of Carrick in Ayrshire. Gilbert Mac Kenedi witnessed a charter granting lands in Carrick to the abbey at Melrose in the early part of the reign of William the Lion, while Gillespie Kennedy is named as senechal of Carrick in charters during the reign of Alexander II. The Kennedys claimed blood kinship with the Earls of Carrick and supported Bruce in the War of Independence. They were rewarded when Robert II confirmed John Kennedy of Dunure as chief of his name and baillie of Carrick in 1372. His direct descendent, Gilbert, created Lord Kennedy around 1457, was one of the regents of the infant James III.

Sir David, 3rd Lord Kennedy, was created Earl of Cassillis in 1509 and died at Flodden in 1513. The 6th Earl of Cassillis, John, was Lord Justice General of Scotland from 1649 to 1651. He was a zealous Protestant, as was his son, the 7th Earl, and both were firm supporters of Parliament during the civil war. When the 8th Earl died without heirs, there was a three-year court dispute to determine the succession. The House of Lords finally found in favour of Sir Thomas Kennedy of Culzean in preference to William, Earl of March and Ruglan. Sir Thomas's brother, David, an advocate, succeeded

him in 1775 as 10th Earl, and was an active improver. He commissioned the architect Robert Adam to build the castle at Culzean, now considered to be Adam's masterpiece.

On the death of the 10th Earl, the title passed to a kinsman who had settled in America, Captain Archibald Kennedy. He tried to be neutral during the American War of Independence, and was accordingly mistrusted by both sides. Half of his New York properties were confiscated, including Number 1, Broadway, which was appropriated by George Washington. His son, the 12th Earl, was a close friend of the Duke of Clarence, who, on his coronation as William IV, created him Marquess of Ailsa.

Lieutenant General Sir Clark Kennedy of Knockgray served throughout the Peninsular War. At Waterloo in 1815, he was in command of the centre squadron of the Royal Dragoons and personally captured the eagle and colours of the 105th Regiment of French Infantry.

The 5th Marquess presented Culzean Castle to the National Trust of Scotland.

Kerr

The Kerrs were one of the great riding clans of the Scottish Borders, and their name is rendered in various forms, including Kerr, Ker, Carr and Carre. It stems from the old Norse, 'kjrr', meaning 'marsh dweller', and came to Scotland from Normandy, the French settlement of the Norsemen. There is a version of the name found on the west coast of Scotland and particularly on the island of Arran, which has a separate derivation, taken from the Gaelic 'ciar', meaning 'dusky'.

In 1451 Andrew Kerr of Cessford received a charter to the barony of Old Roxburgh, and in 1457 he was appointed warden of the marches. The family were confirmed in the barony and castle of Cessford by a charter of 1493. Sir Andrew Kerr of Ferniehurst received a royal charter to the barony of Oxnam, and was appointed warden of the middle marches in 1502. Mark Kerr, grandson of Sir Andrew Kerr of Cessford, had his lands of Newbattle and Prestongrange erected into the barony of Newbattle by a charter of 1591, and in 1606 he was created Earl of Lothian. This title failed when his son died in 1624 without male issue. Sir Andrew Kerr of the Ferniehurst line was created Lord Jedburgh in 1621.

The third peerage to come to the family was the earldom of Ancram, which was bestowed upon Sir Robert Kerr who was descended from a younger son of Sir Andrew Kerr of Ferniehurst. To add to the plethora of honours showered on the family, Sir William Kerr, son of the Earl of Ancram, was granted a new earldom of Lothian in 1631. His son, Robert, who was advanced to the rank of

Marquess, also succeeded to the earldom of Ancram.

The 1st Marquess was Lord Justice General of Scotland. He had five sons and five daughters. One of these, Lord Mark Kerr, was a distinguished professional soldier and is reputed to have had a high sense of personal honour and a quick temper. He fought several duels throughout his military career but rose ultimately to the rank of general, and was appointed governor of Edinburgh Castle in 1745. Robert Kerr, one of the sons of the 3rd Marquess, has the dubious distinction of being the only person of high rank killed on the Hanoverian side at the Battle of Culloden in 1746. His elder brother, later the 4th Marquess, commanded three squadrons of cavalry at Culloden and survived to serve under the Duke of Cumberland in France in 1758. Admiral of the Fleet, Sir Walter Talbot Kerr, a younger son of the 7th Marquess, was a naval lord at the Admiralty from 1899 to 1904.

Ferniehurst Castle still belongs to the chiefs, although the seat is the great mansion house of Monteviot.

Kincaid

CREST
A triple towered castle Argent,
masoned Sable, and issuing from the
centre tower a dexter arm from the
shoulder embowed, vested in the
proper tartan of Kincaid and grasping
a drawn sword all Proper

MOTTO
This I'll defend

The Kincaids are said to descend from the ancient Earls of Lennox,
the Galbraiths of Buthernock, the Grahames and the Comyn Lords
of Badenoch. Their name appears to be territorial in origin, but its
derivation is uncertain. One explanation is that it comes from the
Gaelic, 'ceann cadha', the 'steep place' or 'pass'. A second translation
may be 'of the head of the rock'. An early reference to the name is
found in 1238, when Alexander III granted the lands of the Kincade
to Maldouen, third Earl of Lennox.

Although Kincaids have not made a great mark in Scottish history,
one member of the family distinguished himself by gallant conduct
against the English forces of Edward I, and in his valiant services in
the successful recapture of Edinburgh Castle in 1296. The then
Laird of Kincaid was made constable of Edinburgh Castle, an office
he held until around 1314. It was during Bruce's reign that the castle
on the Kincaid shield was granted as an honourable augmentation to
his armorial bearings as a reference to his feat.

From the late 16th century onwards, the family increased their
landholdings in the east of the country. Firstly, as a result of an
advantageous marriage, the Kincaids gained the estate of
Craiglockhart near Edinburgh. In due course they added to this the
estate of Bantaskin near Falkirk, the grim Blackness Castle near
Linlithgow and the fields of Warriston, now a suburb of Edinburgh.

Malcolm Kincaid, who lost his left arm in a clan skirmish in 1563,
was actively engaged in a feud in the 1570s with the Lennoxes of
Woodhead. The luckless Malcolm was killed by a Stirling of Glorat

in 1581. John Kincaid of Warriston was murdered in 1600 by one of his grooms who was in league with his wife. The conspiracy was detected and the groom forced to confess. The couple both suffered the ultimate penalty for their crime but, although the Lady of Warriston was beheaded in deference to her rank, the hapless groom was 'broken on the wheel'.

The Kincaids fought on the royalist side in the civil wars of the 17th century, campaigning largely in Ireland. The family were later supporters of the Stuart cause in exile, and following the rising in 1715, David Kincaid was obliged to leave Scotland, ultimately settling in Virginia. In 1746 four sons of Alexander Kincaid, Lord Provost of Edinburgh, and the King's Printer, fought a rearguard action after Culloden, but were ultimately taken prisoner and their doom seemed certain. However, they escaped and took ship for America, where they, too, settled in Virginia. At the end of the 18th century the principal line of the Kincaids married into the Lennox family and for most of the next two centuries the families were virtually synonymous. The Kincaid chiefs have since re-established themselves.

Lamont

CREST
A dexter hand couped at
the wrist Proper

MOTTO
Ne parcas nec spernas
(Neither spare nor dispose)

A name of great antiquity in south Argyll, where at one time the
chiefs were described as 'Mac Laomain Mor Chomhail Uile' – 'The
Great MacLamont of All Cowal'. Although some believe the name to
be Norman or French, the family almost certainly originated in
Ulster. Logmaor, meaning, in old Norse, 'lawman' or 'law-giver',
became in Gaelic 'ladhman', and it is from a son of the great O'Neill
princes of Tyrone that the chiefs are said to descend. The Lamonts
were also one time called Macerchar, from Fearchar, the grandfather
of the first Ladhman.

The first certain record of the chiefs is found in charters of the
early 13th century. Laumanus, son of Malcolm, granted to the
monks of Paisley lands at Kilmun, together with the church of
Kilfinan. These grants were confirmed in 1270 and again in 1295 by
Malcolm, the son of Laumanus. In 1456 John Lamond is recorded as
the baillie of Cowal. Later that century the direct line of the chiefs is
believed to have failed, and the representation of the family passed
to the Lamonts of Inveryne, later styled Lamont of Lamont. They
established their chief seats at the strong castles of Toward and
Ascog, which they held until their destruction by the Campbells in
the 17th century.

Sir James Lamont of Lamont, chief of the clan in 1643, was a well
respected and popular leader who was deeply interested in the welfare of his people. He declared for the royalist cause, which brought
his clan into direct confrontation with his powerful Campbell neighbours. In 1646 a powerful Campbell army invaded the Lamont terri-

tory and besieged the castles of Toward and Ascog. Sir James Lamont surrendered the castles, having reached apparently honourable terms with the Campbells. The fortresses were to be handed over but the lives of the Lamonts were to be spared. Sir James was promptly thrown in a dungeon at Dunstaffnage, where he was held in terrible conditions for 5 years. Over 200 clansmen, women and children were massacred, and the castles were reduced to ruins. The Lamont massacre was one of the charges brought against the Marquess of Argyll at his trial in 1661. Argyll was already doomed for his treason, but the Lamont charges were in many ways more damaging to his reputation as a Highland chief. The Lamonts did not receive compensation, and their star remained eclipsed by their Campbell oppressors, whose power continued to grow unabated.

The chiefs took up residence at Ard Lamont, where the last chief to live in Cowal was born in 1854. In 1893 the last of the clan lands were sold and the chiefs later emigrated to Australia.

Lennox

CREST
Two broadswords in saltire behind a
swan's head and neck all Proper

MOTTO
I'll defend

PLANT BADGE
A rose slipped Gules

The ancient earldom which bore this name consisted of the whole of Dunbartonshire, as well as large parts of Renfrewshire, Stirling-shire and Perthshire. The name is Gaelic in origin: 'levenach' in Gaelic meant a 'smooth stream' and from the ancient Celtic Mormaers of Levenax sprang the Earls of Lennox who were to become joined to the royal house of Stewart.

By the end of the 13th century, the Earls of Lennox were among the most powerful nobles in the realm, and Malcolm, the 5th Earl, was one of the nominees supporting the Bruce claim to the crown of Scotland. His son was present at the coronation of Robert II at Scone in 1371, although he died only two years later with no direct male issue. The earldom passed through his only daughter to Walter de Fasselane, who assumed the title of Earl of Lennox. Margaret Lennox and her husband resigned the title to the Crown, who regranted it to their son, Duncan. Duncan's eldest daughter, Isabella, married Murdoch, Duke of Albany and Regent of Scotland between 1419 and 1425. Lennox fell victim to James I's hatred of all those connected with Albany, whose father had murdered the king's broth-er and who had presided over Scotland's decline into disorder. Albany, his heir Walter, and Lennox were all executed. The succes-sion to the title was thereafter disputed, and the lands themselves were divided. The Duchess of Albany's sisters, Margaret and Elizabeth, both left descendants who claimed the vast estates. From Margaret Lennox descended the Menteiths of Rusky, and from Elizabeth, the Stewarts, later Lords Darnley.

John, Lord Darnley assumed the title of Earl of Lennox in 1488 and sat in the first Parliament of James IV. The younger son of the 4th Stewart Earl was Henry, Lord Darnley, the unfortunate husband of Mary, Queen of Scots. The Earldom of Lennox consequently passed to James VI along with the other Darnley estates.

Esmé Stuart, a grandson of the 3rd Stewart Earl of Lennox, was recalled to Scotland by James VI in 1579, and in 1581 he was created Duke of Lennox and High Chamberlain of Scotland. The dukedoms and the estates once more died out in a direct line and devolved on Charles II as the nearest male heir. He conferred the dukedom of Lennox and of Richmond upon Charles Lennox, his illegitimate son by his liaison with Louise de Kerouaille. The present Duke of Richmond, Gordon and Lennox, proprietor of the famous Goodwood racecourse, is Charles Lennox's direct descendant. In the 19th century, the Lennoxes of Woodhead, later of Lennox Castle near Glasgow, claimed the right to succeed to the title and honours of the ancient Earls of Lennox, and although their claim to the peerage was never established, they were recognised as chief of the name.

Leslie

CREST
A demi griffin Proper, beaked,
armed and winged Or

MOTTO
Grip fast

PLANT BADGE
Rue, in flower

The progenitor of this great Scottish family is claimed as Bartolf, a nobleman who came to Scotland in 1067 in the retinue of Edgar the Aetheling, brother of Margaret, later queen of Malcolm III. Malcolm appointed him governor of Edinburgh Castle and bestowed on him estates in Fife, Angus, the Mearns and Aberdeenshire. Bartolf's son, Malcolm, was created constable of the royal castle at Inverury which he held for David II. His great-grandson, Sir Norman Lesley, acquired the lands of Fythkill in Fife, afterwards called Lesley, around 1282.

George Lesley was created a Lord of Parliament in 1445 as Lord Lesley of Leven, and had all his lands united into the barony of Ballinbreich. He was advanced to the title of Earl of Rothes sometime prior to 1458. George, the 4th Earl, died in mysterious circumstances at Dieppe, along with the Earl of Cassillis and two others, returning from the wedding of Mary, Queen of Scots to the Dauphin in 1558.

Thereafter, the Lesleys abandoned politics for a time, for the less hazardous career of professional soldiery. Lesleys fought in Germany, France, Sweden and the Baltic. Perhaps the most famous of the Lesley mercenaries was Alexander Leslie, who was recalled from the Continent to take command of the Army of the Covenant, and was later raised to the peerage as the Earl of Leven. David Lesley, of the Rothes family, was also a Covenanter commander. He was routed by Cromwell's troops at Dunbar in 1650 and imprisoned in the Tower of London until the Restoration in 1660, being created Lord Newark

in the following year. The 7th Earl of Rothes was created a duke in 1680 by Charles II. He was a great favourite of the king and one of the most distinguished statesmen of his time. He was made a Lord of Session and President of the Council. He was a supporter of the ruthless poilcy to suppress forcibly the extreme Protestant movement who met in illegal gatherings known as conventicles. However, the policy became unpopular and Rothes was replaced by the Earl of Lauderdale. The dukedom died with him as he left no male heir, but under the terms of an earlier charter, the earldom could pass through the female line, and thus the title was preserved.

The 9th Earl was Vice Admiral of Scotland and governor of Stirling Castle. He was a supporter of the Hanoverians, and in 1715 he commanded a regiment of cavalry at the Battle of Sheriffmuir. He sold much of the Rothes estates, although the magnificent Leslie House near Fife remained the seat of the earls until 1926.

Lindsay

CREST
Issuing from an antique ducal
coronet Or, the head, neck and
wings of a swan Proper

MOTTO
Endure fort (Endure boldly)

PLANT BADGE
Lime tree

The Lindsays came to prominence both in England and Scotland in the late 11th century. Sir Walter de Lindissie, 'noble and knight' accompanied David, Earl of Huntingdon, brother of Alexander I, to Scotland to claim his throne. His great-grandson, Sir William de Lindesay, sat in the Parliament of 1164 and was afterwards a justiciar. He held the lands of Crawford, the earldom of which was to ultimately be the premier title of the chiefs, but he sat in Parliament as Baron of Luffness in East Lothian. He acquired considerable wealth through his wife, Ethelreda, a granddaughter of the great Cospatrick ruler of most of Northumbria. His son, Sir David, married Marjory, a member of the royal family, and on his death in 1214 he was succeeded as 3rd Lord of Crawford and High Justiciar of Lothian by his son.

Sir David de Lindsay took part in a famous tournament at London Bridge in 1390 in the presence of Richard II of England. Lindsay won the day and the admiration of the English king. On 21 April 1398 he was created Earl of Crawford. He was Lord High Admiral of Scotland in 1403 and sent as ambassador to England in 1406. Alexander, the 4th Earl, joined in the rebellion against James II and fought at the Battle of Brechin in 1452. The royal forces were victorious and the earl was attainted for treason but later pardoned. His daughter, Elizabeth, married John, the 1st Lord Drummond, who was ancestor of Henry, Lord Darnley, the King Consort of Mary, Queen of Scots and the father of James VI.

Ludovic Lindsay, who had learned his trade as a soldier on the

Continent, fought for Charles I during the civil war. He commanded a regiment of cavalry at the Battle of Marston Moor in 1644 and was later with Montrose at Philiphaugh in 1645, where he was captured. He died without issue, having first resigned his earldom of Crawford to the Crown for regrant to his kinsman John, Earl of Lindsay. The title remained in this branch of the family until the 19th century, when it passed to the Earls of Balcarres.

The Lindsays of Balcarres descended from a younger son of the 9th Earl of Crawford, who were created earls in their own right in 1650 for eminent services during the civil war. The 1st Earl of Balcarres was made hereditary governor of Edinburgh Castle, Secretary of State for Scotland and High Commissioner to the General Assembly. His younger son, Colin, later the 3rd Earl, was a staunch Jacobite who fought during the rising of 1715 and only escaped being attainted for treason through the intervention of his life-long friend, the Duke of Marlborough. Alexander, the 6th Earl of Balcarres, became the 23rd Earl of Crawford, and the chiefs are now styled Earls of Crawford and Balcarres.

Livingstone

CREST
A demi savage, wreathed about the
head and middle with laurel,
holding on his dexter shoulder
a club and in his sinister hand
a serpent nowed all Proper

MOTTO
Si je puis (If I can)

This name is probably territorial in origin, deriving from lands of the same name in West Lothian. According to one legend, the lands were named after a Saxon called Leving. There is record of one Livingus living during the reigns of Alexander I and David I. Sir William Livingstone, believed to be his great grandson, had three sons. Two of his younger sons appear on the Ragman Rolls swearing fealty to Edward I of England in 1296. His eldest son followed David II on his invasion of England in 1346 and was taken prisoner at the Battle of Durham. He was one of the commissioners to England who negotiated the release of the king and was thereafter granted the barony of Callendar.

Sir Alexander Livingstone of Callendar was one of the guardians of the infant James II, a post he extorted from the king's mother, Queen Joan, whilst she was under his control in Stirling Cstle. In 1440 the Livingstones were instrumental in persuading the young Earl of Douglas and his brother to attend a banquet of reconciliation in Edinburgh Castle. The Douglases were promptly seized and executed. In revenge, the Douglases imprisoned Livingstone and killed one of his sons. Another son, Sir James Livingstone, was created captain of Stirling Castle and later Great Chamberlain of Scotland. He was raised to the peerage as Lord Livingstone in 1458. He died without issue and the title devolved upon his nephew, John. In 1543 Alexander, the 5th Lord Livingstone, was one of the noblemen chosen to educate the young Mary, Queen of Scots. He accompanied the young queen to France and died there. William, his son who suc-

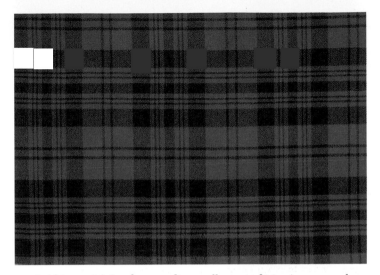

ceeded him as 6th Lord, was a fierce adherent of Mary's cause and fought for her at the Battle of Langside in 1568. In 1600 Livingstone was raised to the rank of Earl of Linlithgow and the 2nd Earl was created Hereditary Constable of the Royal Palace of Linlithgow. His son, George, remained loyal to the Crown during the civil war and the estates suffered, first at the hands of the Army of the Covenant and later the forces of Oliver Cromwell. The family supported the Jacobite cause, and for their part in the 1715 rising the titles were forfeited.

The Livingstones of Bachuil had received in early times a grant of lands on the island of Lismore as hereditary keepers of the crozier, or Bachull Mor, of St Moluag. The Celtic barony attached to the hereditary keepership was recognised by Parliament. The Barons of Bachuil are still the keepers of this sacred relic and live on their ancient lands on Lismore.

Lumsden

CREST
Issuant from a crest coronet Or a
naked arm grasping a sword Proper

MOTTO
Amor patitur moras
(Love endures delays)

PLANT BADGE
Sprig of hazel fructed Proper

The manor of Lumsdene is first mentioned in 1098 when Edgar, King of Scots, and son of Malcolm III and Margaret, refounded Coldingham Priory in the county of Berwick, endowing it with the villages of Coldingham, Lumsdene, Renton and Swinewood. The first recorded possessors of the land, divided into Easter and Wester Lumsden, were Gillem and Cren de Lummisden who, between 1166 and 1182, attested a charter to the priory of Coldingham by Waldeve, Earl of Dunbar. Gilbert de Lumisden appears as witness to charters between 1249 and 1262. The common ancestor of the Lumsdens, Adam de Lumisden of that Ilk, and his son, Roger de Lummesdene, did homage to Edward I of England in 1296, and their names appear, with the variations of spelling, on the Ragman Rolls.

When the Act of Parliament establishing the *Public Register of All Arms and Bearings in Scotland* was passed in 1672, the senior line of Lumsden did not register their arms, althought two cadet houses, of Alexander Lumsden of Cushnie and Sir James Lumsden of Innergellie, did so.

Lumsdens appear in Scottish history as soldiers, scholars and statesmen, and also included merchants, barristers, surgeons, churchmen and soldiers. Sir James Lumsden served under King Gustavus Adolphus of Sweden during the Thirty Years' War, and he and his brother, William, returned to fight for the royalists in the civil war, after the Battle of Marston Moor in 1644. The Lumsdens of Cushnie sat as barons of the north in Parliament.

Andrew Lumsden, descended from Andrew, third son of Robert Lumsden, Baron of Cushnie, was secretary to Prince Charles Edward Stuart during the 1745 rising. Attainted after Culloden, he fled to Rome where he became Secretary and later Secretary of State to James VIII, the 'Old Pretender', until the latter's death in 1766, when he rejoined Prince Charles until 1768. He returned to Scotland in 1773 and was fully pardoned in 1778 by the Hanoverian Government. His tartan waistcoat is preserved at Pitcaple Castle.

Another cadet of Cushnie, Sir Harry Burnett Lumsden of Belhelvie, founded the elite Lumsden's Guides, who served on the North-West Frontier of India. He was the first to use 'khaki' (an Urdu word meaning 'dust-coloured') uniforms.

The House of Lumsden Association was formed in 1972, and their work to gather together those of the name throughout the world reached a pinnacle in 1985, when the claim of the hereditary chief was established in the Court of the Lord Lyon.

Macalister

CREST
A dexter arm in armour erect,
the hand holding a dagger
in pale all Proper

MOTTO
Fortiter
(Boldly)

Some doubt exists as to the exact progenitor of this clan, but it is generally accepted they are the descendants of Alasdair Mor, son of Donald of Islay and great-grandson of Somerled, King of the Isles. The lands of Lowb, later to be the chiefly designation of Loup, are mentioned in a charter by James III confirming lands in Kintyre to the Lord of the Isles. In 1481, Charles Macalister was made constable of the Castle of Tarbert, and received a grant of land. Charles was succeeded as chief by his son, John, who was the first to be styled 'of the Lowb'. Clan Alister occupied an influential position, although they were by no means a numerous clan and therefore sought to secure their position by alliances with other houses. In 1591, Godfrey Macalister of Loup received a charter from the Earl of Argyll in relation to lands at Tarbert which they held until after 1745.

In 1602, Archibald Macalister, the heir of Tarbert, led his men, along with other clans of north Kintyre, to raid the prosperous island of Bute, for which act he was denounced as a rebel. In 1605 Archibald and his kinsman, John Macalister, Tutor of Loup, were ordered to appear before the Privy Council and find surety on pain of being outlawed. Alexander Macalister, along with Angus Og, leader of the Macdonalds of Islay, was found guilty of treason and, after incarceration in the Tolbooth prison in Edinburgh, they were hanged. However, by 1623 Macalister of Loup is named as one of the justices of the peace for Argyllshire.

The Macalisters came to Stirlingshire some time in the 14th centu-

ry, and during generations that followed their Celtic name was anglicised into its more familiar lowland version, Alexander. By the 16th century they settled on the estates of Menstrie only a few miles north-east of the mighty royal castle of Stirling. William Alexander of Menstrie became a courtier under the patronage of the Earl of Argyll. He was instrumental in promoting the colonisation of the Scottish territories in Canada, known as Nova Scotia, and devised the scheme whereby those investing in the colony would receive the honour known as a Baronetecy of Nova Scotia.

By 1706 Tarbert had passed from the Macalisters into the possession of the Macleans. The chiefs continued to flourish on their lands of Loup and a younger son, Duncan, settled in Holland in 1717, where he rose to high rank in the army; his descendants can still be traced to this day. The chiefly family eventually sold off their estates in Kintyre, and the present chief lives in England. Glenbarr Abbey is the modern clan centre, displaying many interesting artifacts and momentoes of the name.

Macarthur

CREST
Two laurel branches in orle Proper

MOTTO
Fide et opera
(By fidelity and labour)

The sons of Arthur are one of the oldest clans in Argyll. They probably spring from the same ancient British or Celtic stock as the Campbells with whom they were to become strongly identified. The Macarthurs supported Robert the Bruce in the struggle for the independence of Scotland, and their leader, Mac-ic-Artair, was rewarded with lands in mid Argyll, which had belonged to those who had opposed the king. However, in 1427, Iain Macarthur was beheaded for treason by James I and his lands were forfeited, signalling the decline of the clan as an independent force.

Over the years many descendants of Arthur dispersed, some settling in Skye where one family of Macarthurs established a famous piping school and were for several generations hereditary pipers to the Macdonalds of Sleat. Another branch of the family became armourers to the Macdonalds of Islay. Two families of Macarthurs came to the fore in the late 1400s around Loch Awe. There has been a good deal of confusion between the Macarthurs of Loch Awe and the Macarthur Campbells of Strachur on Loch Fyne. The names of some Macarthurs holding prominent positions appear in the 15th century in mid Argyll, and by the latter half of the 16th century they had gained so much land and power that their neighbours became jealous. Duncan Macarthur and his son were drowned in Loch Awe during a skirmish in 1567. The Earl of Argyll ordered compensation to be made and appointed a nephew, John, son of Finlay, to be leader of the Loch Awe Macarthurs. The direct male line appears to have died out somewhere round about 1780.

The Macarthurs of Milton, at Dunoon, had by the middle of the 1680s produced a baillie in Kintyre and a chamberlain to the Marquess of Montrose in Cowal. A large number of the clan, many of whom fought on both sides during the various Jacobite risings, left Scotland, particularly after the disaster of Culloden in 1746, eventually to settle in the West Indies, America and Canada. John Macarthur went to New South Wales with the 102nd Regiment and became commandant at Parramatta until 1804. He is credited with the foundation of the great Australian wool industry by first crossing Bengal and Irish sheep and later introducing the Merino breed from South Africa. His sons planted the first Australian vineyard. A Macarthur migrant from Strathclyde landed in America in 1840. His son, Arthur, fought in the civil war and was promoted to lieutenant general in the Union army, while his son, Douglas, became even more well known as the US military commander of the Pacific theatre during the Second World War.

Clan Arthur is at present without a chief, but in 1991 the Lord Lyon appointed James Macarthur of Milton as commander.

Macaulay

CREST
A boot couped at the ankle
and thereon a spur Proper

MOTTO
Dulce periculum
(Danger is sweet)

Some historians attribute this clan to one of the branches of the Siol Alpin, from whom also descend the Macgregors. It has equally been asserted that they stem from Amalghaidh, a younger son of the Earl of Lennox. The 19th-century heraldic authority, Nisbet, in his commentary on the Ragman Rolls of 1296, states that Maurice de Arncaple, who submitted to Edward I of England, was the ancestor of the Lairds of Ardincaple, which was to become the principal Macaulay seat.

In 1587 Sir Aulay Macaulay of Ardincaple was noted as a principal vassal of the Earls of Lennox. Whether the connection between the Macgregors and the Macaulays was one of descent or not, they became closely connected, and a bond of manrent was entered into on 27 May 1591 between Macgregor of Glen Strae and the Laird of Ardincaple; in it, Macaulay acknowledged the superiority of Macgregor and agreed to pay him tribute in cattle. The historian Skene, while sceptical about the claim that the Macaulays were a sept of Macgregor, stated that 'their connection with the Macgregors led them to take some part in the feuds that that unfortunate race were at all times engaged in, but the protection of the Earls of Lennox seems to have relieved the Macaulays from the conse-quences which fell so heavily upon the Macgregors'. The Macaulays were certainly keen to renounce any connection with the Macgregors when that family was declared outlaw, and Ardincaple was required to find surety for the good behaviour of his clan in 1610.

The fortunes of the family declined, however, and the 12th and last chief of the Macaulays sold off the estates to the Campbells around 1767.

The Macaulays of Lewis asserted that they were of Norse descent, their name meaning simply, 'son of Olaf'. One of the chiefs of the Lewis Macaulays in the 16th century was known as Donald Camm, meaning Donald One-Eye. He was renowned for his great strength and quarrelsome nature. The son of Donald Camm followed the Marquess of Montrose in his campaign for Charles I during the civil war, and died at the Battle of Aldern in 1645.

Thomas Babington Macaulay, the 19th-century politician and historian, was descended from the line of Donald Camm. He is best remembered for his works, *A History of England*, which is still read by historians today, and *Lays of Ancient Rome*. He appears to have made little reference during his life to his distinguished Highland background. He was MP for Edinburgh for a number of years and received many honours; he was raised to the peerage as Lord Macaulay in September 1857.

Macbain

CREST
A grey demi-cat-a-mountain
salient, on his sinister foreleg
a Highland targe Gules

MOTTO
Touch not a catt bot a targe

PLANT BADGE
Boxwood plants

There are several possible Gaelic origins for this name, but the most likely appears to be 'bheathain', meaning 'lively one'. According to tradition, the ancestor of the Macbains, a noble scion of the royal house of Macbeth, sought out his kin among the descendants of Gillichattan Mor, more commonly called the Clan Chattan after Malcolm IV finally broke the unruly remnants of the Mormaers of Moray. It is believed that Macbain formed part of the wedding party that accompanied Eva, daughter of Dougal Dall, 6th in line from Gillichattan Mor, on her marriage to Angus, chief of the Mackintoshes, in 1291.

The Macbains supported Robert the Bruce in the struggle for Scottish independence, and they are credited with the killing of the steward of the Red Comyn, whose master had been stabbed to death by Bruce himself in Greyfriars Church at Dumfries in 1306. They fought at the Battle of Harlaw in 1411 along with the rest of the Chattan confederation in the last serious attempt to wrest the ancient Lordship of the Isles from the grip of the king of Scots. Paul Macbean, the 12th chief, was weighed down by heavy debts and was forced to relinquish his lands around 1685. The present chiefly line descends from his younger son, the elder line having ended in a daughter, Elizabeth Margaret Macbean, who married Dougald Stuart around 1790, but died without issue.

The Macbains supported the Jacobite rising of 1715, and many were transported to the plantations in Virginia, Maryland and South Carolina after the Stuart defeat. This did not deter Gillies Mor

Macbean, grandson of the 12th chief, from taking up a commission as major to fight for Bonnie Prince Charlie, the 'Young Pretender'. At the Battle of Culloden in 1746, Gillies, a giant of a man said to be at least 6 ft 4 in, distinguished himself as he personally attempted to prevent Government dragoons breaking through to assault the Highlanders in the flank. He died in the attempt but not before he had taken 14 of the enemy with him. After Culloden the chief struggled to keep the remaining clan lands together, and they were finally sold in 1760.

The military prowess of the clan continued unabated. Lieutenant General Forbes Macbean was appointed commander of artillery in Canada in 1778. William Macbean had an extraordinary military career, rising from the rank of private to that of major general, earning the Victoria Cross for gallantry during the Indian Mutiny of 1858. It was a Macbain who commanded the Gordon Highlanders against the Boers of South Africa in 1881. In this century, the chiefly line has flourished, first in Canada and now in the United States. The chiefs have retrieved some of the clan lands, establishing a memorial park on the shores of Loch Ness.

Maccallum (Malcolm)

CREST
A tower Argent, window
and port Azure

MOTTO
In ardua tendit
(He has attempted
difficult things)

The Maccallums derive their name from 'Mac Ghille Chaluim', 'son of the disciple of Columba'. They settled in Lorn, probably towards the end of the 13th century. 'Maol', or 'shavenhead', became synonymous in Gaelic for 'monk', and thus 'Maol Chaluim' can also be translated as 'monk' or 'disciple of Columba'.

Ronald Maccallum of Corbarron was appointed constable of Craignish Castle in 1414. Donald McGillespie Vich O'Challum received a charter of the lands of Poltalloch in the parish of Kilmartin in Argyll from Duncan Campbell of Duntrune in May 1562. Zachary, the 5th of Poltalloch, was a noted swordsman who had been educated at St Andrews University. Zachary also succeeded to the estates of Corbarron, which were left to him by a kinsman. Neil Maccallum, son of Zachary's younger brother, Duncan, served in the French navy, and was reputed to have been the natural father of the Marquis de Montcalm, who was later to defend Quebec against what may well have been his own kin.

John Malcolm of Balbedie, Lochore and Innerneil, chamberlain of Fife in the reign of Charles I, had four sons: Sir John, created a Baronet of Nova Scotia in 1665; Alexander, later the judge, Lord Lochore; James, who fought with Viscount Dundee at Killiecrankie in 1689, and Michael. In the late 18th century, Dugald Maccallum, 9th of Poltalloch, changed his surname to Malcolm, according to the late Sir Iain Moncreiffe, for purely aesthetic reasons.

John Winfield Malcolm, who succeeded to the chiefship in 1893, had a distinguished parliamentary career, representing first Boston in

Lincolnshire in England, and then Argyll, from 1886 to 1892. In June 1896 he was raised to the peerage as Baron Malcolm of Poltalloch, but the title became extinct when he died without issue. He was succeeded by his brother, Edward, who was an engineer and much involved in local government. He had two sons, Major General Sir Neil Malcolm, who served in India and Africa, and throughout the First World War, and Sir Iain, who succeeded to the chiefship. In 1902 he married Jeanne Langtry, daughter of Émilie (Lillie) Langtry, the famous Edwardian actress and friend of Edward VII. It was widely believed that Jeanne was, in fact, the daughter of Prince Louis of Battenberg, a name now famous in its anglicized form of Mountbatten.

The chief's seat is still at Duntrune Castle, where the family have lived for centuries.

Macdonald

CREST
On a crest coronet Or, a hand
in armour fessways couped at
the elbow Proper holding a
cross crosslet fitchée Gules

MOTTO
Per mare per terras
(By sea and by land)

The Clan Donald hold as their eponymous ancestor Donald of Islay, who succeeded his father Reginald or Ranald, son of Somerled, King of the Isles in 1207. Somerled's campaigns spanned over 40 years, during which time he gained a kingdom and the hand of Ragnhild, daughter of King Olav the Red, Norse king of Man and the Isles. On Somerled's death, his realm was partitioned between his heirs: Dugall received Lorne, Mull and Jura; Angus had Bute, Arran and Garmoran, and Reginald fell heir to Islay and Kintyre. Reginald's son, Donald, was a fierce warrior who perpetrated so many black deeds in defence of his possessions that he feared for his eternal salvation and went to Rome to seek absolution for his sins from the pope. He was succeeded by Angus Mor, around 1269

When Alexander III determined to oppose the nominal suzerainty of Norway over the Hebrides, Angus Mor and his uncle, Ruari, fought with him at the Battle of Largs in 1263. Angus's son, Angus Og, came to the aid of Robert the Bruce, and led his clansmen at Bannockburn in 1314. The king rewarded his friend with extensive grants of land in the Islands and west Highlands. Angus Og was succeeded by his son, John, 'the Good', who assumed the title of Lord of the Isles. John's second marriage, to Princess Margaret, daughter of Robert II, produced the next Lord of the Isles, Donald, who fought at the Battle of Harlaw in 1411. The battle, fought to secure the Macdonald claim to the earldom of Ross, was indecisive but Donald's losses were heavy and he withdrew from the campaign.

The power of the lordship reached its peak under John, Earl of

Ross and Lord of the Isles. He entered into the Treaty of Ardtornish with Henry VII of England in 1462, agreeing to accept the English king as overlord once James IV had been defeated. James, with customary decisiveness, acted swiftly, invading the isles the following year and ultimately stripping John of all his titles. Attempts were made over the next two generations to revive the lordship, but by 1545, this had become a forlorn hope. The various branches of the descendants of Donald gradually accepted Crown charters and recognition of their separate holdings.

Various claims were made to the chiefship of the whole Clan Donald, but by the late 17th century, Hugh Macdonald of Sleat on Skye was recognized by the Privy Council as Laird of Macdonald. The lairds were first created baronets and then, in 1776, Lords Macdonald in the Irish peerage. The 3rd Lord Macdonald settled the chiefship and peerage on his younger son and obtained an Act of Parliament in 1847 to confirm this (see Macdonald of Sleat). The dispute was resolved in 1947, when the Lord Lyon recognized Lord Macdonald as high chief of Clan Donald, under whom are recognized the chiefs of Sleat, Clanranald and Glengarry.

Macdonald of Clanranald

CREST
A triple-towered castle Argent
masoned Sable, and issuing from
the centre tower a dexter arm in
armour embowed grasping a
sword all Proper

MOTTO
My hope is constant in thee

On a broken cross shaft found on the island of Texa off Islay is carved what is probably the oldest surviving likeness of a Macdonald. It depicts a typical 14th-century Celtic prince, armed with a great sword and a battle-axe. This is the cross of Ranald, son of John of Islay, Lord of the Isles, by his marriage to Amy Macruari, the heiress to the great Lordship of Garmoran. There now seems little doubt that Ranald was heir to the chiefship, but the succession did not pass to him, but to Donald, his younger half-brother, whose mother was a Stewart princess. Clan historians believe this was part of an amicable arrangement which saw Ranald receive a charter from his father for the greater part of the Macruari inheritance in return for being passed over as high chief.

Ranald had five sons, including Alan, the eldest, who was to succeed as chief of Clanranald, and Donald, who founded the line of Glengarry. Clanranald appears to have adjusted quickly to the realities of the extension of royal power throughout the Highlands, and on the first visit of James IV to the north, Ranald's grandson, Alan Macruari, was one of the few chiefs to render him homage.

James V annulled all charters given to chiefs while he was still a minor and, amongst others, Clanranald rebelled. James led an expedition to the isles and John Moidartach, the Clanranald chief, was arrested. In his absence, Ranald Gallda, another descendant of Alan Macruari, occupied Castle Tirrim. When the king died in 1542 the Earl of Arran became regent to the infant Mary, Queen of Scots, and promptly released the imprisoned island chiefs to use them as a

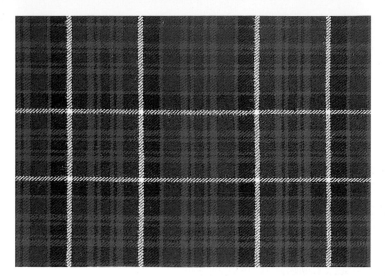

counterbalance to the powerful Argyll. John gathered his forces to oppose Ranald. They met to the north of Loch Lochy in 1544 at the Battle of Blar-na-leine. Ranald was killed during this stuggle.

The chiefs of Clanranald were staunch supporters of Charles I, and played a distinguished part in Montrose's great victory at Inverlochy in 1645. When the Stuart royal standard was unfurled on the Braes of Mar in 1715, Alan, the 14th chief, hurried to be first to rally to the Jacobite cause. His grateful monarch created him Lord Clanranald. He was killed at the head of his clan at Sheriffmuir later that year. His brother, Ranald, assumed the chiefship, but spent the rest of his life in exile in France. Succession passed to Donald of Benbecula, who had fought at Killiecrankie. It was his son, Ranald, who became famous during the rising of 1745 as Old Clanranald, to distinguish him from his dashing son, Ranald, Younger of Clanranald, who led the clan out. After Culloden, young Clanranald escaped to France but was allowed to return to Scotland in 1754.

The line of 'Young Clanranald of the Forty-five' died out in 1944, and the chiefship, or captaincy, passed to the heirs of Alexander Macdonald of Boisdale, a younger brother of the 17th chief.

Macdonald of Sleat

CRESTS
A hand in armour fesswise
holding a cross crosslet
fitchée Gules

MOTTO
Per mare per terras
(By sea and by land)

The Macdonalds of Sleat descend from Uisdein or Hugh, younger son of Alexander, Lord of the Isles, who had died at Dingwall in 1449. Hugh was a man of power and ability, and sat on his brother's Council of the Isles. In 1495, after the Lords of the Isles had been forfeited, Hugh obtained a Crown charter to the lands he held.

Donald Gorm, whose father had been proclaimed chief of all Clan Donald around 1518, attempted to restore the ancient Lordship of the Isles. He was proclaimed chief and Lord of the Isles, and in 1539 he led his men against the great Mackenzie castle at Eilean Donan in Kintail. Macdonald's galleys came under fire from the castle which was commanded by Duncan Macrae. Donald Gorm was shot in the leg by an arrow, and died from loss of blood. The feud with the Mackenzies was settled by the Council of Perth in 1539.

In 1608 Donald, grandson of Donald Gorm, along with his kinsman Clanranald and other leading chiefs, was invited to meet the king's representative, Lord Ochiltree, to discuss the royal policy for the isles. The meeting was a trap, and Donald was confined in Blackness Castle, only being released when he agreed to submit to the king. He died in December 1616, when he was succeeded by his nephew, Sir Donald Macleod, later 1st Baronet of Sleat. He supported the royalist cause in the civil war, and when he died in 1643, his son sent 400 of his clansmen to join Montrose.

Sleat remained loyal to the Stuart cause and fought with his clansmen at Killiecrankie and Sheriffmuir in 1715. Despite strong Jacobite sympathies, they took no part in the rising of 1745 and the

Sleat estates remained intact. The 9th Baronet was created Lord Macdonald in July 1776.

Sir Godfrey, the 11th Baronet and 3rd Lord Macdonald, married Louisa, natural daughter of the Duke of Gloucester, brother of George III. He did not, however, contract a marriage which was legally recognized in England until 1803 and, although Lord Macdonald's eldest son was legitimate in Scots law, he was not so under the law of England. He decreed that his eldest son should change his name to Bosville and have his mother's substantial English estates, while the eldest son born after the marriage was recognized in England should have the chiefship of Clan Donald and the peerage. A private Act of Parliament was procured in 1847 to regulate the position in accordance with the chief's wishes. However, in 1910, Alexander Bosville, grandson of Macdonald's eldest son, obtained a declarator in the Court of Session that his grandfather was legitimate and he was therefore entitled to resume the name of Macdonald and the Sleat baronetcy, a decision which partly overturned the settlement imposed in the previous century.

Macdonell of Glengarry

CREST
A raven Proper perching
on a rock Azure

MOTTO
Cragan an Fhithich
(The rock of the raven)

Ranald, son of a 14th-century Lord of the Isles, had five sons, including Alan, the progenitor of Clanranald, and Donald. Donald took as his second wife a daughter of Fraser of Lovat, and had two further sons, Alexander and Angus. Alexander is considered by some historians to be the first true chief of Glengarry, but usually counted as the 4th.

It was not until the late 15th century that Glengarry played an independent part in the politics of Clan Donald. Royal policy to pacify the Gael required that the traditional rights of chiefs should be replaced with feudal relationships, in which the Crown was acknowledged as ultimate superior. On 6 March 1539, the chief received a Crown charter to his lands of Glengarry and Morar, half the lands of Lochalsh, Lochcarron and Lochbroom, together with the castle of Strome. However, this did not stop Glengarry from following Donald Gorm of Sleat in his attempt to reclaim the Lordship of the Isles. The rebellion swiftly collapsed when Donald was killed while attacking Eilean Donan Castle. Glengarry was among the island chiefs tricked into attending on James V at Portree, whereupon they were seized and imprisoned in Edinburgh. Glengarry remained in the castle until the king's death in 1542.

Donald, 8th of Glengarry, is reputed to have lived for more than 100 years and ruled his clan for more than 70 of these. He obtained a charter under the Great Seal in 1627, erecting his lands of Glengarry into a free barony. However, he had not always enjoyed such royal favour. In 1609, Donald was warned by the Privy Council

to stop harbouring fugitives from the isles, and to appear before them that year to answer for his conduct. He failed to appear, and was denounced as a rebel.

Aeneas, the 9th chief, fought for Charles I at Inverlochy, Dundee and Auldearn. He followed Charles II to the final Royalist defeat at Worcester in 1651. The Glengarry estates were forfeited by Cromwell, but at the Restoration, the chief was created Lord Macdonell and Aros. The honour was short-lived; when he died in 1680 without issue, his peerage became extinct. The Stuart monarchs called upon the Macdonells again in their struggle to regain their throne from the house of Hanover. Alasdair, the 11th chief, fought at Sheriffmuir in 1715, faring rather better than the 13th chief, who was captured by an English frigate when hurrying from France to join the Forty-five. He languished in the Tower of London until 1747.

The chiefs of Glengarry have served their country ably in the field over the last two centuries, with perhaps the most famous being General Sir James Macdonell, brother of the 14th chief, who was one of the heroes of the Battle of Waterloo in 1815.

Macdougall

CREST
(On a chapeau Gules furred Ermine)
a dexter arm in armour embowed
fessways couped Proper, holding a
cross crosslet fitchée erect Gules

MOTTO
Buaidh no bas
(To conquer or die)

This clan takes its name from Dugall, son of Somerled, King of the Isles, who, after his father's death in 1164, held most of Argyll together with the islands of Mull, Lismore, Jura, Tiree, Coll and many others. He styled himself 'King of the South Isles and Lord of Lorne'. His son, Duncan, and his grandson, Ewan, built castles to defend their broad dominions, including Dunstaffnage, Dunollie and Duntrune.

The Macdougalls were vassals of the Norwegian kings, but opposed their overlords at the Battle of Largs in 1263. The Norsemen were defeated, and three years later, all of the Hebrides were ceded by Norway to Scotland.

The Macdougalls influence in Argyll brought them into conflict with the Campbells, and in 1294, John Macdougall, 'the Lame', led the clan against them. At the Path of Lorn, between Loch Avich and Scammadale, the Macdougalls were intercepted by the Argyll men and there was considerable slaughter on both sides.

Because of marriage ties with the Comyns, the Macdougalls came into conflict with the Bruces, in spite of previously having supported Wallace and the cause of Scottish independence. In 1308, Robert the Bruce led a large force into Argyll against the Macdougalls. John of Lorne set an ambush for the king's army at the narrow Pass of Brander, but after a savage engagement the Macdougalls were broken and forced to flee. The king formally forfeited the Macdougall lands, most of which passed to the Campbells.

The Macdougalls were never to regain their island possessions, but

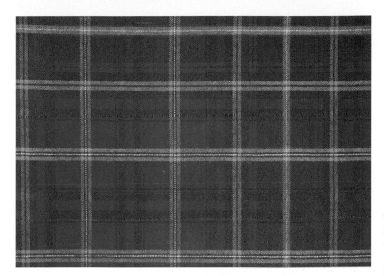

to a large degree their fortunes were restored when Euan Macdougall married a granddaughter of Robert the Bruce. Most of the mainland estates were re-granted by a royal charter of David II.

During the troubled times of the early 17th century, the Macdougalls were generally royalist, and in 1645 Alexander Macdougall led 500 of his clansmen into battle. After the defeat of the Marquess of Montrose, a Covenanting army under David Leslie was sent to Argyll to deal with royalist sympathisers.

With the re-establishment of the monarchy in 1660, the Macdougall lands were again restored. Their loyalty to the Stuarts was proved again when the 22nd chief, Iain Ciar, fought in the rising of 1715 at the Battle of Sheriffmuir. The chief was forced into exile, but later returned to Scotland to live as a fugitive until he was pardoned in 1727. His son, Alexander, although certainly a Jacobite sympathizer, did not join the Forty-five, although his brother and some clansmen fought at Culloden. Alexander built a more modern house behind Dunollie Castle which was extended in the mid-19th century by the 25th chief, Vice Admiral Sir John Macdougall of Macdougall.

Macduff

CREST
A demi-lion Gules holding in the
dexter paw a broadsword erected
in pale Proper, hilted and
pommelled Or

MOTTO
Deus juvat
(God assists)

Clan Duff claims descent from the royal Scoto-Pictish line through Queen Gruoch, wife of Macbeth. After the death of the king, her second husband, her son Lulach was murdered in 1058. Malcolm III seized the Crown and his son, Aedh, married Queen Gruoch's only living granddaughter. He was created Earl of Fife and hereditary abbot of Abernethy. Fife, symbolically representing the ancient royal line of his wife, became the undisputed second man of the kingdom. He bore on his shield the red lion rampant and was accorded the right to enthrone the king of Scots at his coronation.

In 1306 Duncan Macduff, Earl of Fife, was a minor held by Edward I of England as his ward, and so his sister, Isabel, Countess of Buchan, placed the golden circlet upon the head of Robert the Bruce. For this act, she was imprisoned in a cage suspended from the walls of Berwick Castle when she later fell into the hands of the English army.

The earldom was forfeited in 1336 for treason, and passed into the hands of Robert Stewart, later Duke of Albany and Regent of Scotland. In 1404, David Duff received a charter from Robert III to the lands of Muldavit in Banffshire. John Duff sold Muldavit in 1626, but his half-brother, Adam, was a man of ability who acquired considerable wealth and laid the foundation for the ultimate prosperity of the family. His son, Alexander, improved the family's estates in Banffshire, which he further extended by marriage to Helen, the daughter of Archibald Grant of Ballentomb. William Duff, MP for the county of Banff, was created Earl Fife and Viscount Macduff in

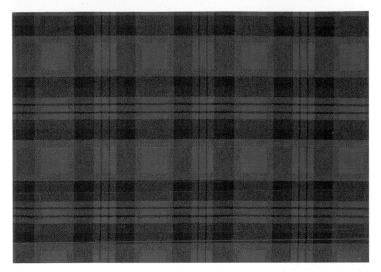

1759. The new earl's claim of descent from the great Macduffs had some merit but has never been genealogically established.

James, the 4th Earl Fife, fought with distinction during the Peninsular War of 1808–14 and was honoured for his services with the Order of the Thistle. The 6th Earl Fife, married Princess Louise, the Princess Royal, eldest daughter of the Prince of Wales, the future King Edward VII. He was advanced to the highest rank of the peerage as Duke of Fife in 1889. By a special reservation in the patent creating the dukedom, the title was to pass, in default of a male heir, to the duke's eldest daughter, Princess Alexandra, and if she produced no male heirs, to her sister Princess Maude. In 1923, Princess Maude married Lord Carnegie, who was later to succeed to his father's title as Earl of Southesk and chief of the Carnegies. The dukedom of Fife has now passed to the Carnegie chiefs. The ancient red lion on gold of Fife is today borne on the shield of Wemyss of Wemyss, direct descendents of the ancient Macduff earls.

Macewen

CREST
The trunk of an oak tree
sprouting Proper

MOTTO
Reviresco
(I grow strong again)

There are numerous spellings of this name, which is rendered in Gaelic as 'Maceoghainn'. The sons of Ewen hold that they descend from Ewen of Otter on the shores of Loch Fyne in Argyll. Malcolm MacEwen witnessed a charter by the Earl of Atholl to the church of St Andrews around 1174. The chiefs of the clan seem to have stayed around Loch Fyne and shared a common heritage with the Maclachlans and the Macneils until around 1432, when by a charter of James I, the barony of Otter was confirmed to Sween Macewen with a destination to the heirs of Duncan Campbell of Loch Awe. Sween is the last Macewen chief on record, and thereafter they appear only as dependents of the Campbells or as broken (clanless) men. In 1598 200 Macewens were described as broken Highlandmen heavily armed and living by robbery. They are listed in an Act of Parliament in 1602, along with other broken clans as subjects of the Earl of Argyll who was made answerable for their good behaviour. Some of this name seem to have become poets or bards, and found patrons among the Campbells and the Macdougalls; Neil Macewen composed a poem on the death of Campbell of Glenorchy in 1630. The Macewens seem to have supported the Jacobite cause, but only as individuals, as they were lacking a chief to call them out as a clan.

The Macewens were true to their motto and grew strong again in the south west of Scotland. They made their home at Bardrochat in Ayrshire, sometime in the early 17th century. However, the name is listed by Black in his *Surnames of Scotland* in this region as early as

the 14th century; Patrick McEwyn was provost of Wigtown in 1331. There may be no connection between the Argyll and Ayrshire Macewens other than their names.

The lairds of Bardrochat rose to prominence in their own right and were created baronets. The sister of the 3rd Baronet is Christian, Lady Hesketh, the author of a significant study of tartan. Sir William Macewan, who was born in Rothesay in 1848, was a distinguished surgeon who performed the first operation to remove a brain tumour in 1879.

Sir Alexander Macewan, a provost of Inverness, was a noted advocate of Gaelic education. He was elected president of the Scottish National Party and, shortly before his death in 1941, stood unsuccessfully for Parliament.

The Macewens are presently without a chief but, in the spirit of their motto, there is an active clan association, particularly in the USA.

Macfarlane

CREST
A demi-savage brandishing in his
dexter hand a broad sword Proper
and pointing with his sinister to an
Imperial Crown Or standing by
him on the Wreath

MOTTO
This I'll defend

The Macfarlanes are descended from Alwyn, Celtic Earl of Lennox, whose younger son, Gilchrist, received lands at Arrochar on the shores of Loch Long at the end of the 12th century. Gilchrist's grandson, Malduin, sheltered Robert the Bruce when he was forced to flee through Loch Lomondside to reach the safety of the west Highlands. The Macfarlanes also fought at Bannockburn in 1314.

Malduin's son, Parlan, provided the chief's patronymic, and Iain Macpharlain received a charter of confirmation to Arrochar in 1420. Duncan, the last Celtic Earl of Lennox, was executed by James I, and although the Macfarlanes had a valid claim to the earldom, the title was given to John Stewart, Lord Darnley. The Macfarlanes sought to oppose the Stewarts but they proved too powerful and Andrew Macfarlane, the 10th chief, married a younger daughter of Lord Darnley, cementing a new alliance.

The 11th chief and many of his clansmen fell at Flodden in 1513. When the Earl of Lennox threw in his lot with Henry VII of England, the clan followed him, capturing Bute and Arran, but they met with stout resistance at the royal castle of Dumbarton. The Macfarlanes later opposed the invading English at the Battle of Pinkie in 1547 where Duncan, the 13th chief, and his brother were both killed.

After the murder of Lord Darnley, Mary, Queen of Scots' second husband, the Macfarlanes opposed the queen and were noted for their gallantry at the Battle of Langside in 1568. The clan's crest and motto alludes to the defence of the crown of the infant James VI

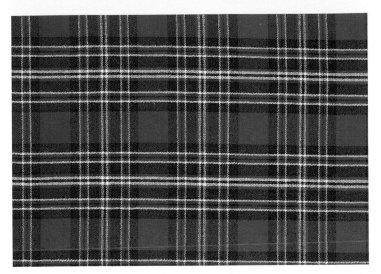

which was secured by the victory at Langside. Their loyalty to the Stuarts brought Macfarlane swords to the aid of the Marquess of Montrose when Walter Macfarlane, the 16th chief, declared for Charles I. They fought at Montrose's great victory at Inverlochy in 1645. In spite of their attachment to the Stuarts, they could not support James VII, and the chief declared for Queen Mary and her husband, William of Orange, in 1688.

The clan does not seem to have played any major part in the Jacobite risings of 1715 and 1745 which may have been because the 20th chief, Walter Macfarlane, a noted antiquary and scholar, lived in Edinburgh for most of his life. The clan lands at Arrochar were sold off after Walter's death in 1767, and the direct male line of the chiefs failed in 1886.

Macfie

CREST
A demi lion rampant Proper

MOTTO
Pro rege
(For the king)

In modern Gaelic, this name is written as 'Maca'phi'. It is usually rendered in English, Macfie, Macphee or Macafie. The name appears to be derived from 'MacDhuibhshith', meaning 'son of the dark fairy' although the origin of this name has been remains a mystery. Tradition asserts, however, that the Macfies are descended from a seal-woman who was prevented from returning to the sea

In 1164 a Duibhshith was known to have been 'ferleighinn', or 'reader', at Iona when Malcolm IV was king. The Macphees of Colonsay were the hereditary keepers of the records of the Lords of the Isles and there is a tradition that one of the chiefs of Colonsay, serving in the retinue of the Lord of the Isles, fought and overcame Sir Gile de Argentine at the Battle of Bannockburn in 1314.

In the 15th century, the Stewart kings, and particularly James IV, were determined to bring the isles under direct royal control – a process naturally opposed by the Macdonalds and their allies. In 1615 Malcolm Macphee of Colonsay joined Sir James Macdonald in his rebellion against the Earl of Argyll, who represented royal authority. Macphee and 18 other leading conspirators were betrayed to the Campbells and were forced to submit to royal authority. (Colonsay was later murdered in 1623 while ignominiously hiding under piles of seaweed.)

The Macphees were dispossessed, and most went to the mainland where they found shelter in Lochaber. Many Macphees followed Cameron of Lochiel at the ill-fated Battle of Culloden in 1746. In the middle of the 19th century Ewan Macphee became famous as the

last Scottish outlaw, when he settled with his band on Eilean Mhic Phee in Loch Quoich. He recognised no law and was an inveterate sheep stealer. Comtemporary accounts describe him as a man of ferocious appearance and stature who was heavily armed at all times. He raised a family in atrocious conditions and in later years became a local, if eccentric, celebrity. He was allowed to live out his life in peace and was sustained by gifts, even from neighbouring lairds

Macfie of Dreghorn matriculated arms in the Lyon Register in 1864. He was a member of a powerful merchant family with considerable interests in the sugar-refining industry. The company was eventually to be taken over by the present sugar giants, Tate & Lyle.

There is an active Macfie Society worldwide and the Lord Lyon has recognized this by granting a commission for the appointment of a clan commander.

Macgillivray

CREST
A cat-a-mountain sejant guardant
Proper, his dexter fore-paw on the
ground, his sinister fore-paw in a
guardant posture and his tail reflexed
under his sinister paw

MOTTO
Touch not this cat

This name is derived from the Gaelic, Mhic Gille-brath , which means 'son of the servant of judgement'. This may indicate a clerical origin and indeed many early references to the name are found in church records. Tradition asserts that Gillivray, the progenitor of the clan, placed himself under the protection of the chiefs of the Clan Mackintosh, and through them joined the Clan Chattan confederation.

The Macgillivrays were first accurately recorded in Dunmaglas in 1549. At a great gathering of the Clan Chattan in 1609, the 'haill kin and race of Macgillivray' was represented by Malcolm of Dalcrombie and Duncan Macfarquhar of Dunmaglas. The Macgillivrays were supporters of episcopacy in the church, and this caused them to be persecuted by their Calvinist and presbyterian neighbours.

In common with most of the confederated Clan Chattan families, the Macgillivrays were staunch Jacobites, and they fought in both the Fifteen and in the Forty-five rebellions. In 1745, the chief of the Mackintoshes was an officer in a Hanoverian regiment. His wife, a formidable lady with distinct Jacobite sympathies, summoned Alexander Macgillivray and placed him in command of the regiment raised by Clan Chattan. Macgillivray was at the head of his men at Culloden where he fell along with many of his followers, and the graveyard at Dunlichity commemorates the many clan dead.

After Culloden, many emigrated across the Atlantic where their spirit of independence and fortitude made many successful, particularly as traders. William Macgillivray became head of the Canadian Northwest Company and member of the Legislative Council of

Lower Canada. Another William became a leading Victorian naturalist. Raised in Harris, Macgillivray was educated at Aberdeen University from where he graduated in 1815. In 1841, he was appointed professor of natural history at his alma mater and is generally regarded as the father of British ornithology, publishing a seminal five-volume collection, *The History of British Birds*, between 1837 and 1852.

The estates in Dunmaglas were sold off in 1890 and the last chief is believed to have died in Canada. However, the Macgillivrays have become organized and active once more, and there are clan societies throughout the world.

Macgregor

CREST
A lion's head erased Proper,
crowned with an antique crown Or

MOTTO
'S rioghal mo dhream
(My race is royal)

PLANT BADGE
Scots pine

The Clan Gregor held lands in Glenstrae, Glenlochy and Glenorchy. Most modern historians agree that the first certain chief was Gregor 'of the golden bridles'. Gregor's son, Iain Camm, One-eye, succeeded as the 2nd chief sometime prior to 1390. Robert the Bruce granted the barony of Loch Awe, which included much of the Macgregor lands, to the chief of the Campbells who harried the Macgregors. The clan were forced to retire deeper into their territories until they were largely restricted to Glenstrae.

Iain of Glenstrae died in 1519 with no direct heirs. The Campbells supported the succession of Eian, who was married to the daughter of Sir Colin Campbell of Glenorchy. Eian's son, Alistair, fought the English at the Battle of Pinkie in 1547 but died shortly thereafter. Colin Campbell of Glenorchy, who had bought the superiority from his kinsman, Argyll, refused to recognize the claim of Gregor Roy Macgregor to the estates. For 10 years Gregor waged war against the Campbells. He had little choice but to become an outlaw, raiding cattle and sheltering in the high glens. In 1570 the Campbells eventually captured and killed him.

In April 1603 James VI issued an edict proclaiming the name of Macgregor 'altogidder abolisheed' – any who bore the name must renounce it or suffer death. Macgregor and 11 of his chieftains, were hanged at Edinburgh's Mercat Cross in January 1604. Clan Gregor was scattered, with many taking other names, such as Murray or Grant. They became known as the 'Children of the Mist'.

Rob Roy Macgregor, born in 1671, a younger son of Macgregor of

Glengyle, was forced to assume his mother's name of Campbell. His adventures have been immortalized and romanticized by Sir Walter Scott's novel, *Rob Roy*, but there is little doubt that he was a thorn in the Government's flesh. When the Stuart standard was raised in 1715, he attached himself to the Jacobite cause, although he acted largely independently. After the indecisive Battle of Sheriffmuir, he set about plundering at will. He died in 1734 and is buried in the churchyard at Balquhidder.

The persecution of Clan Gregor ended in 1774, when the laws against them were repealed. A petition subscribed by over eight hundred Macgregors declared General John Murray of Lanrick to be the proper and true chief. He was, in fact, a Macgregor, being a descendant of Duncan Macgregor of Ardchoille, who died in 1552. The general had served extensively in India before being created a baronet in 1795. His son, Sir Evan, was also a general and later Governor of Dominica. He played a prominent part in the 1822 visit of George IV to Scotland, when his clansmen guarded the Scottish Crown regalia, the 'Honours of Scotland'. He proposed the toast to the 'chief of chiefs' at the royal banquet in Edinburgh.

Macinnes

CREST
A sinister arm from the shoulder bend-
ways, attired in a close sleeve of the
proper tartan of Clan Aonghais, cuff
flashes yellow with three buttons Or,
grasping a bow Vert, stringed Gules

MOTTO
Ghift dhe Agus an righ
(By the grace of God and king)

This Celtic name is derived from the Gaelic 'Macaonghais', meaning 'son of Angus'. The historian, Ian Grimble, notes the earliest reference to the sons of Angus is given in the 7th-century chronicle,
Senchus Fer n'Alban (*History of the Men of Scotland*). The Scots of
Dalriada appear to have been divided into three kindreds: those of
Gabran, of Lorne and of Angus. The kindred of Angus are said to
have possessed Islay, later to be the seat of the Lordship of the Isles.
There is, however, little concrete evidence to connect all of this to
the Macinneses as a distinct family.

It seems reasonable to assume that the Macinnes were in some way
descended from the early rulers of Dalriada and that they were kin
to the lords of Lorne. They were later to become largely dependants
of the Campbells who secured hegemony over much of what had
been the old kingdom of Dalriada. The Macinnes appear to have
become established in Morven around the castle at Kinlochaline.
Clan tradition asserts that they once held this fortress in their own
right under the Lords of the Isles but it is more likely that they were
captains or hereditary keepers for their more powerful kin. In 1645,
the Macinnes held Kinlochaline against the forces of Alasdair
Maccolla Macdonald (known as Colkitto, meaning left-handed).
Colkitto was plundering Morven in support of Montrose and
Charles I and his forces stormed the castle, burning it to the ground.

Another section of this family were noted as hereditary archers to
the Mackinnon chiefs on Skye, and this is alluded to in the most
common crest of this name, which is an arm holding a bow.

In the Jacobite stuggles of the 18th century, the main body of the clan followed the Campbells in supporting the Hanoverian cause against the Stuart exiles. However, one branch, which had become connected with the Stewarts of Ardsheal, fought for the Jacobite cause.

In common with many fragmented families, the Macinneses scattered worldwide during the great periods of emigration and the name is commonly found throughout the English-speaking world, particularly in Canada and New Zealand.

Macintyre

CREST
A dexter hand holding a dagger
in pale Proper

MOTTO
Per ardua
(Through difficulties)

PLANT BADGE
White heather

In Gaelic, the name Macintyre is rendered 'Mac-an t'saor', meaning 'son of the carpenter'. A traditional account dates the origins of the name to the early 12th century, when Somerled was establishing his lordship in the Western Isles. Somerled's nephew, Macarill, promised to aid his uncle to win the hand of the daughter of King Olav. He sabotaged the king's galley by boring holes in the hull, which he only plugged when Olav agreed to the marriage. Macarill was thereafter known as the 'wright' or 'carpenter', and found high favour with his uncle. Macarill's descendants later established themselves on the mainland at Glen 'Oe by Ben Cruachan on Loch Etiveside. By the end of the 13th century, the Macintyres were foresters to the Lord of Lorn, an office they held through the passing of the lordship from the Macdougalls to the Stewarts and finally to the Campbells.

The Macintyre chiefs cannot be listed with any accuracy, but the 1st chief of modern record was Duncan, who married a daughter of Campbell of Barcaldine and died in 1695. Duncan had led his clan through the dangerous times of the early 17th century as Charles I struggled to impose his religious practices on his Scottish subjects. Although many Macinnes supported Archibald Campbell, 8th Earl of Argyll, the leader of the Covenanter faction in the Scottish Parliament, in his opposition to the Crown, others joined the royalist forces commanded by Alasdair Macdonald, 'Colkitto', including the chief's piper. The chief, however, was with Argyll at Inverlochy in February 1645 when the Campbells were surprised by Montrose and routed.

James, the 3rd chief, was born around 1727. When Prince Charles Edward Stuart raised his father's standard at Glenfinnan in 1745, James would have joined him but for the influence of his Campbell wife and neighbours. Many clansmen, however, slipped away and fought under Stewart of Appin at Culloden.

The Macintyres originally held their lands by right of the sword, but they had acquired feudal obligations to the Campbells. The payments were purely symbolic until the early 18th century, when Campbell of Breadalbane persuaded the Macintyre chief to pay a cash rent. The rent was then progressively raised to a point where Donald, the 4th recorded chief, was unable to pay, and he emigrated to America in 1783, leaving his brother, Duncan, to manage the estate. Duncan struggled on until 1806, when he, too, left the glen. The chiefly line continued to honour their Scottish origins in America, preserving the armorial great seal, signet ring and quaffing cup.

In 1991, James Wallace Macintyre of Glenoe, 9th of the recorded chiefs, was formally recognized by the Lord Lyon, King of Arms, and admitted to the Standing Council of Scottish Chiefs.

Maciver

CREST
A boar's head couped Or

MOTTO
Nunquam obliviscar
(I will never forget)

This family of very ancient heritage takes its name from the Gaelic 'Maciomhar', meaning 'son of Ivar'. This is a Norse personal name and it is therefore extremely difficult to determine with any certainty the progenitor after whom this family is named. Doenaldus, son of Makbeth Macyvar, is recorded as one of the perambulators of the boundary between the lands of Arbroath Abbey and the barony of Kynblathmund in 1219. In 1292 the lands of Malcolm McIuyr and others in Lorne were erected into the sheriffdom of Lorne by Act of Parliament.

However, it is asserted that Iver was a son of Duncan, Lord of Lochow, and therefore the Macivers were part of the progeny from which was to spring the mighty Clan Campbell. Indeed, it has been suggested that Iver was the elder son and that the Macivers were truly the senior line. In practical terms, this seems to have been of little significance, as the Campbell Lords of Lochow succeeded in acquiring the lordship of Lorne, thereafter becoming earls, and ultimately dukes, of Argyll. Their ascendency over their cousins, the Macivers, does not seem to have gone undisputed, and it is recorded that in 1564 the 5th Earl, in return for Maciver acknowledgment of his title, resigned all claims he might have to receive calps (tribute in cattle or other livestock) from them.

The Macivers held the estates of Asknish, and the deeds to their estates bound them to use that name. They remained trusted allies of the Campbells, and in 1572 Duncan Maciver, chief of Asknish, was captain or keeper of Inveraray Castle. His cousin, Charles, the

Laird of Ballochyle, is said to have used the names Campbell and Maciver quite indiscriminately, but in May 1589 he is recorded as holding the powerful post of chamberlain of Argyll. Thereafter the fortunes of the Macivers were largely those of the great house of Argyll and they followed Campbell interests throughout the 17th and 18th centuries.

Some historians have suggested that it was after the restoration of the Campbell fortunes, after the defeat of James VII in 1690, that the Earls of Argyll imposed upon their Maciver supporters the condition that they adopt the surname of Campbell in return for the restoration of their forfeited estates. However, because there had been so much intermarriage with other Campbell cadets, including the houses of Dunstaffnage, Ardkinglass and others, the use of the name and the quartering of arms would have taken place in any event. The principal houses bore into this century the compound surnames of Maciver-Campbell of Asknish and Maciver-Campbell of Ballochyle.

There is now an active Maciver Society which has established its headquarters at Strathendry Castle in Fife, and which seeks to promote awareness of the distinctive character of the name.

Mackay

CREST
A dexter arm erect couped at the
elbow the hand grasping a dagger
also erect all Proper

MOTTO
Manu forti
(With a strong hand)

PLANT BADGE
Great bullrush

In Gaelic this name is rendered as 'Macaodh', 'son of Hugh'. Exactly who Hugh was is uncertain. It is suggested that the name comes from a branch of the ancient Celtic royal house. Aodh, or Hugh, was the abbot of Dunkeld, 1st Earl of Fife, and the elder brother of Alexander I. Aodh's wife was the granddaughter of Queen Gruoch, wife of Macbeth. Malcolm Macaodh, who died in 1168, was married to a sister of Somerled of the Isles, became Earl of Ross. Malcolm's son-in-law became Earl of Caithness and was also lord of the lands of Strathnaver where, by the 14th century, the clan appears to have become established in its recognized form.

Angus Dubh, Macaodh, married Elizabeth, sister of Donald, Lord of the Isles, and granddaughter of Robert II, around 1415. Angus was an extremely powerful figure and is said to have been able to call out 4000 men from his lands at Strathnaver. From this pinnacle of power, the clan spent the next five centuries fending off their predatory neighbours, the Earls of Sutherland. They were ultimately to lose the lands to the Sutherlands in 1829 through debt.

By the end of the 16th century, the Mackay chiefs were largely dependant on the Earls of Sutherland and sought a better future as professional soldiers on the Continent. The Mackay Regiment was renowned for its martial prowess during the Thirty Years War under the command of Donald Mackay who was created a Baronet of Nova Scotia on 28 March 1627. A year later he was elevated to the peerage as Baron Reay. Lord Reay fought for Charles I in the civil war and was to have been created Earl of Strathnaver, but the royal patent

was not completed. He went into exile in Denmark, where he died in February 1649. His elder son, John, the 2nd Lord Reay, also fought for Charles I. His second wife was Barbara, daughter of Hugh Mackay of Scouri, who commanded the forces of William and Mary at Killiecrankie in 1689. John's second son, Aenas, was Brigadier General of Mackay's Scotch Regiment in the service of the States General of Holland. The family settled in the Netherlands, where they prospered. Barthold Mackay was created Baron Ophemert in the Netherlands in June 1822.

Eric, the 9th Lord Reay, died unmarried in 1875. The succession passed to his cousin, the Baron Ophemert, who became 10th Lord Reay. The family maintained their links with the Netherlands, and on the 11th Baron's death, the title passed to his cousin, whose father had been prime minister of that country. Lord Reay died within months of succeeding to the title, which then passed to his 15-year-old son. The new chief became a British subject in 1938 and worked in the Foreign Office during the Second World War.

Mackenzie

CREST
A mount in flames Proper

MOTTO
Luceo non uro
(I shine, not burn)

PLANT BADGE
Stagshorn clubmoss

This name is rendered in Gaelic as 'Maccoinneach', meaning 'son of the bright one'. It has been suggested that the name alludes to the pagan god, Cernunnos, who is often depicted as having a stag's head or antlers; this may be one explanation of the chief's shield which bears a stag's head. The Mackenzies are believed to descend from Gillean of the Aird, the 12th-century ancestor of the earls of Ross. By 1267 the clan were settled at Eilean Donan, the great castle at Loch Duich.

By the 15th century, the earldom of Ross formed part of the patrimony of the lordship of the isles. By acknowledging allegiance to the Crown, the Mackenzies weathered the storms which the Stewarts unleashed on the Lordship of the Isles, so that their fortunes waxed as the Macdonalds' waned. In 1463, the chiefs received a royal charter to their lands of Kintail and when Alasdair of Kintail raised his clan against the rebellious earl of Ross, he was rewarded by James III with a grant of extensive lands. In 1508, Kintail was erected into a free barony.

By the beginning of the 17th century, the Mackenzie territory extended from the Black Isles to the Outer Hebrides. They gained the island of Lewis from its former Macleod rulers and Lochalsh from the Macdonells. In 1609 the chief was raised to the peerage as Lord Mackenzie of Kintail and in 1625, his son was created Earl of Seaforth. Lord Mackenzie's brother, Sir Roderick Mackenzie of Coigach, founded the line created baronets in 1628 and later, earls of Cromartie.

While the Seaforths embraced the reformed church and were signatories of the National Covenant in 1638, the execution of Charles I appalled Seaforth, who hurried to join Charles II in exile in Holland. He died before Oliver Cromwell's final victory at Worcester in 1651.

The family continued their support of the Stuarts, and Seaforth fought for James VIII at the Battle of the Boyne in 1690. Already a Knight of the Thistle, the exiled king made him a Jacobite marquess. The 5th Earl was charged with treason for his participation in the rising of 1715 and his titles were forfeited. Although his grandson was made Earl of Seaforth again, the male line came to an end in 1815.

The earls of Cromartie were also Jacobites, and George, the 3rd Earl, fought at the Battle of Falkirk. He and his son, Lord Macleod, were captured at Dunrobin Castle in April 1746 and the earl's titles were forfeit. The forfeited estates, but not the title, were subsequently restored. His descendant, Anne, was created Countess of Cromartie in her own right in 1861, with a special destination of the earldom in favour of her second son, Francis. The re-created earls were recognized by the Lord Lyon as chiefs of Mackenzie.

Mackinnon

CREST
A boar's head erased and holding
in its mouth the shank of a deer
all Proper

MOTTO
Audentes fortuna juvat
(Fortune assists the daring)

The Mackinnons are a branch of the great Siol Alpin, the descendants of Kenneth Macalpin, who reigned in the 9th century.

The Mackinnons on Arran gave shelter to Robert the Bruce during his time as a fugitive, helping him make his escape to Carrick. After the king's victory at Bannockburn they were rewarded with land on Skye. A branch of the chiefly family became hereditary abbots of Iona. The last hereditary abbot was John Mackinnon, the 9th chief, who was also Bishop of the Isles. He died around 1500.

The Scots kings since the reign of James IV had slowly undermined the power of the island chiefs. In 1606 James VI sent Lord Ochiltree to Mull to make proposals to the chiefs on his plans for government of the isles. When they disagreed with Ochiltree's plans, he seized the chiefs and imprisoned them in castles on the mainland. In 1609, Lachlan Mackinnon of that Ilk and other chiefs were forced to subscribe to the Statutes of Iona, which placed many restrictions upon their power.

Despite this, the Mackinnons were loyal to the Stuarts, and fought in the army of Montrose at the Battle of Inverlochy in 1645. Their young chief, Lachlan Mor, was at the time in the custody of Argyll. In 1650, Lachlan raised a regiment which fought on the royalist side at the Battle of Worcester in 1651. The chief was created a knight banneret by Charles II on the field of battle.

The clan remained loyal to the Stuarts in the next century, and sent 150 men to join the Earl of Mar at the Battle of Sheriffmuir in 1715. For this act the chief was declared forfeit for treason. The Mackin-

nons were also out during the Forty-five, marching to Edinburgh to join Prince Charles. They fought at Culloden, where the Stuarts' dreams of regaining their crown were crushed. The prince was sheltered by the Mackinnons in a cave, and Iain Og, who was over 70-years-old, sent for his galley to take the prince to Mallaig, avoiding two Gover-nment warships on the way. He was less fortunate on the return voyage, however, and was captured in Morar. He was incarcerated in a prison ship at Tilbury, where he languished until 1750. When Iain Og died in 1756, his son, Charles, succeeded, but this line died out in 1808.

In 1811, William Mackinnon, MP for Dunwich in England, matriculated arms in the Lyon Court, showing his descent from Daniel, second son of Lachlan Mor, who had emigrated to Antigua. The new chief was a prominent parliamentarian, and sat for 35 years. His second son, Sir William Mackinnon, served in the Grenadier Guards, becoming Director of Recruitment at the War Office during the First World War.

Mackintosh

CREST
A cat-a-mountain salient
guardant Proper

MOTTO
Touch not the cat bot a glove

PLANT BADGE
Red whortleberry fructed Proper

The word 'toisech', meaning 'leader' can also be translated as 'chief' or 'captain'. According to the Mackintosh seanachies, the first chief was Shaw, second son of Duncan Macduff, Earl of Fife, of the royal house of Dalriada. He was made constable of Inverness Castle around 1163, and granted land in the Findhorn valley. Farquhar, the 5th chief, led his clan against the army of King Haakon of Norway at the Battle of Largs in 1263. He was killed in a duel in 1265, leaving his infant son, Angus, as heir. Angus was brought up at the court of his uncle, Alexander of Islay, the Lord of the Isles. A splendid match was arranged for him in 1291, when he married Eva, the only daughter of Dougal Dal, chief of Clan Chattan in Lochaber. Thereafter, the Clan Chattan, which developed into a confederation of what were later to become independent clans, was generally led by Mackintosh chiefs. Mackintosh and Chattan history is thus inextricably entwined.

The 6th chief supported Robert the Bruce during the War of the Independence. Ferquhar, the 9th chief, was induced to surrender the chiefship, in his own right and for those of his successors, in favour of Malcolm, the son by a second marriage of William, the 7th chief. He was a strong leader who greatly extended the influence of the clan and his lands stretched from Petty far into Lochaber.

The Mackintoshes fought for Montrose throughout his campaigns in support of Charles I. They remained loyal to the Stuarts in 1715, and Lachlan Mackintosh led 800 clansmen to swell the Jacobite ranks under the command of his cousin, Brigadier William

Mackintosh of Borlum. After the defeat at the Battle of Preston, many clansmen were transported to the Americas.

Angus, 22nd chief of the Mackintoshes, was a captain in the Black Watch Regiment when Prince Charles Edward Stuart landed in Scotland in 1745. However, in her husband's absence, the chief's wife, Lady Anne, daughter of Farquharson of Invercauld, raised men for the prince, the command of whom was given to MacGillivray of Dunmaglas. They contributed to the victory at Falkirk, following which the prince arrived at Moy in February 1746 to be received by Lady Mackintosh. The prince's bed is still in the modern Moy Hall. An attempt was made by a force of 1500 Government troops to capture the prince at Moy, but they were deceived by five of Lady Anne's retainers into believing that they had blundered in the midst of the entire Jacobite army, and they fled. The Mackintoshes and their Clan Chattan allies suffered heavy losses at Culloden.

On the death of the 28th chief in 1938, the title passed to his cousin, Vice Admiral Lachlan Mackintosh of Mackintosh. In a complicated decision by the Lyon Court in 1942, the leadership of Clan Chattan passed to Mackintosh of Torcastle.

Maclachlan

CREST
(Issuant from a crest coronet of four
(three visible) strawberry leaves Or)
a castle set upon a rock all Proper

MOTTO
Fortis et fidus
(Brave and faithful)

PLANT BADGE
Rowan seedlings fructed Proper

Lochlainn was the name of the senior branch in Tirconnell of the Ui'neill descendants of the pagan King Niall of the Nine Hostages. Until 1241 the MacLochlainns were virtual rulers of Ulster, until they suffered defeat at the hands of King Brian O'Neill. The name was known in Scotland by the 13th century, when the great warrior, Lachlan Mor, is recorded as living on the shores of Loch Fyne.

In 1292, Archibald Maclachlan was one of the 12 barons whose lands were formed into the sheriffdom of Argyll. Gillespie, probably the son of the chief, supported Robert the Bruce and attended his first Parliament at St Andrews in 1308. By the early 15th century the chiefs were described as 'Lords of Strathlachlan'. The Maclachlans recognized the rising power of the Campbells in Argyll, and allied themselves to them. Iain Maclachlan witnessed a bond by Stewart of Appin in favour of the 1st Earl of Argyll in 1485.

In 1615, the Maclachlan chief, Lachlan Og, led his clan in Argyll's foray against the Macdonalds of Islay. He had previously obtained a charter to his lands from James VI in 1591, but in 1633 he procured an Act of Parliament confirming him as 'Laird of Maclachlin'.

The civil war allowed many clans an opportunity to settle old scores, and the Maclachlans savaged their neighbours, the Lamonts. Lachlan Maclachlan of that Ilk accepted a commission in 1656 from Oliver Cromwell, the Lord Protector, to be justice of the peace for Argyllshire. His son, Archibald, the 15th chief, received a charter in 1680, erecting his whole lands into the Barony of Strathlachlan with Castle Lachlan as its seat.

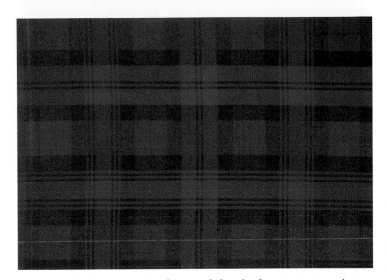

The Maclachlans were Jacobites and the chief was present at the raising of the standard of James VIII, the 'Old Pretender', in Scotland in 1715 and fought at Sheriffmuir. In 1745 the Maclachlans rallied to Prince Charles Edward Stuart's cause, the chief being appointed to the prince's staff as commissary-general. When the Jacobite army invaded England, it was Maclachlan who was sent north to Perth to summon reinforcements. His strongest entreaties for haste were of no avail, and fresh troops idled at Perth while the tide of fortune turned against the prince. The retreat from Derby did not dismay the Maclachlan, who led 300 of his clansmen to Culloden. He was riding to order the Highland advance when he was killed by a stray cannon shot. Castle Lachlan was ruined and the chief's family was forced to flee. Lachlan was declared forfeit for treason, but as the estates had been conveyed to his son more than a decade before the rising, they escaped untouched. A new mansion house was built in the 19th century in sight of the ruins of the ancient castle.

During the Second World War, the chiefship was assumed by Marjory Maclachlan of Maclachlan, the 24th chief.

Maclaine of Lochbuie

CREST
A branch of laurel and a branch of
cypress in saltire surmounted of a
battle axe in pale all Proper

MOTTO
Vincere vel mori
(To conquer or die)

The Maclaines of Lochbuie are descended from Gilleathan Na Tuaidh, 'Gillan of the Battleaxe', a renowned 13th-century warrior who held lands in Mull and Morven. Gillean and his three sons fought at the Battle of Largs in 1263 against the Norse, and they were well rewarded by Alexander II. Gillean was succeeded by Gille-Iosa, whose son, Malcolm, fought at Bannockburn in 1314. Iain Dhu, Malcolm's son, was the father of Eachainn Reaganach (Hector the Stern), founder of the Maclaines of Lochbuie, and also of Lachlan Lubanach, who founded the Macleans of Duart.

Hector was granted lands in Mull by the Lords of the Isles around 1350 and built his castle at the head of Loch Buie. Lands were also granted in Duror and Glencoe but they were never taken into possession. In 1542 the lands held by the sixth Lochbuie chief were united into the barony of Moy.

John Mor, 7th chief, was renowned as an excellent swordsman. When an Italian master-at-arms challenged Scottish nobles to meet him in duel, John Mor accepted the challenge, and fought and killed him, to the delight of the king and the court. His son, Hector, initiated the spelling of the surname 'Maclaine', which became the accepted spelling by subsequent chiefs. Murdoch Mor, 10th chief, fought for the royalist cause alongside the Marquess of Montrose in 1645 and subsequently forfeited his lands, which were not restored until 1661. In 1689, the 12th chief, Hector, was the victor in the first battle of the Jacobite campaign of James VII at Knockbreck in Badenoch.

John, 17th chief, was host to Dr Samuel Johnson and James Boswell on the last stop of their famous tour of the Hebrides in 1773. Boswell said of John, 'Lochbuie proved to be a bluff, comely, noisy old gentleman, proud of his hereditary consequence and a very hearty and hospitable landlord'. John had a plaque placed above the door of Lochbuie House to commemorate the visit.

Murdoch, 23rd of Lochbuie, was born in 1814. He, along with the Duke of Argyll, founded the Argyllshire Gathering and Ball in 1871. He had a distinguished military career and, while serving as military correspondent of *The Times* during the Franco–Prussian War in 1871, was awarded the Iron Cross by the Kaiser. Murdoch's son and heir, Kenneth Maclaine, the 24th chief, made a mark for himself by going on the stage as a singer to try to forestall for closure of the Lochbuie estates. Unfortunately, the onset of the First World War made it impossible for him to avoid the inevitable, and the entire estates of some 30,000 acres were lost. The chief now lives in South Africa.

Maclaren

CREST
A lion's head erased Sable crowned
with an antique crown of six (four
visible) points Or, between two
branches of laurel issuing from
the Wreath at either side of
the head both Proper

MOTTO
Creag an Tuirc (The boar's rock)

It is possible that there are two quite separate origins of this name, one arising in Perthshire around Balquhidder, and the other in Tiree in Argyll. In Argyll, the family are said to descend from Lorn, son of Fergus MacErc, founder of the kingdom of Dalriada in the 6th century. In Gaelic, they are Clann Labhruinn. However, the eponymous ancestor is generally given as Laurence, a 13th-century abbot of Achtow in Balquhidder, which was part of the ancient princedom of Strathearn.

Three Maclaren nobles are recorded as signing the Ragman Rolls in 1296, swearing allegiance to Edward I of England although the Maclarens probably fought at Bannockburn in 1314 under the standard of Malise, Earl of Strathearn. In 1344, when the last Celtic Earl of Strathearn was deprived of his title, the Maclarens came under pressure from their more powerful neighbours. Balquhidder passed into the hands of the Crown and in 1500 James IV granted the lordship to his mistress, Janet Kennedy, and the Maclaren chief found that his land had become part of another barony. When the Campbell persecution of the Macgregors drove them from their own lands into Balquhidder, they plundered those of the Maclarens, bringing fire and death in their wake. The chiefs appealed to the Campbells who demanded, as the price of their protection, that the Maclarens acknowledge them as feudal superiors.

The Maclarens fought for Montrose, in the cause of Charles I, at Inverlochy, Auldearn, Alford and Kilsyth. At the end of the century, when the Stuarts again called for aid, the Maclarens joined James

Graham of Claverhouse, Viscount Dundee, who was mustering resistance for James VII, following him to fight at Killiecrankie in 1689. The Maclarens were out in the Fifteen, taking part in the Battle of Sheriffmuir. They also flocked to the standard of Prince Charles Edward Stuart, the 'Young Pretender', in 1745 following the prince from his victories at Prestonpans and Falkirk to the ill-fated Battle of Culloden in 1746. At the battle they were on the right of the line with the Appin regiment under Lord George Murray, brother of the Duke of Atholl. Donald Maclaren was captured and carried off to Edinburgh. Balquhidder was ravaged by Hanoverian troops. Donald escaped while being taken to Carlisle for trial by hurling himself down a track, a route none of the Redcoats dared to follow. He remained a fugitive in Balquhidder until the amnesty of 1757.

In more recent times the chiefs have recovered some of the clan lands including the clan heartland, Creag an Tuirc – the Boar's Rock – the rallying point or 'duthus' from which the clan's war cry is derived.

Maclean

CREST
A tower embattled Argent

MOTTO
Virtue mine honour

*T*his name in Gaelic is rendered as 'MacGille Eoin', 'son of the servant of St John'. It has also been suggested that there is an alternative derivation from 'leathan', meaning 'broad' or 'broad-shouldered'. The Macleans descend from Gilleathan Na Tuaidh, 'Gillean of the Battleaxe'. Gillean fought at the Battle of Largs in 1263 when the army of Haakon IV was defeated, effectively ending the Norse hegemony over the Hebrides. Gillean's great-great-grandson, Iain Dhu Maclean, settled in Mull. Of his sons, Lachlan Lubanach was progenitor of the Macleans of Duart and Eachainn Reaganach (Hector) founded the Maclaines of Lochbuie. By the end of the 15th century, the Macleans owned most of Mull, Tiree, Islay, Jura and Knapdale, with Morvern in Argyllshire and Lochaber.

Lachlan Lubanach's son, 'Red Hector of the Battles', was a renowned warrior who fought for the Lord of the Isles at Harlaw in 1411. Red Hector and Sir Alexander Irvine of Drum met in single combat. After the duel, in which neither was dishonoured, they both died of their wounds. Lachlan of Duart was killed with the king at Flodden in 1513.

The Campbells and the Macleans, who vied for control of Mull, were at least united in their Protestant faith and their dislike of the Macdonalds. Sir Lachlan Mor Maclean harried the Macdonalds of Islay, causing such carnage that, in 1594, he and the Macdonald chief were declared outlaws by the Privy Council.

Sir Lachlan Maclean was created a Baronet of Nova Scotia on 3 September 1631. He was passionately devoted to Charles I and

called his clan out to join Montrose. He died in 1649, after which his son, Sir Hector, took up the cause, losing his life at the Battle of Inverkeithing in 1651. The estates fell heavily in debt and by 1679 the Campbells had gained possession of Duart and most of the Maclean estates. When the Stuarts once again called for aid against their rebellious subjects, the Maclean chief hurried to their standard. Sir John, the 5th Baronet, fought for James VII at Killiecrankie in 1689.

The Macleans were out in the rising of 1715, and Sir Hector Maclean was given a Jacobite peerage a year later. Sir Hector returned to Edinburgh in 1745 to pave the way for the rising of that year but was arrested and imprisoned in the Tower of London until 1747; he died in Rome in 1750. The clan was led throughout the Forty-five by Maclean of Drimmin, who was killed in the Highland charge at Culloden.

Duart Castle subsequently fell into ruins but was reclaimed by the chiefs in 1911 and has been restored as their seat.

Maclennan

CREST
A demi-piper all Proper, garbed
in the proper tartan of the
Clan Maclennan

MOTTO
Dum spiro spero
(While I breathe I hope)

PLANT BADGE
Furze

In Gaelic this name is rendered as 'MacGille Finnan', 'son of the fol-lower of St Finnan'. Some historians maintain that the clan was orig-inally known as Logan and only adopted their new name in the 15th century. According to this version of the family's origins, Gillegorm Logan led his men towards Inverness to prosecute a feud against the Frasers. Gillegorm was ambushed at Kessock and he and most of his men were slain. The Frasers captured Logan's pregnant wife, intend-ing either to kill the child, or perhaps to raise him as a fosterling, a common Highland method of obtaining influence over a rival clan. The son was born, but was deformed and placed with the monks at Beaul. He entered the church in due course but disregarded the decree of Pope Innocent III enjoining the celibacy of the clergy, pre-ferring to follow the ancient Celtic practice of marrying; he subse-quently had several children. He was the 'Gille Finnan', and his sons honoured his memory by adopting a new name. The heraldry of the Lowland Logans and the Maclennans is certainly similar but this is of doubtful assistance to the historian and no real genealogical evi-dence exists to support this story.

The Maclennans, along with the Macraes, were staunch supporters of the Mackenzies, and may at one time have been custodians of the great castle at Eilean Donan. It was in the service of the Mackenzie chief that the clan came to great prominence. The Marquess of Montrose had rallied many Highland clans to the royalist cause in 1645. He was, however, equally opposed by many, including the Covenanter Earl of Seaforth, then chief of the Mackenzies. The men

of Kintail, led by the Maclennan chief, Ruaridh, a red-bearded giant standing well over 6 ft tall, carried Lord Seaforth's standard.

The forces of the Covenant engaged Montrose at Auldearn in May 1645. The marquess was heavily outnumbered but his strategy rose to the occasion, massing his banners in the hope of deceiving the enemy as to the location of his main force. The ruse succeeded and the Covenanters massed their army for a full assault. Montrose outflanked and attacked Seaforth, turning the tide of battle in his favour. The Maclennans were sent an order to withdraw, but it was never delivered. Ruaridh and his men fought to the last, defending Seaforth's standard before being cut down by Gordon cavalry.

The decimated clan played little part in the Jacobite risings in 11715 and 1745, although a number of Maclennans are recorded as being taken prisoner after Culloden.

More recently, Ronald Maclennan of Maclennan was recognized by the Lord Lyon, King of Arms, as chief of this name under the process of selection known as the 'ad hoc derbhfine'. He was not a bloodline chief, although he was a member of the only Maclennan family to have matriculated arms since 1672.

Macleod

CREST
A bull's head cabossed Sable,
horned Or, between two flags
Gules, staved of the First

MOTTO
Hold fast

PLANT BADGE
Juniper

It is generally held that Leod was the younger son of Olaf the Black, one of the last Norse kings of Man and the North Isles. Olaf died around 1237, and Leod inherited the islands of Lewis and Harris, with part of Skye. Marriage to the daughter of the Norse seneschal or steward of Skye brought the family to Dunvegan, which remains the chief's seat to this day. The clan consisted of two main branches, the Macleods of Lewis, later 'of the Lewes', named after a son or grandson of Leod, Thorkil or Torquil (the 'Siol Torquil'), and the Macleods of Skye, named after another of Leod's sons, Tormod (the 'Siol Tormod'), who established their seat at Dunvegan.

The Macleods followed the Macdonald Lord of the Isles to the Battle of Harlaw in 1411, but when James IV set out to break Macdonald power the Macleods were successful in steering a path through the tortuous politics of the time. Alasdair Crotach, 'Humpbacked', the eighth Dunvegan chief, secured a title to Trotternish in 1542 which had long been disputed with the Macdonalds of Sleat. The famous fairy tower at Dunvegan Castle was constructed on Alasdair Crotach's orders, and he also rebuilt the church of Rodel in Harris where he was later entombed. The church and his tomb are considered two of the finest monuments in the Hebrides.

Ruaraidh Mor succeeded as the 15th chief in 1595. He was knighted by James VI and he continued the work of Alasdair Crotach, establishing Dunvegan as the cultural centre of the isles. He was described in a contemporary report as 'a very lordly ruler'. No chief of the Macleods can avoid at least once calling Rory Mor to memory.

A great drinking horn, named after the 15th chief, is kept at Dunvegan and forms an integral part of the rite of passage of every Macleod chief. The horn, which holds a bottle and a half of claret, must be drained at one draft 'without setting down or falling down'.

The Macleods of the Lewes, leaders of the 'Siol Torquil', who had never fully accepted the ascendancy of their cousins at Dunvegan, were forced to do so when the head of that family, Torquil Macleod of the Lewes, was killed in 1597, and the barony passed to Sir Rory Mackenzie of Cogeach, husband of Torquil's daughter, Margaret. The representation of the 'Siol Torquil' passed to the Macleods of Raasay, senior cadets of the Lewes house. In 1988 Torquil Macleod of Raasay rematriculated his arms to be recognized by the Lord Lyon as Macleod of the Lewes, 'Chief and Head of that Baronial House under the MacLeod of MacLeod'.

Dunvegan Castle was renovated and remodelled during the Victorian era and it remains the chief's home. An active clan society promotes the fellowship of clansmen throughout the world.

Macmillan

CREST
A dexter and a sinister hand issuing
from the Wreath grasping and
brandishing aloft a two-handed
sword Proper

MOTTO
Miseris succurrere disco
(I learn to succour the unfortunate)

The Macmillans are Celts descended from an ancient royal house and from the orders of the Celtic church. In the early 12th century, Cormac, a Celtic priest, was appointed by Alexander I as bishop of Dunkeld. Cormac had numerous sons, one of whom, Gillie Chriosd, was the progenitor of the Macmillans. As a Celtic priest, the bishop's son would have had a distinctive tonsure: the Celts shaved their hair over the front of the head, rather than in the Roman manner of a ring around the crown. The Celtic tonsure was described as that of St John, which is rendered in Gaelic, 'Mhaoil-Iain'. Macmillan is therefore 'son of one who bore the tonsure of St John'. An alternative form, 'Mac Ghillemhaoil', 'son of the tonsured servant', was favoured by the Lochaber branch of the clan.

The clan appears to have moved to the shores of Loch Archaig in Lochaber when David I abolished the mormaership of Moray, and settled the region with Norman knights. When Bruce was forced into hiding in the Highlands, he was sheltered by Maolmuire, the Macmillan chief, at his home at Ben Lawers and the clan fought at Bannockburn with Bruce in 1314. John of Islay, Lord of the Isles, granted them lands at Knapdale around 1360. Alexander, 5th of Knap, and 12th chief of the clan, has left the two most enduring Macmillan memorials, a round tower near to Castle Sween, known as Macmillan's Tower, and a fine Celtic cross in the church yard at Kilmory. In time, the direct line became extinct and the chiefship passed, in 1742, to Macmillan of Dunmore, whose lands lay on the side of Loch Tarbert.

The Macmillans were not noted Jacobites. John Macmillan of Murlaggan, whose line were later to head the Lochaber Macmillans, refused to join Prince Charles Edward unless the Stuarts renounced the Catholic faith. Murlaggan's eldest son defied his father and the Macmillans formed a company of Locheil's regiment which fought at Culloden; both sons died in the battle. Donald Macmillan of Tulloch was induced to surrender to the Duke of Cumberland under the impression that he and his men had been promised protection, but they were subsequently transported to the Caribbean without trial.

The chiefship passed through a series of lawyers and soldiers, who did not really seem to grasp clearly their status as Highland chiefs, until the 20th century, when General Sir Gordon Macmillan of Macmillan was recognized by the Lyon Court and established his seat at Finlaystone House in Renfrewshire. An active clan association now gathers there regularly.

Macnab

CREST
The head of a savage
affrontée Proper

MOTTO
Timor omnis abesto
(Let fear be far from all)

PLANT BADGE
Stone-bramble

The name Macnab derives from the Gaelic 'Mac An Aba', 'child of the abbot'. According to tradition, the progenitor of this great clan was the abbot of Glendochart and Strathearn, younger son of King Kenneth Macalpin. Abaruadh, the 'Red Abbot', was descended from a nephew of St Fillan, founder of the monastery in Glendochart in the 7th century.

Angus Macnab was brother-in-law of John Comyn, murdered in 1306 by Robert the Bruce, and he joined with the Macdougalls in opposition to the king. When Bruce's power was consolidated by his victory at Bannockburn in 1314, the Macnab lands were forfeit and their charters destroyed. The fortunes of the clan were to some degree restored in 1336, when Angus' grandson, Gilbert, received a charter from David II. When the Lord Lyon considered the succession of the Macnab chiefs in 1954, he ruled that Gilbert be considered the first undisputed chief (although he was perhaps the 20th).

The Macnabs were loyal to the Stuarts, and their chief, 'Smooth John', led them to join Montrose and contributed to the royal victory at Kilsyth. He was appointed to garrison Montrose's own castle at Kincardine. General Lesley besieged the castle, but the whole garrison broke through the Covenanter lines and fought their way clear. John was, however, captured and taken to Edinburgh, where he was sentenced to death. He contrived to escape on the eve of his execution and led 300 of his clansmen at the Battle of Worcester in 1651.

The chiefs did not support the later Stuarts, although many clansmen drew their swords for the 'Old Pretender'. However, the 15th

chief was a major in the Hanoverian army and was taken prisoner by Jacobite forces after the Battle of Prestonpans in 1745 and confined in Doune Castle.

Francis Macnab succeeded as 16th chief, and although within the clan he is renowned as a notable producer and consumer of whisky, he is more generally known as 'The Macnab' of Raeburn's outstanding portrait. He was succeeded by his nephew, Archibald, who made desperate efforts to extricate the estate from debt. In 1823 a writ of foreclosure was issued, and Archibald fled to Canada to avoid the estates' debts. Sarah Anne, the eldest of his children, was recognized as the 18th chief, but she died unmarried in Italy in 1894.

The de jure chiefship passed to James William Macnab. He served in the East India Company and was succeeded by his eldest son, James Frederick, rector of Bolton Abbey. His only son, James Alexander, succeeded as 21st de jure chief. In 1954, he relinquished the chiefship to his uncle, Archibald Corrie Macnab, who had acquired the Killin estate to enable him to become the 22nd de facto chief. Archibald died in 1970 when the succession reverted to James Charles, the eldest son of James Alexander, 23rd chief.

Macnaghten

CREST
A tower embattled Gules

MOTTO
I hoip in God

PLANT BADGE
Trailing azalea Proper

The Macnaughtens are one of the clans who claimed decsent from the great Pictish rulers of Moray. The name Nechtan, which may mean 'pure' or 'clear', was popular in at least one branch of the Pictish royal line. In the 13th century, there are records of three brothers, Gilchrist, Athe and Gilbert, the sons of Malcolm Macnachten. Gilchrist received from Alexander III a charter in 1267 granting him the keepership of a castle warding the narrow Pass of Brander, the gateway to the west Highlands.

The Macnachtens were slow to support the claim of Robert the Bruce, at first opposing him in conjuction with the Macdougals but later switching allegiance and fighting for Bruce at Bannockburn in 1314. They gained little from this late change of heart. Duncan, whose father fought at Bannockburn, made his seat at Dunderave, which was thereafter the territorial designation of the chiefs. In 1478, his grandson, Alexander, was knighted by James IV and followed the king to Flodden in 1513, where he was one of the few survivors; he died two years later. He had married twice and had six sons, the eldest of whom succeeded his grandfather in 1527. The second son, Ian, acted as tutor to his nephew and was the father of Iain, or John, Dubh, who may be the 'Shane Dhu' credited with founding the Irish branch of the family.

In 1548 Gilbert Macnachten succeeded as chief. When he died without issue, the succession devolved upon his younger brother, Alexander. He started the rebuilding of Dunderave Castle on Loch Fyne and it was completed by his son, Iain, in 1596.

Malcolm of Killearn, who succeeded to the chiefship around 1630, was a fervent royalist, and called out his clansmen, accompanied by Argyll's son, for the abortive rising against the Cromwellian occupation led by the Earl of Glencairn in 1653. The expedition was sheer folly, and earned Macnachten the enmity of Argyll. He was knighted after the Restoration in 1660, but through Argyll's influence, he was later denounced as an outlaw. Iain, the next chief, who succeeded in 1685, inherited little more than an empty title. He joined the forces of Graham of Claverhouse, the 'Bonnie' Viscount Dundee, fighting for James VII at Killiecrankie in 1689. He was denounced as a Jacobite rebel, and his remaining lands were forfeited.

On the extinction of the main line in the mid-18th century, the chiefship passed to an Irish branch, descendants of 'Shane Dhu'. Francis Macnaghten of Dunderave was created a baronet in 1836. Sir Edward, 4th Baronet, was a distinguished lawyer who became a Lord of Appeal in 1887 with the life peerage of 'Baron Macnaghten of Runkerry'. He was succeeded by his son, Sir Edward, whose sons both succeeded to the title, but were killed in the First World War. The 8th Baronet, Sir Francis, succeeded his nephews.

Macneil

CREST
On a chapeau Gules furred
Ermine, a rock Proper

MOTTO
Buaidh no bas
(To conquer or die)

PLANT BADGE
Plants of dryas

The Clan Macneil claims descent from Niall, a descendant of Aodh O'Neil, king of the North of Ireland at the beginning of the 11th century. Aodh was twentieth in descent from Niall of the Nine Hostages, the pagan 5th-century founder of the mighty U'Neill dynasty. Niall came to the island of Barra in the Outer Hebrides around 1049, and is identified as the first chief. 'Barra' means the 'isle of St Barr', but it is uncertain whether this is St Fionnbharr, the founder of Cork, or St Barr, great-grandson of Niall of the Nine Hostages.

Neil Macneil, 5th of Barra, was described as a prince at a Council of the Isles in 1252 and he was still the chief when Haakon IV's army was defeated at Largs in 1263, effectively ending the Norse domination of the Hebrides. His son, Neil Og Macneil, is believed to have fought with Robert the Bruce at Bannockburn in 1314. For this, he was rewarded with lands in north Kintyre, which were added to his barony of Barra.

The Macneils were largely independent-minded, with scant respect for any authority save their own. However, by the 17th century, they had accepted the inevitability of central government, and Neil Og, the 16th chief was made a colonel of horse by Charles II and fought at Worcester in 1651. Ruari Dubh received a Crown charter of all the lands of Barra erected into a free barony in 1688.

The Macneils were Jacobites, and Black Ruari led his clansmen to fight for James VII at Killiecrankie in 1689. He remained loyal to the cause and rallied to the 'Old Pretender' at the rising in 1715. His two

sons, Roderick and James, went into exile in France. They returned to Scotland on their father's death. The Macneils supported the rising in 1745 and for his Jacobite sympathies, Roderick was consigned to a prison ship, the *Royal Sovereign*. He was later taken to London and was not released until July 1747. The estates, however, were not forfeited.

The clan prospered until the time of the 21st chief, General Roderick Macneil who was forced to sell Barra in 1838. The general, who died in England in 1863, had no children and the chiefship passed to a cousin, whose line had emigrated to America at the beginning of the 19th century.

It was from the New World that Robert Lister Macneil of Barra came to reclaim Kisimul, together with the greater part of the island of Barra, in 1937. He was the second son of Roderick Ambrose Macneil of Barra who nominated him as chief by the process known as 'tanistry'. This title was recognised by the Lyon Court and he has since been succeeded by his son. Robert devoted a great part of his life to the restoration of Kisimul Castle, which is once more the seat of the Macneil chiefs.

Macnicol

CREST
A hawk's head erased Gules

MOTTO
Sgorr-a-bhreac

It seems likely that, as with the Macleods, the MacNicols were originally of high Norse descent. The name-father of the Clan Nicail or
Nicolson, a name popular in Scandinavia, is believed to have flourished in the mid-13th century with the ancestral Nicail living on
Lewis around this time.

The first chief on record, early in the 14th century, is John, son of
Nicail. He appears in the company of leading Hebridean chiefs,
Macdonald, Macdougald and Macruairi, descendants of Somerled,
King of the Isles, who had rested control of the southern Hebrides.
In the next generation, most of the clan lands passed to the Lewis
Macleods, but the main line continued, finding a home at
Scorrybreac in Skye. Later, they followed the Macdonald Lords of
the Isles and sat on their council. Tradition maintains that James V
was entertained at Scorrybreac during his expedition in 1540 to sub-
due the island chiefs.

After the collapse of the Lordship of the Isles, the clan followed the
Macdonalds of Sleat, and fought alongside them during the civil war.
Later in the 17th century, the chief, Donald, was minister of Kilmuir
in Skye, and many of his descendants also followed into the
Protestant ministry. It was around this time that the surname
became generally anglicized as Nicolson, although it remained
Macneacail in Gaelic.

The Macdonalds of Sleat were Jacobites, and participated in the rising of 1715. After the Stuart defeat, they were forfeited, and were
more cautious in the Forty-five, when neither they nor the Macleods

of Dunvegan came out for the 'Young Pretender'. However, many
Skye men did follow the prince, including the Macleods of Raasay
and a band of Nicolsons who joined the Stuarts of Appin and fought
at Culloden in 1746.

In the 19th century, the clan was badly affected by the Highland
clearances; the chief was forced to abandon Scorrybreac and his family settled in Tasmania.

Until a decision of the Lyon Court in 1989, there had been much
confusion between the west Highland, or Hebridean clan, and those
who became established on the mainland and anglicized their name
to 'Nicholson'. A petition was brought forward by Lord Carnock, to
be recognized as chief of the name and arms of Nicholson. This was
granted, but thereafter the Lord Lyon additionally granted a petition
of Iain Nicholson of Scorrybreac to be recognized as Macneacail of
Macneacail and Scorrybreac, Chief of the West Highland Clan
Macnicol. In 1989, the chief unveiled a cairn at Portree in memory
of the Nicolsons of Scorrybreac and their place in 700 years of
Hebridean history. The portion of ancient Scorrybreac acquired by
the clan is presently being developed as a national park.

Macpherson

CREST
A cat sejant Proper

MOTTO
Touch not the cat but a glove

PLANT BADGE
White heather

This is a name derived from the Gaelic 'Mac-a Phearsain', meaning 'son of the parson'. The old Celtic church had married clergy, and the Clan Macpherson is believed to have been founded by Muireach (or Murdo) Cattenach, who was prior or parson of Kingussie in Badenoch. The Macphersons formed part of the great Clan Chattan confederation.

Macpherson tradition has it that in 1309 Robert the Bruce proposed granting the lands of Badenoch to the chief of the Macphersons (perhaps Ewan Ban MacMhuirich), on condition that he destroyed Bruce's enemies, the Comyns; they duly carried out the king's wishes with alacrity. Ewan Ban had three sons: Kenneth of Clunie, Iain of Pitmain and Gillies of Invereshie, and the Macphersons are sometimes known as the Clan of the Three Brothers.

Andrew Macpherson, reckoned as the 8th chief, acquired the abbey-castle grange in Strathisla in 1618. His son, Euan, was a great royalist, and fought with Montrose during the civil war. Duncan Macpherson of Cluny, the 10th chief, lost his claim to lead Clan Chattan in 1672 when the Privy Council and the Lord Lyon, King of Arms, ruled in favour of a Mackintosh. As Duncan had no sons, he was succeeded as chief of the Macphersons by Lachlan Macpherson, 4th Laird of Nuid, in 1722.

His son, Euan of Cluny, became a famous Highland leader in the Forty-five. During the retreat from Derby, he defeated a numerically superior force at Clifton Moor in Westmorland. After the defeat at Culloden, Cluny was able, through the faithful support of his clans-

men, to escape capture by Hanoverian troops for nine years, despite a reward of £1,000 for his capture. He finally escaped to France in 1755. William Macpherson the Purser, ancestor of the present chief, was killed at Falkirk in 1746. The Purser's nephew, James Macpherson of Balavil, witnessed the Government forces' burning of Cluny's castle in 1746.

Duncan Macpherson of Cluny, 'Duncan of the Kiln', was born in 1748 while his mother took refuge in a corn kiln. He accepted the ultimate defeat of the Jacobites, and fought for the Government during the American Wars of Independence. The Macpherson estates were returned to him in 1784, 20 years after his father's forfeiture but due to a faulty lease and debts incurred by a son, the Cluny estate was bankrupt by the end of the 19th century. Macphersons, however, continued to serve the country in many parts of the world, and thanks to the co-operation of clan members, the principal relics of the chiefs were purchased to form the basis of the clan museum.

Macrae

CREST
A cubit arm grasping a
sword all Proper

MOTTO
Fortitudine
(With fortitude)

This Celtic name stems from the Gaelic, 'son of Grace'. The clan appears to have inhabited the lands of Clunes around Beauly in the 12th and 13th centuries, prior to moving to Kintail in Wester Ross some time in the 14th century.

The Macraes were staunch allies of the Mackenzies. Duncan Macrae was constable of the Mackenzie stonghold of Eilean Donan Castle and acquired for himself the lands of Inverinate. The Macraes were so fierce in adherence to their Mackenzie overlord that they became known as 'Mackenzie's shirt of mail'. In 1539 the Macdonalds, under Donald Grumach, 4th of Sleat, besieged Eilean Donan Castle as part of their attempt to revive the shattered Lordship of the Isles. Macrae is credited with slaying the Macdonald chief with an arrow, bringing the siege to an end.

The fortunes of the Mackenzies prospered and they obtained for themselves the title of'Earl of Seaforth. The Macraes basked in reflected glory and were invested with the hereditary constableship of Eilean Donan Castle and also created chamberlains of Kintail. Numerous cadet houses were crerated including the Macraes of Conchra, Clunes and Feoirlinn.

During the turbulent years of the civil wars in the early 17th century, the Macraes played a full part in the conflict and in 1715 were conspicuous for their bravery at Sherrifmuir, fighting for the Jacobite cause. They did not take part in the 1745 rising as a clan although many individual clansmen flocked to join Prince Charles Edward Stuart.

The clan was not only renowned for its military prowess. Duncan
Macrae of Inverinate, born around 1640, was educated at Edinburgh
University and composed Gaelic poetry; he was the compiler of the
important anthology of Gaelic poetry known as the Fernaig
Manuscript. A cultured Highland aristocrat, Duncan was known as
Donnchadh nam Pios, 'Duncan of the Silver Cups', due to the mag-
nificence of his table service.

Lieutenant Colonel John Macrae, born in 1861, served in the Black
Watch, and was both deputy keeper of the Palace of Holyroodhouse
and a member of the Royal Company of Archers (the bodyguard of
the monarch in Scotland). Colonel Sir Colin Macrae of Feoirlinn
served with distinction througout the Boer War and was not only a
member of the Royal Company of Archers, but also a lieutenant in
the monarch's English bodyguard, the Yeomen of the Guard.

The splendid castle at Eilean Donan was restored in the 1930s by a
Macrae descendent and is now perhaps the most photographed
fortress in the Highlands.

Macthomas

CREST
A demi-cat-a-mountain rampant
guardant Proper, grasping in his
dexter paw a serpent Vert, langued
Gules, its tail environing the
sinister paw

MOTTO
Deo juvante invidiam superabo
(I will overcome envy with God's help)

Thomas, a Gaelic-speaking Highlander known as Tomaidh Mor, from whom the clan takes its name, was a descendant of the Clan Chattan Mackintoshes, his grandfather having been a son of William, 8th chief of the Clan Chattan. Thomas lived in the 15th century, at a time when the Clan Chattan confederation had become large and unmanageable, and he took his kinsmen and followers across the Grampians from Badenoch to Glenshee, where they settled and flourished, being known as Mccomie, a phonetic form of the Gaelic, as well as Mccolm and Mccomas. To the Government in Edinburgh, they were known as Macthomas, and are so described in the roll of the clans in the Acts of Parliament of 1587 and 1595.

The early chiefs ruled from the Thom, on the east bank of the Shee Water, opposite the Spittal of Glenshee. In about 1600, when the 4th chief Robert Mccomie of Thom was murdered, the chiefship passed to his brother, John Mccomie of Finegand, who made Finegand the seat of the chiefs. The 7th chief, John Mccomie, more properly known as Iain Mor, has passed into the folklore of Perthshire and Angus as McComie Mor. Tax collectors appear to have been particularly offensive to him, especially those of the Earl of Atholl.

The Macthomases supported Charles I, and Iain Mor joined Montrose at Dundee in 1644. When Aberdeen fell to royalist forces it was Iain Mor who captured Sir William Forbes of Craigievar, the sheriff of Aberdeen and Covenant cavalry commander. After Montrose's defeat at Philiphaugh, the chief withdrew his men from the struggle and devoted his energies to his lands and people,

extending his influence into Glen Prosen and Strathardle. Despite his earlier royalist sympathies, Iain Mor admired the stability of the government brought by the Commonwealth, with the attendant prosperity it brought to Scotland. This soured his relationship with his royalist neighbours, including Lord Airlie. At the Restoration in 1660, the local royalists took their revenge. Crippling law suits and fines ultimately ruined the Macthomases, and after Iain Mor's death in 1676, his remaining sons were forced to sell their lands.

From the late 17th century the clan began to drift apart, moving south into the Tay valley, or to Angus.in Fife and seeing their name anglicised as Thomas, Thomson, Thom or Thoms.

William Mccombie of Tillifour, descended from the youngest of Iain Mor's sons, was MP for South Aberdeenshire at the end of the 19th century, and is today regarded as the father of Aberdeen-Angus cattle breeding. The 15th chief, Patrick Hunter Macthomas Thoms of Aberlemon, was Provost of Dundee from 1847 to 1853. He was succeeded by his son, George, an advocate and a great philanthropist. In 1967 George's great-nephew was officially recognized by the Lyon Court as MacThomas of Finegand, 18th chief.

Mar

CREST
On a chapeau Gules furred Ermine,
two wings, each of ten pen feathers,
erected and addorsed,
both blazoned as in the Arms

MOTTO
Pans plus
(Think more)

Mar was one of the seven ancient kingdoms or provinces of Scotland whose rulers were known by the title of 'mormaer'. In the charter erecting the Abbey of Scone in 1114, the Mormaer of Mar is named as Rothri. Rothri was succeeded by Morgund, 2nd Earl of Mar, who witnessed, some time before 1152, charters to the abbey of Dunfermline. William, the 5th Earl, was one of the regents of Scotland and Great Chamberlain of the Realm in 1264. The Earls of Mar supported the Bruce claim to the throne, and Donald's eldest daughter, Isabel of Mar, became the first wife of Robert the Bruce.

Thomas, the 9th Earl, died without issue, and the title passed to his sister, Margaret, and through her, to her daughter, Isabel. She took as her second husband Alexander Stewart, the natural son of the feared Wolf of Badenoch. She granted the life-rent of the earldom to her Stewart husband, but reserved succession to her own lawful heirs. She died without issue around 1407, and her kinsman, Robert, a descendant of Elyne, daughter of the 7th Earl, became de jure 13th Earl of Mar. His son, Thomas, was denied his lawful title when James II claimed the earldom through the alleged rights of Alexander Stewart, Countess Isabel's husband. The title was then bestowed firstly on the king's son, Prince John, and later, in 1562, on James Stewart, the illegitimate half-brother of Mary, Queen of Scots. In 1565 Mary granted a charter to John, 18th Earl, restoring the title.

The earls were not supporters of Charles I's religious policies, but when it became clear that support of the Covenant meant armed

opposition to the king, both the earl and his eldest son, John, Lord Erskine, took up arms in the royalist cause. The earl entertained Montrose in 1645 in his castle at Alloa. Lord Erskine accompanied the king's captain general and rode at the Battle of Kilsyth in August 1645. As a result, the family estates were forfeited until Charles II was restored to the throne in 1660. John, the 23rd Earl, was created Duke of Mar in 1715 by the exiled James VIII, although for his Jacobite loyalties all his Scottish honours were ultimately forfeited.

The earldom was restored to John, 24th of Mar, by Act of Parliament in 1824. John's grandson succeeded to the earldom of Kellie in 1835 but he died without issue and the succession became so complex that a second Act of Parliament was required to resolve it. The outcome, which causes some understandable confusion, was that the ancient earldom of Mar passed to the descendents of the 26th Earl's sister whilst a separate earldom of Mar (with precedence only from 1565) passed to the Earl of Kellie, the chief of the Erskines.

Matheson

CREST
Issuant from an antique crown Or,
a hand brandishing a scimitar
fessways all Proper

MOTTO
Fac et spera
(Do and hope)

In common with many clans, the Mathesons suffer from the anglicization of their name from more than one possible Gaelic derivation. 'Mic Mhathghamhuin' means 'son of the bear' (from this
derivation, the chiefs' arms carry two bears as supporters), whilst
'MacMhathain' means 'son of the heroes'. There is also, of course, a
Lowland derivation, which is simply 'son of Matthew'.

It is not known whether the Mathesons are of pure Celtic descent,
but given the immense influence of the Norse over the Western
Isles, it is perfectly possible that some of their blood was intermin-
gled. They seemed to have settled around Lochalsh, Lochcarron and
Kintail, where they were granted lands by the great Celtic Earls of
Ross.

As the power of the Lords of the Isles waned, so did the fortunes of
the Mathesons. They found themselves uncomfortably set between
the powerful and feuding Macdonalds and Mackenzies. In 1539 Iain
Dubh was killed defending Eilean Donan Castle. He had become
constable of the great Mackenzie stronghold after marrying the
widow of Sir Dugald Mackenzie. The Mathesons were baillies to the
Earls of Sutherland in the late 15th century, and they settled on the
north side of Loch Shin. Donald Matheson of Shiness fought against
the Jacobites during the rising of 1715. Alexander Matheson joined,
with his uncle James, the merchant adventurers engaged in trade in
India and China and in 1827, they founded the trading house of
Jardine Matheson.

Meanwhile, the chiefship had descended through the line of Dugal

of Balmacara's elder brother, Roderick. His family acquired
Bennetsfield in the Black Isle in 1688. John, second of Bennetsfield,
was, unlike his Sutherland cousins, a Jacobite and fought at
Culloden in 1745, escaping unscathed from the debacle. The chiefship passed to his nephew and subsequently to a cousin, Heylan
Matheson. His son, Colonel Bertram Matheson of that Ilk, was confirmed in the chiefship by the Lord Lyon in 1963. The Matheson
baronets had continued to prosper, and Sir Torquhil, 5th Baronet,
was a distinguished soldier. The chief, Colonel Bertram, nominated
General Sir Torquhil as 'tanastair' (successor). Major Sir Torquil succeeded his father as 6th Baronet in 1963 and Colonel Bertram as
chief in 1975, thus uniting the baronetcy and the chiefship.

The chiefship has since passed to Sir Torquil's brother, Sir Fergus
Matheson of Matheson, Baronet, who has rematriculated his arms at
the Lyon Court for himself and his son, thereby securing the chiefly
line for the foreseeable future.

Maxwell

CREST
A stag Proper, attired Argent,
couchant before a holly
bush proper

MOTTO
Reviresco
(I grow strong again)

Maccus Well, a pool in the River Tweed by Kelso, is claimed as the origin for this name. The eponymous Maccus was believed to be a Norse chief who lived in the reign of David I. However, it was from the family of Aymer Maxwell, brother of a chamberlain of Scotland, that the many branches of this family throughout the south-west of Scotland sprang. Sir Herbert Maxwell is recorded as swearing fealty to Edward I of England in the Ragman Rolls of 1296 and his son, Eustace, held Caerlaverock Castle as a vassal of the English, although he later followed Robert the Bruce to Bannockburn in 1314.

Eustace's descendant, another Sir Herbert, was created Lord Maxwell around 1440, taking his seat as Lord of Parliament. From his second son descended the Maxwells of Monrieth, who were later to be created baronets in 1681. The 5th Lord intrigued with Henry VII of England, although by 1542 James V had appointed him warden of the marches. Maxwell was captured at the Battle of Solway Moss in the same year.

John, the 7th Lord, remained a devout Catholic throughout the Reformation, and his name was linked with a number of plots to restore Mary, Queen of Scots to her throne. After Mary's execution in England in 1587 and the defeat of the Spanish Armada the following year, Lord Maxwell continued to correspond with Philip of Spain, seeking support for a Catholic revolution. Maxwell was killed in 1593 during a feud between his family and the Johnstons, near Lockerbie. The feud continued, however, and the next Lord Maxwell

shot Sir James Johnston, who was attempting to reconcile the two warring factions. His brother, Robert, succeeded to the Maxwell title and additionally was created Earl of Nithsdale. His descendant, the 5th Earl of Nithsdale, was a staunch Jacobite who was captured at the Battle of Preston during the ill-fated rising of 1715. He was taken to London, tried and sentenced to death for treason. On the eve of his execution, with the assistance of his wife, he escaped from the Tower of London, disguised as a serving woman. The couple fled to Rome, where the earl died in 1744.

A number of the cadet branches rose to prominence in their own right, including the Maxwells of Cardoness, Monreith, Sprinkel and Pollok, each achieving the rank of baronet. Pollok House, the seat of the Maxwell Baronets of Pollok, was gifted to the city of Glasgow in 1967; in its grounds is the world-famous Burrell Collection of art.

Menzies

CREST
A savage head erased Proper

MOTTO
Vil God I Zal

PLANT BADGE
Menzies heath

Mesnières in Normandy was the original home of the Norman family who in England rendered their name as Manners, and who were ancestors of the present Dukes of Rutland. Sir Robert de Meyneris appeared at the court of Alexander II, where he gained royal patronage, rising to become chamberlain in 1249. Sir Robert received grants of lands in Glen Lyon and Atholl, reinforced by a grant to his son, Alexander, of Aberfeldy in Strathtay, in 1296. Alexander also acquired the lands of Weem and made a splendid marriage to Egidia, daughter of James, the High Steward of Scotland. His son, Sir Robert, was a companion-in-arms of Robert the Bruce, and was rewarded with lands in Glendochart, Finlarig, Glenorchy, and Durisdeer. It was the 8th chief, another Sir Robert Menzies, who built the castle at Weem around 1488. James IV erected the Menzies lands into the free barony of Menzies in 1510.

In 1665, Sir Alexander Menzies was created a Baronet of Nova Scotia. His brother, Colonel James Menzies of Culdares, ancestor of the present chiefly line, was a veteran of the civil war who, it was claimed, had survived no fewer than nine serious wounds. Another of Sir Alexander's brothers had died fighting for the royalists at the Battle of Worcester in 1651. Clan loyalties were divided by the exile of James VII and, although Major Duncan Menzies of Fornock led his Highlanders in the charge which broke the Government troops at the Battle of Killiecrankie in 1689, they faced in the ranks of General Mackay's army, hundreds of their Perthshire kinsmen.

In 1715, Menzies of Culdares quickly rallied to the standard of the

'Old Pretender'. Culdares was captured at Dunblane after the rising and spent many years in exile. When the 'Young Pretender' landed in Scotland in 1745, Culdares was beyond active campaigning, but sent the prince a fine horse. However, the clan was out in force under Menzies of Shian who, with his son, was killed during the campaign. The Menzies lands at Glen Lyon provided shelter for refugees from Culloden, including members of the prince's personal staff.

The Menzies baronetcy became extinct on the death of Sir Neil Menzies of Menzies, 8th Baronet, in 1910. His sister, Miss Egidia Menzies, succeeded to the estates, but on her death in 1918, they were sold. Menzies Castle fell into a dilapidated state, and during the Second World War was used as a Polish army medical stores depot. It was saved from ruin in 1957, when it was purchased by the Menzies Clan Society and has now been extensively restored as the clan heritage centre. The present chief lives in Australia.

Moncreiffe

CREST
Issuing from a crest coronet Or,
a demi-lion rampant Gules,
armed and langued Azure

MOTTO
Sur esperance
(Upon hope)

PLANT BADGE
Oak

This name is derived from the feudal barony of Moncreiffe in Perthshire. The lands themselves take their name from the Gaelic 'Monadh croibhe', 'Hill of the sacred bough'. The plant badge of the clan is the oak, presumably the sacred tree. Moncreiffe Hill, which dominates the south-east Perth valley, was a stronghold of the Pictish kings. It is believed that the family can trace its links to the royal households of Duncan I in Scotland and of Naill of the Nine Hostages in Ireland.

In a charter of 1248, Sir Matthew de Muncrephe received lands in Perthshire from Alexander II. Malcolm Moncreiffe of that Ilk, the 6th Laird, was a member of the council of James II, and received a new charter incorporating his Highland and Lowland estates into the barony of Moncreiffe. He died around 1465, when he was succeeded by his son, the 7th Laird, chamberlain and shield-bearer to James III. His grandson, Sir John Moncreiffe, was killed at the Battle of Flodden in 1513.

The three main branches of the family descend from the 8th Laird, who died around 1496: the Moncreiffes of Moncreiffe are the chiefly line, while the principal cadets are the Lords Moncreiff of Tulliebole and Moncreiff of Bandirran.

William, the 10th Laird, was captured at the rout of Solway Moss in 1542 and imprisoned in the Tower of London. Thereafter, he embraced the Protestant religion and was one of the barons who subscribed to the Articles in the General Assembly of the Church of Scotland in 1567. The 12th Laird, Sir John Moncreiffe, was Sheriff of

Perthshire, and in April 1626 he was created a Baronet of Nova Scotia. His son, John, was heavily in debt, and in 1667 he secured a Crown charter confirming a family arrangement whereby the barony of Moncreiffe was sold to his kinsman, Thomas, a descendant of the 8th Laird. Thomas succeeded in 1683 to the chiefship of the name, while the baronetcy passed to Sir John's brother In 1685 a second Moncreiffe baronetcy was created when Thomas, now the 14th Laird, was himself created a baronet by James VII, as Moncreiffe of that Ilk. He commissioned a new seat at Moncreiffe in 1679, the first major country house completed by Sir William Bruce. The house remained the family seat until it was destroyed by fire in November 1957, claiming the life of Sir David Moncreiffe of that Ilk, Baronet, the 23rd Laird. It was this tragedy which led to the chiefship of Sir Iain Moncreiffe, the great Scottish herald and historian. The 24th Laird's sister, Miss Elizabeth Moncreiffe of Moncreiffe, was entitled to succeed to the chiefship but she declared that it was her wish that it be assumed by her cousin, Sir Iain, while she retained the feudal barony of Moncreiffe.

Montgomery

CRESTS
A lady dressed in ancient apparel
Azure holding in her dexter hand
an anchor and in her sinister the
head of a savage couped suspended
by the hair all Proper

MOTTO
Garde bien
(Watch well)

Although the actual derivation of this name is obscure, the Norman family who bore it held the castle of Sainte Foy de Montgomery at Lisieux. Roger de Mundegumbrie, whose mother was the niece of the great-grandmother of William the Conqueror, accompanied his kinsman on the invasion of England and commanded the van at Hastings in 1066 and was rewarded with the Earldom of Shrewsbury.

The first Montgomery who appears on record in Scotland is Robert, who obtained the lands of Eaglesham in Renfrewshire. It is generally supposed that Robert, a grandson of Earl Roger, accompanied Walter Fitzalan, the first high steward of Scotland when he came to Scotland around 1147 to take possession of lands conferred upon him by David I. Sir John, the 7th Baron of Eaglesham, was one of the heroes of the Battle of Otterburn in 1388, capturing Sir Henry Percy, the renowned Hotspur. The Percy's paid a great ransom for the release of Hotspur, building for Montgomery the castle of Polnoon. The hero of Otterburn cemented his good fortune by marrying the heiress of Sir Hugh Eglinton, thereby acquiring the Barony of Eglinton and Ardrossan.

Sir John's grandson, Alexander, was created Lord Montgomery around 1449. Hugh, the 3rd Lord Montgomery, supported Prince James in rebellion against his father, James III, and fought at the Battle of Sauchieburn in 1488. Montgomery was rewarded with the grant for life of the island of Arran and the keepership of Brodick Castle. In 1507, Lord Montgomery was created Earl of Eglinton. He

escaped the carnage of Flodden in 1513 and was part of the Parliament at Perth in October of that year which proclaimed the infant James V king.

The 3rd Earl rejected the Reformation and remained a devout Catholic. He staunchly supported Mary, Queen of Scots throughout her troubled reign. He fought for her at the Battle of Langside in 1568, where he was taken prisoner. He was imprisoned and declared guilty of treason, but remained unrepentant until 1571, when he was convinced to accept James VI.

When the 5th Earl died without issue, the Eglinton title passed to Sir Alexander Seton as heir of line. A rigid Protestant, the new Earl of Eglinton could not accept the religious policies of Charles I, and he fought in the Army of the Covenant during the civil war. He was able to accept Charles II, who had agreed to his Scottish subjects' terms concerning religion. He was captured at Dumbarton and remained imprisoned in Berwick until the Restoration in 1660.

The 13th Earl organized the Eglinton Tournament in 1839 which set out to recapture the spectacle of medieval jousting. He also became Earl of Winton in 1859.

Morrison

CREST
Issuant from waves of the sea Azure
crested Argent, a mount Vert, thereon
a battlemented wall Azure masoned
Argent, and issuing therefrom a
cubit arm naked Proper, the hand
grasping a dagger hilted Or

MOTTO
Teaghlach Phabbay (Pabbay family)

This ancient name highlights the problems created by the anglicization of Gaelic names. It seems quite likely that there are three quite distinct origins – two Hebridean and one mainland. In Co. Donegal in Ireland, the O'Muirgheasains, whose name means 'sea valour', were bards and keepers of the holy relics of St Columcille at Clonmany. It is believed that a branch of this family found its way to Habost on the north-east coast of Lewis. Meanwhile, further to the south, Ghille Mhuire, or 'servant of the Virgin Mary', was, according to tradition, washed ashore, having survived a shipwreck by clinging to a piece of driftwood; this is commemorated in the clan's plant badge. The Virgin's servant has been claimed as a natural son of King Olav, and therefore half-brother of Leod, the progenitor of the Macleods. However Olav's son came ashore, he married the heiress of the Gows, or Clan Igaa, who held Pabbay in the Sound of Harris.

In 1493 the Crown finally broke the power of the Macdonald Lords of the Isles, but was in no position to establish royal justice. There followed almost two centuries of feuds and unrest. The Morrisons were not a numerous clan and tried to live at peace with their more aggressive neighbours. The Macaulays of Uig killed Donald Ban, the brother of John Morrison, 'the Brehon' or 'traditional judge', at Habost. When the Morrisons retaliated by raiding Uig, the Macaulays appealed to their allies, the Macleods of Lewes. The Brehon was soundly defeated at the Caws of Tarbert, whereupon a strong force of Macaulays and Macleods invaded the Morrison lands. The feud was carried on by the next chief, Uisdean, or Hucheon,

who invaded north Harris only to be heavily defeated once more.

Hucheon, on his death bed in 1566, confessed to being the natural father of Torquil, until then accepted as the lawful son of Roderick Macleod of Lewes and his wife, Janet Mackenzie. Macleod disinherited Torquil, set aside Janet as an adulteress and took a third wife. She bore two sons, Torquil Dubh and Tormod. The older Torquil, now half-brother to the Morrison chiefs, allied himself to the Mackenzies of Kintail who, through him, claimed the island of Lewis. In the bloody war which followed, the Morrisons sided with the Mackenzies against the Macleods, and both Hucheon's successor, Iain Dubh, and his son, Malcolm Mor, were killed. The Morrisons were driven from their lands and their power as a fighting force was broken forever.

On the mainland the Morrisons, whose senior representatives were the Morrisons of Bognie in Aberdeenshire, appear to have no connection whatsoever with their Hebridean namesakes, but are descendants of Maurice, a Norman name derived from the Latin, 'Mauricius', meaning 'dark-skinned' or 'swarthy'. In the 20th century, the chiefship was vested in the Morrisons of Ruchdi.

Munro

CREST
An eagle perching Proper

MOTTO
Dread God

PLANT BADGE
Common club moss

The country of the Munros lies on the north side of the Cromarty Firth. The clan occupied the fertile coastal strip along the firth and spread up the river valleys into the upland around Ben Wyvis. By the 14th century, the Munros of Foulis had acquired lands on the west coast in Loch Broom and northwards in the border between Ross and Sutherland.

Donald, ancestor of the Munros of Foulis is said to have received his lands in Ross-shire as a reward for helping Malcolm II against invaders from Scandinavia. Members of the family are also said to have fallen in the Scots armies at Bannockburn in 1314 and at Halidon Hill in 1333. The chiefs held public office under the Stewart monarchs: Sir William Munro was killed in 1505 on the king's business in Wester Ross and his son was the royal lieutenant there ten years later. In 1547 the chief was slain at the Battle of Pinkie together with many of his men, resisting an English invasion.

When more peaceful times came, military service abroad had its attractions, and many Munros fought under Gustavus Adolphus of Sweden in the Thirty Years' War in Germany. Two successive chiefs, Robert Dubh and Sir Hector, died on the Continent, the latter shortly after having been created a Baronet of Nova Scotia.

A long minority in the chiefship from 1635 to 1651 coincided with the period of civil war. During these years, General Robert Munro commanded the army sent by the Scottish Parliament to Ireland in 1642 while Sir Robert Munro was sheriff of Ross under the Commonwealth and Protectorate, and had his lands raided and his

tenants abused. Sir Robert's brother, George, later commanded the king's forces in Scotland from 1674 to 1677.

The Revolution of 1688, which brought William and Mary to the throne of the deposed James VII, was supported by Sir John Munro of Foulis, a devout presbyterian. The clan followed their chief, and throughout the period of Jacobite unrest from 1689 to 1746, supported the Government.

Events during the Forty-five had left Foulis Castle a semi-ruin, but when Sir Hector Munro inherited the estate in 1884 he once more made it a family home. Sir Hector's grandson, Captain Patrick Munro of Foulis, completed a programme of restoration begun in 1955, and Foulis now stands much as it did when it took its present form over two centuries ago. Another Sir Hector Munro, son of Hugh Munro of Novar, was a distinguished soldier who made his name in India. His victories there led to the establishment of a real political base for frontier influence to extend later to empire. He also served as MP for Inverness for over thirty years.

Murray

CREST
On a Wreath Or and Sable a
demi-savage Proper wreathed
about the temples and waist with
laurel, his arms extended and holding in the right hand a dagger,
in the left a key all Proper

MOTTO
Furth fortune and fill the fetters

The ancient Pictish kingdom of Moray, in Gaelic 'Moireabh', was given to Freskin, probably a Flemish knight, as part of David I's policy to use ruthless professional warlords to pacify the northern provinces of his kingdom. In charters, Freskin's descendants were designated 'de Moravia', which, in Lowland Scots, became 'Murray'.

Sir Walter Murray, who became Lord of Bothwell in Clydesdale, was one of the regents of Scotland in 1255. Sir Andrew Murray, heir to the 3rd took up the cause of Scottish independence and rose against Edward I of England in 1297. He was joined by Sir William Wallace who, when Murray was killed at the great victory of Stirling Bridge, assumed command. Sir Andrew's heir, the 4th Lord, fell at the Battle of Halidon Hill in 1333 and the lordship of Bothwell passed out of family control in 1360 when the widow of the 5th Lord married the 3rd Earl of Douglas.

There were many branches of the name who disputed the right to the chiefship, and it was not until the 16th century that the Murrays of Tullibardine are recorded using the undifferenced Murray arms in Lord Lyon Lindsay's armorial of 1542. Sir John Murray of Tullibardine was created 1st Earl of Tullibardine in 1606. His son and heir married Dorothea Stewart, heiress to the Earls of Atholl. She brought with her a vast estate of over 200,000 acres. The Stewart earldom of Atholl became a Murray earldom in 1629, and a marquessate in 1676.

In 1703 the Murrays reached the pinnacle of the peerage when they were created Dukes of Atholl. The 1st Duke's younger son,

Lord George Murray, was the great Jacobite general and the architect of the early successes of the rising of 1745. His elder brother, the duke, supported the Hanoverian Government. Lord George led a charge at Culloden which broke the Hanoverian ranks, although this was not enough to prevent the overall defeat. He died in exile in the Netherlands in 1760. Culloden was the last time that the Highlanders of Atholl went to war, but the ceremonial guard of the chiefs – which became known as the Atholl Highlanders – still has the unique honour of being the only private army in the realm.

Sir David Murray was created Lord Scone in 1600, and later Viscount of Stormont. His descendants became the Earls of Mansfield who built the magnificent palace at Scone which is their home today. The 1st Earl of Mansfield was one of the greatest jurists of his time, and rose to become Lord Chief Justice of England. His direct descendant, the 7th Earl of Mansfield, has held high Government office as a minister for Scottish affairs.

Although the Dukes of Atholl have three separate heraldic crests, that illustrated opposite has been designated by the chief as the clansman's badge.

Napier

CREST
A dexter arm erect couped below
the elbow Proper, grasping a
crescent Argent

MOTTO
Sans tache
(Without stain)

The Napiers have a long and ancient history and are descended, through the Earls of Lennox, from the Celtic royal families of Scotland and Ireland. One suggested derivation of the name is from the officer of the royal household who was in charge of linen, the 'naperer'. The earliest certain reference to the name appears in a charter of Malcolm, Earl of Lennox, sometime prior to 1290, which granted lands at Kilmahew in Dunbartonshire to John de Naper. The Napiers were to hold lands at Kilmahew for 18 generations, until the estate was sold in 1820.

The 1st Laird of Merchiston, Alexander Napier, was a prominent Edinburgh merchant who amassed a fortune and became Lord Provost of the city. His son, Sir Alexander Napier, rose high in royal favour. He was wounded while rescuing the widow of James I and her second husband, Sir James Stewart, from rebels. James II honoured Napier by making him Comptroller of the Royal Household in 1440, and Vice Admiral of Scotland in 1461. His son, John, the son-in-law of the Earl of Lennox who was executed in 1444, did not press his family's claim to the earldom. He was killed at the Battle of Sauchieburn in 1488. His heir, Alexander, and his grandson were both killed at Flodden in 1513.

The most famous of the name is the 7th Laird of Merchiston, John Napier, who developed the system of logarithms. His son, Archibald, who succeeded to Merchiston in 1617, accompanied James VI when he travelled to England to claim his new throne, and was sworn a member of the Privy Council in 1615. He became a judge and was

Lord Justice Clerk of Scotland from 1623 to 1624. He was first created a Baronet of Nova Scotia in 1627, and later in that year raised to
the peerage as Baron Napier of Merchiston. A brother-in-law of
Montrose, he naturally supported Charles I throughout the civil war.
He died in 1645 and his only son, Archibald, 2nd Baron Napier, was
forced into exile when Scotland became part of the Commonwealth.
He died in the Netherlands in 1660.

Three grandsons of the 6th Lord Napier served throughout the
Napoleonic Wars, each attaining the rank of general and the Order
of the Bath. Francis, the 8th Lord, was an ensign when he was captured during the American War of Independence. He survived the
ordeal, and later sat in Parliament as a representative Scottish peer,
from 1796 to 1823. Francis, the 10th Lord Napier, was a friend of
Jefferson Davis, later to be the only president of the Confederate
States of America. He was ambassador to the Netherlands, Russia
and Prussia and served as acting Viceroy of India in 1872. A Knight
of the Thistle, he was created Baron Ettrick of Ettrick in the peerage
of the United Kingdom in July 1872.

Nicolson

CREST
A lion issuant Or armed
and langued Gules

MOTTO
Generositate
(By generosity)

PLANT BADGE
Sprig of juniper

The Nicolsons are of Norse descent, perhaps derived from the personal name Olsen, 'Nic' in Gaelic signifying 'daughter of'. It could also be a corruption of Nicolassen. Haakon IV, the last Norse king to invade Scotland, sent an advance party under Anders Nicolassen, his foster brother and one of his chief barons. Nicolassen plundered Bute before joining the main fleet off Largs in 1263. The Norsemen were defeated, but there is a persistent tradition that Nicolassen eventually settled in Scotland after he was sent as an envoy from Norway to conclude the Treaty of Perth in 1266, which finally ceded sovereignty of the Hebrides to the kings of Scots.

James Nicolson was a lawyer in Edinburgh who died around 1580. He married Janet Swinton of the ancient Borders family, and they had two sons. John, the heir, became an advocate, while his brother, James, entered the Church, briefly becoming the bishop of Dunkeld in 1606. John acquired the lands of Lasswade by a charter of 1592 from Sinclair of Dryden. His son, John, was created a Baronet of Nova Scotia as Nicolson of that Ilk and Lasswade on 27 July 1629. The direct male line failed in 1826 and passed to a branch established in Shetland by Bishop James' grandson.

Another baronetcy had been conferred on the family in 1637, when Thomas Nicolson, a son of John Nicolson of Edinburgh, became the 1st Baronet of Carnock near Stirling. The last of this line, Sir David Nicolson, died at Breda in 1808.

The Carnock title then passed to Major General Sir William Nicolson, only son of George Nicolson of Tarviston. The general saw

service in America, India, Ireland and Mauritius. He died in 1820, to be succeeded by his son, Admiral Sir Frederick Nicolson. The admiral's eldest son, Frederick, was killed fighting the Zulus in 1879, and it was his second son, Arthur, who succeeded. He was ambassador to the imperial court at St Petersburg from 1906 to 1910, when he was appointed Permanent Under Secretary of State for Foreign Affairs, a post he held until 1916. He was showered with honours during his distinguished career, and in June 1916 he was created Baron Carnock of Carnock.

The 4th Lord Carnock, who had inherited not only the peerage and baronetcy of Carnock, but also the baronetcy of Lasswade and of that Ilk, followed his ancestors into the law, practising as a solicitor in London. In 1985 he matriculated his arms, and was recognized by the Lord Lyon, King of Arms as Nicolson of that Ilk, chief of the Clan Nicolson. The Lord Lyon also recognised Nicolson of Scorrybreac as Macnicol of Macnicol, the chief of the independent west Highland Clan Macnicol who had hitherto been a cadet of the Nicholsons (see pp. 226–227).

Ogilvy

CREST
A lady affrontée from the middle
upward Proper in Azure vestments
richly attired holding a portcullis
Gules

MOTTO
A Fin
(To the end)

This name derives from the Old English 'Ocel-fa', meaning high plain. The lands of Ogilvy are in Angus, once a Pictish kingdom ruled by a mormaer, one of the ancient Celtic nobles of Scotland who became the first earls. Gillebride, Earl of Angus, gave the lands of Ogilvy to his son, Gilbert, some time before 1177.

The Ogilvys became hereditary sheriffs of Angus in the 14th and 15th centuries. When Sir Patrick Ogilvy commanded the Scottish forces fighting with Joan of Arc against the English, he was styled 'Viscomte d'Angus'. Sir Walter Ogilvy, younger son of Ogilvy of Wester Powrie, was appointed Lord High Treasurer of Scotland in 1425. In 1430, he was an ambassador to England, and four years later attended Princess Margaret on her marriage to the Dauphin, heir to the throne of France. He had numerous sons, including his namesake, Walter, who was to become ancestor of the Earls of Seafield and Deskford. His eldest son, Sir John Ogilvy of Lintrathern received a charter to the castle and lands of Airlie in 1459. Sir John's son, Sir James Ogilvy of Airlie, was appointed ambassador to Denmark in 1491 and advanced to the ranks of the peerage as Lord Ogilvy of Airlie in the same year. The 7th Lord Ogilvy was created Earl of Airlie in April 1639.

The family was to suffer much in the service of the Stuart monarchs. The 1st Earl and his sons joined Montrose to oppose the enemies of Charles I; Sir Thomas, the earl's second son, was killed at Inverlochy, in February 1645.

In the following century, Lord Ogilvy was attainted for his part in

the 1715 Jacobite rising, but was allowed to return home in 1725. His titles were not restored and he died in 1730, when his younger brother, John, assumed the style 'Earl of Airlie'. His son, David, raised a regiment comprising mostly of Ogilvys to fight for the 'Young Pretender' in 1745. It fought at Culloden the following year and after the Jacobite defeat, Ogilvy escaped to France, entering royal service there and rising to the rank of general.

The Ogilvys also held the earldoms of Findlater and Seafield. James Ogilvy, younger son of the 3rd Earl of Findlater, was created Earl of Seafield in 1701 and in 1711, inherited his father's title of Findlater. However, it was not until 1896 that an Act of Parliament confirmed the restoration of the Airlie earldom to David Ogilvie who became the 6th Earl.

The present chief serves as Lord Chamberlain to Her Majesty The Queen, as did his father. This royal link was reinforced when the Honourable Angus Ogilvie, the chief's brother, married Her Royal Highness Princess Alexandra.

Oliphant

CREST
A unicorn's head couped Argent
armed and maned Or

MOTTO
Tout pourvoir
(Provide for all)

The Oliphants were a Norman family who first held lands in England around Northampton. It is said that David de Olifard rescued David, Earl of Huntingdon, later David I of Scotland, at the siege of Winchester Castle in 1141. He travelled north when the earl came to Sotland in 1124 to claim his kingdom, and was granted lands in Roxburghshire and made justiciar of Lothian.

The Oliphant name appears on the Ragman Rolls of 1296 amongst the ranks of the Scottish nobility acknowledging the overlordship of Edward I of England. However, in common with many of those forced to swear fealty in 1296, the Oliphants quickly took up the cause of Scottish independence and were prominent in the defence of Stirling Castle. The Oliphants later fixed their seal to the famous Declaration of Arbroath in 1320, asserting to the pope the historic independence of Scotland.

The family received the lands of Gask in Perthshire which were erected into a barony. Sir John Oliphant was knighted by Robert II and his son, Sir Laurence of Aberdalgy, was created a Lord of Parliament by James II in 1458. His grandson was killed following James IV at the Battle of Flodden in 1513, and his great-grandson was captured at the Battle of Solway Moss in 1542.

The 4th Lord Oliphant was a staunch supporter of Mary, Queen of Scots, and fought for her at the Battle of Langside in 1568. The Oliphants were also devoted to the Jacobite cause; the 9th Lord fought at the Battle of Killiecrankie in 1689 and was afterwards imprisoned. He joined with his cousin, Oliphant of Gask, in the ris-

ing of 1715. The 10th and last Lord Oliphant played an active role in the campaign of Bonnie Prince Charlie in the Forty-five, escaping first to Sweden and then to France after the defeat at Culloden in 1746. He was allowed to return to Scotland in 1763, but never relented in his opposition to the Hanoverians. Lady Nairne, the Jacobite poet, was Carolina Oliphant, daughter of the Laird of Gask. She is credited with writing the lyrics of *Charlie is My Darling* and the equally famous *Will Ye No' Come Back Again?*

The principal seat of the family is now at Ardblair Castle, the home of a direct descendant of the 1st Lord Oliphant.

Ramsay

CREST
A unicorn's head couped
Argent armed Or

MOTTO
Ora et labora
(Pray and work)

The Norman knight, Sir Symon de Ramesie, is believed to have been in the retinue of David 1 when he travelled to Scotland in 1124 to claim his kingdom. Sir Symon received a grant of land in Midlothian and witnessed several important charters, including one to the monks of Holyrood in 1140. The de Ramesie family prospered, and by the 13th century, there were five major branches: Dalhousie; Auchterhouse; Banff; Forfar; and Clatto.

In 1400, Sir Alexander Ramsay held Dalhousie Castle in Midlothian against a siege by Henry IV of England, and resisted so resolutely that the English were forced to withdraw. His descendant and namesake, Alexander Ramsay, was killed at Flodden in 1513, when Dalhousie passed to his son, Nicolas, who was to be a staunch supporter of Mary, Queen of Scots. After Mary's final defeat in 1568, the Ramsays acknowledged her son as James VI.

In 1600 John Ramsay, one of Nicolas's great-grandsons, killed the Earl of Gowrie and his brother, Alexander Ruthven, who were apparently attempting to kidnap the king in what became known as the Gowrie Conspiracy. John was created Earl of Holderness and Viscount Haddington by his grateful monarch. George Ramsay, the new earl's eldest brother, also attained high rank when he was created Lord Ramsay in 1618. Ramsay's eldest son, William, opposed the religious policies of Charles I and raised a cavalry regiment for Parliament. He fought at Marston Moor in 1644, and was part of General Lesley's force which surprised Montrose at Philiphaugh the following year. He had been created Earl of Dalhousie in 1633.

The Ramsays were thereafter to continue in military and public service down to the present day. They served in all the great campaigns of the 18th and 19th centuries on the Continent, in Canada and in India. The 9th Earl was Governor of Canada from 1819 to 1828, and commander-in-chief of India from 1829 to 1832. His son also served as Governor General of India from 1847 to 1856, during a period of great expansion of British interest on the sub-continent. He was created Marquess of Dalhousie in 1849, but this title died with him in 1860, although the older earldom passed to a cousin from whom the present Earl descends. Dalhousie Castle is now a hotel and the chief's seat is Brechin Castle in Angus.

Allan Ramsay, born in 1686, was a celebrated figure in Edinburgh's literary 'Enlightenment' of the 18th century, both as a poet and as a publisher. His best-known work, *The Gentle Shepherd*, was universally admired. His son, also Allan, was to become one of the greatest portrait painters of his time and received much royal and society patronage.

Robertson

CREST
A dexter hand holding up an
imperial crown Proper

MOTTO
Virtutis gloria merces
(Glory is the reward of valour)

PLANT BADGE
Bracken

The Robertsons can trace a path of descent from Crinan, Lord of Atholl, the royal house of Duncan I, and the Earls of Atholl. They are more properly called Clan Donnachaidh, from Duncan, fifth in descent from Conan of Glenerochie, a younger son of Henry, Earl of Atholl. Duncan supported Robert the Bruce, and his clan fought at Bannockburn in 1314. Duncan later seems to have fallen into the hands of the English, at either Durham or Neville's Cross in 1346. He died in 1355, succeeded by Robert, from whom the general surname of the clan is taken.

The clan's fame and fortune was assured in 1437, following the murder of James I at Perth. Robert, known as Riach (the Grizzled), captured Sir Robert Graham, the king's assassin, who was later put to death with considerable savagery. The chief received the tangible reward of having his lands of Struan erected into a free barony.

The clan feuded with their neighbours, the Stewarts of Atholl. William, the 6th chief, was killed trying to recover lands seized by them and the 8th chief was murdered. His brother inherited an estate riddled with debt and consequently, a large part of the family lands were sold off. However, in 1606, a prosperous Edinburgh merchant, John Robertson (who claimed kinship to the chiefly family) succeeded in transferring the title of the lands to Robertson of Struan.

When the chiefship passed to an infant, Alexander, in 1636, the leadership of the clan devolved upon his uncle, Donald. Donald, who was generally known as the Tutor of Struan, was a staunch

adherent to the royalist cause, and he fought with the Marquess of Montrose in all of his campaigns.

The gallant Alexander, 'the Poet Chief', followed James VII into exile in France in 1690. He called out his clan in 1715 when the standard of the 'Old Pretender' was raised. He was twice captured by Government forces, and on each occasion contrived to escape, finally fleeing to exile again in France. He returned to Scotland in 1725 under the terms of a general amnesty but would swear no oath of allegiance to the Hanoverians. Despite all he had suffered for the Stuart cause, he hastened to the side of Prince Charles Edward Stuart in 1745, although his age precluded him from active campaigning. He died in 1749 without issue.

The chiefship passed to his kinsman, Duncan Robertson of Drumachuine, but he could not take up the family estate as he had been forfeited in his own right for his participation in the rising of 1745. His son, Alexander, the 15th chief, had the barony of Struan restored to him by the Crown in 1784. Struan was sold by George, the 18th chief, in 1854 and for many years, his successors lived in Jamaica although they have since returned to live in England.

Rose

CREST
On a chapeau Gules furred
Ermine, a harp Azure

MOTTO
Constant and true

PLANT BADGE
Wild rosemary

This name is Norman in origin, originating from Ros near Caen in Normandy, a fief of William the Conqueror's brother, Odo, the bishop famous for his war-like character and for the tapestry named after his see of Bayeux. It has no connection with the ancient Celtic family of Ross.

The de Ros family appear to have been strongly connected with two other Norman families, the de Boscos and the de Bissets. All three families disappear from records in Wiltshire and Dorset where they first settled after the Conquest, and re-appear in the middle of the 13th century around the Moray Firth area. Elizabeth de Bisset, whose family owned the lands of Kilravock, married Andrew de Bosco, and their daughter, Marie, married around 1290, Hugo de Ros, whose family lands were at Geddes. Hugh's father had been witness to the foundation charter of the priory of Beauly erected by Sir John Bisset of Lovat. Hugh and Marie established their home at Kilravock, which has remained the designation of the chief and the family's home to this day.

Around 1460 the 7th Baron built the present Tower of Kilravock, as he lived in unsettled times with unruly neighbours. When the Earls of Ross were forfeited in 1474, the following year Hugh Rose received a charter under the Great Seal of his lands of Kilravock and Geddes.

Mary, Queen of Scots, stayed at Kilravock, as did her son, James VI, and regarded Hugh, the 10th Laird with great affection. The Roses had supported the Reformation and the 13th Baron opposed

the religious policies of Charles I. He led his clan against Montrose at the Battle of Auldearn in 1645. However, when the king was handed over to Parliament by the Scots army, Rose led a regiment of dragoons in the Duke of Hamilton's expedition which planned to rescue him.

At the outbreak of the Jacobite rising of 1715, the Roses declared for the Government. Arthur Rose was killed leading a detachment of the clan to seize Inverness. On the eve of the Battle of Culloden on 14 April 1746, Kilravock entertained Prince Charles Edward Stuart, while the Duke of Cumberland occupied the Rose's town house at Nairn.

Lieutenant Colonel Hugh Rose, 24th Baron of Kilravock, had a distinguished military career, commanding the 1st Battalion, the Black Watch. His son was killed at El Alamein in 1942. He himself died in 1946, to be succeeded by his daughter, Elizabeth.

Kilravock is still the clan seat and the chief's family home.

Ross

CREST
A hand holding a garland
of juniper Proper

MOTTO
Spem successus alit
(Success nourishes hope)

PLANT BADGE
Juniper plant fructed Proper

In the ancient Celtic tongue, a ros was a promontory, such as the fertile land between the Cromarty and Dornoch Firths. Those who bore the name rose to be Earls of Ross, and it is believed that the first earl, Malcolm, who lived in the early 12th century, allied his family to O'Beolan of the great Irish royal house of Tara, through the marriage of his daughter. The clan was sometimes also referred to as Clan Anrias, or Gille Andras, alluding to Anrias, a distinguished O'Beolan ancestor. It has also been suggested that another variation, 'MicGille Andras', 'son of the follower of St Andrew', derives from one of the ancient earls who was devoted to Scotland's patron saint.

In 1214, Alexander II led his army to the north to put down the rebellion of the son of Donald Bane, a rival claimant to the throne. He was aided by the chief of Clan Ross, Fearchar Mac an t'sagirt. Fearchar was knighted by his king, and by 1234 he was formally recognized in the title of Earl of Ross.

The Rosses were prominent in medieval Scottish affairs. They fought at the Battle of Largs against the Norse in 1263 and through-out the struggle for independence. The clan fought with distinction at Bannockburn in 1314, and the earl's seal was affixed to the great Declaration of Arbroath in 1320. Hugh Ross, the brother-in-law of Bruce, fell at the Battle of Halidon Hill in 1333.

The last chief to hold the earldom was another William, who died in 1372. Euphemia, his only daughter, claimed the earldom as Countess of Ross, but it eventually passed through the Macdonalds of the Isles into the hands of the Crown in 1476. The chiefship

devolved upon William's younger half-brother, Hugh of Balnagowan.

The Rosses were royalists in the civil war, and David, the 12th chief, led almost a thousand of his clansmen against Cromwell at the Battle of Worcester in 1651. However, the chief was captured and imprisoned in the Tower of London and many of his clansmen were transported to the colonies in New England. His son, another David, succeeded to the chiefship when he was only nine years of age.

David died, without an heir, in 1711, and the chiefship rightfully passed to his kinsman, Malcolm Ross of Pitcalnie. However, General Charles Ross, brother of Lord Ross of Hawkhead, whose family were from the Lowlands and were truly 'de Roos' of Norman descent, obtained Lyon Court recognition of a specious claim to chiefship.

In the risings of 1715 and 1745 the clan as a whole avoided Jacobite intrigues, although Malcolm, the Younger of Pitcalnie, joined the 'Old Pretender'.

The chiefship was restored to the true line in 1903, when Miss Ross of Pitcalnie rematriculated the chiefly arms. The chiefship passed in 1968 to her heir, David Ross of Ross and Shandwick, a descendant in the direct male line of Mac an t'sagirt.

Scott

CREST
A stag trippant Proper,
attired and unguled Or

MOTTO
Amo
(I love)

While likely to be Celtic in origin, the exact derivation of this name is unclear. The Latin word 'Scotti' was used originally to denote the Irish Celts and, later, Gaels in general although an early written record of the name is accompanied by a Saxon personal name. In another early record of the name, a Henricus le Scotte witnessed a charter by David, Earl of Strathearn, around 1195. Four generations later, Sir Richard Scott married the daughter and heiress of Murthockstone, and thereby acquired her estates. Sir Richard was appointed ranger of Ettrick Forest. The new laird built his residence at Buccleuch. His son, Sir Michael, 2nd Laird of Buccleuch, proved a staunch supporter of Robert the Bruce, and later distinguished himself at the Battle of Halidon Hill in 1333. He was one of the few that escaped the carnage of that disastrous day, but he later fell at Durham in 1346.

By the end of the 15th century, the Scotts were among the most powerful of the Borders clans, and the chief could easily call upon a thousand spears to enforce his will. In common with most Borders families, the Scotts quarrelled with their neighbours, particularly the Kerrs of Cessford. The feud resulted in the deaths of chiefs on both sides and was only settled by marriage during the chiefship of the 10th Laird, who died in 1574.

James VI's accession to the English throne in 1603 led to a vigorous royal policy to pacify the Borders, and as a result, Lord Scott sought military adventure on the Continent, fighting for the Prince of Orange in the Netherlands. His son, Walter, was advanced to the

268

title of Earl of Buccleuch in 1619. The 2nd Earl, Francis, supported the National Covenant and opposed the religious policies of Charles I. He died in 1651 at the early age of 25, and was succeeded by his 4-year-old daughter, Mary, Countess of Buccleuch. She was succeeded by her sister, Anne whose hand in marriage was sought by Charles II for his illegitimate son, James, Duke of Monmouth. On the day of the marriage in April 1663, the couple were also created Duke and Duchess of Buccleuch. Monmouth later rose in rebellion against the Crown, and was executed in July 1685. His titles were forfeit, but as Anne Scott had been specifically created Duchess of Buccleuch, her title was unaffected. The duchess was succeeded by her grandson, Francis, 2nd Duke of Buccleuch.

The Buccleuch art collection, maintained in the family's three great houses of Drumlanrig, Bowhill and Boughton, is internationally renowned.

Shaw of Tordarroch

CREST
A dexter cubit arm couped and
holding a dagger erect all Proper

MOTTO
Fide et fortitudine
(By faith and fortitude)

Shaw Macduff, a younger son of Duncan, Earl, or Thane of Fife
and a descendant of Kenneth Macalpin, rode north with his royal
cousin, Malcolm IV, in response to a rising in Moray. Shaw was made
keeper of the strategic royal castle at Inverness. His heirs, the 'Mhic
an Toiseach', the 'sons of the Thane', consolidated their power
around Inverness in support of the royal government. Shaw's grandson, Shaw Macwilliam, acquired important lands at Rothiemurchus
in 1236. His son, Ferquhard, sought alliance with the powerful
Macdonalds by marrying Mora, daughter of Angus Mhor, Lord of
Islay. In 1291, Ferquhard's son, Angus, 6th chief of Mackintosh,
married Eva, daughter of Dougall Dall, the descendant of
Ghillechattan Mhor. From this union emerged the large tribal confederation to be known as the Clan Chattan and the first chief of
Clan Shaw, John, the second son of Angus and Eva's .

The 2nd chief, Shaw Macghillechrist Mhic Iain, a great-grandson of
Angus and Eva, was generally known as 'Sgorfhiaclach', meaning
'bucktooth'. He was raised with his cousins at the Mackintosh seat at
Moy, and it seems certain that he was present at the Battle of
Invernahavon in 1370.

Aedh, the grandson of Shaw 'Bucktooth', settled at Tordarroch in
1468. Occupying a strategic site above the fort on the River Nairn,
he and his followers became a powerful force in their own right,
known as Clan Aedh or Ay. The Torrdarrochs were signatories to
Clan Chattan bands of union and manrent in 1543 and 1609 on
behalf of Clan Ay

William Mackintosh of Borlum called out Clan Chattan to fight for the Jacobite cause on 15 September 1715 at Farr near Tordarroch. Robert, the Younger of Tordarroch, and his brother, Angus, led the Shaw contingent. After the collapse of the rising at Preston, both Robert and Angus were imprisoned, and as a result of the rigours he experienced, Robert died soon after his release in 1718. Angus was transported to Virginia until he was pardoned in 1722. He never recovered from his experience or the death of his brother, and although a Jacobite, he refused to call out his clan for Bonnie Prince Charlie in 1745. Many Shaws, however, rallied to the prince's standard.

The tartan illustrated is Shaw of Tordarroch. However, it is equally correct to wear the green Shaw (which is, in fact, the regimental tartan of the former 43rd Highlanders) in memory of Fearchar Shaw who was executed at Towerhill in 1743 for refusing to serve overseas when the regiment had been promised that no such service would be demanded of it. Fearchar and two comrades were made an example of to discourage further mutiny and quickly became heroes in their native Highlands.

Sinclair

CREST
A cock Proper,
armed and beaked Or

MOTTO
Commit thy work to God

PLANT BADGE
Whin

St Clair lay in Pont d'Eveque in Normandy, and was the birthplace of this great clan. One of the earliest records of the name in Scotland is found in 1162, when Henry de St Clair received a charter to lands of Herdmanston near Haddington. The St Clairs of Herdmanston were created peers with the title Lord Sinclair in 1449, and this line still flourishes today.

The chiefs descend from Sir William Sinclair, a sheriff of Edinburgh, who was granted the barony of Roslin in 1280. His eldest son, Sir Henry, fought at Bannockburn and received a grant of lands around Pentland in 1317 as his reward. Sir Henry's son, Sir William, was a favourite of Bruce, and he accompanied Sir James Douglas on his expedition to the Holy Land with the heart of the king. En route, the Scots joined the king of Aragon in his fight against the Spanish Moors and Sinclair and Douglas were both killed. William's grandson, Henry, became Earl of Orkney through his mother, Isabel. Henry conquered the Faroe Islands in 1391 and discovered Greenland. He is now believed to have voyaged as far as the Americas, possibly landing in both Nova Scotia and Massachusetts.

The 3rd Earl was High Chancellor of Scotland between 1454 and 1458. He was granted the earldom of Caithness in 1455 in compensation for the loss of his claim to the lordship of Nithsdale. The Caithness title was settled on the eldest son of his second marriage, and the Roslin lands on his younger son. It was around this time that the spelling 'Sinclair' came into general use, although the Earls

of Rosslyn still prefer the older form. The 2nd Earl of Caithness died at Flodden in 1513.

George, the 6th Earl of Caithness, was forced to sell off much of the family lands in 1672, being greatly burdened with debt. He died without issue in 1676, and Sir John Campbell of Glenorchy claimed the earldom, being in possession of most of the mortgaged estates. Glenorchy promptly married the widowed countess. The right to the title in the estates was disputed by George Sinclair of Keiss, a descendant of a younger son of the 5th Earl. Keiss took possession of the estates by force, but when he met the Campbells in a pitched battle on the banks of Altimarlech near Wick, it is said so many Sinclairs were killed that the Campbells were able to cross the water without getting their feet wet. The Sinclairs regained the earldom in 1681 by an order of Parliament.

The remains of Rosslyn Castle near Edinburgh and the splendid chapel associated with it are still in family hands. In 1805, the earldom of Rosslyn passed to Sir James St Clair Erskine, Baronet, whose descendants care for these jewels of Scottish architecture today.

Skene

CREST
A dexter arm issuing from
the shoulder out of a cloud,
holding forth in the hand
a triumphal crown, Proper

MOTTO
Virtutis regia merces
(A palace the reward of bravery)

The traditional origin of this name is found in an 11th-century legend of the Robertsons. It is said that a younger son of Robertson of Struan saved the life of the king by killing a savage wolf with only his small dagger, or 'sgian'. He was rewarded with a grant of lands in Aberdeenshire which he named after the weapon which had brought him the good fortune, and the family thereafter were named for their ownership of this land. The feat is commemorated in the chief's shield, which displays three wolves' heads impaled on daggers, or as they have now been blazoned, 'durks'.

The first recorded bearer of the name was John de Skeen, who lived during the reign of Malcolm III in the late 11th century. After Malcolm's death, he supported Donald Bane, a rival to the succession of King Edgar. His lands were forfeited, and they were only restored when the Skenes joined the army of Alexander I marching against rebels in the north in 1118. His great-grandson, John de Skene, held the lands during the reign of Alexander III, and his son, Patrick, appears on the Ragman Rolls in 1296, submitting to Edward I of England. However, the Skenes staunchly supported Robert the Bruce, and after his victory, their lands were erected into a barony. Adam de Skene was killed at the Battle of Harlaw in 1411 and four generations later, Alexander Skene de Skene is listed among the dead on the ill-fated field of Flodden in 1513. Yet another Skene laird fell at the Battle of Pinkie in 1547.

The Skenes were not Covenanters, and for their support of Charles I they were forced into exile. The chief took service with the

Swedish armies under King Gustavus Adolphus. In 1827 the direct line of the Skenes of Skene died out and the estates passed to a nephew, James, Earl of Fife.

Other prominent branches of the family include the Skenes of Dyce, Halyards, Rubislaw and Curriehill. Sir John Skene of Curriehill was a prominent 16th-century lawyer who was appointed to the Supreme Court Bench in 1594, taking the title of Lord Curriehill. He was knighted by James VI, and his son was created a Baronet of Nova Scotia in 1626. Sir John's second son, John Skene of Halyards, also rose to high judicial office as the Lord Clerk Register. One of the Skenes of Halyards later founded Skeneborough on the shores of Lake Camplain in Canada. James Skene of Rubislaw was a close friend of the novelist Sir Walter Scott, and is said to have provided Scott with some inspiration for both *Quentin Durward* and *Ivanhoe*. William Forbes Skene, the celebrated writer and historian, was appointed historiographer royal for Scotland in 1881.

On 17 February 1994, the Lord Lyon, King of Arms recognized Danus George Moncrieffe Skene of Halyards as chief of the name and arms of Skene.

Stewart

CREST
A pelican Argent, winged Or, in her
nest feeding her young Proper

MOTTO
Virescit vulnere virtus
(Courage grows strong at a wound)

The Stewarts, who were to become monarchs of the Scots, descended from a family who were seneschals of Dol in Brittany. Walter Flaad, the Steward, moved to Scotland when David I claimed his throne in 1124. He was created Steward of Scotland and granted extensive estates in Renfrewshire and East Lothian. Walter, the High Steward, married Marjory, Robert the Bruce's daughter, and when Bruce's son, David II, died childless, he was succeeded by Bruce's grandson, Robert Stewart, who reigned as Robert II. The royal line of male Stewarts continued uninterrupted until the reign of Mary, Queen of Scots, and as a family they held the throne of Scotland and later that of England in the direct line until the death of Queen Anne in 1714.

Apart from the royal house, three main branches of the Stewarts settled in the Highlands during the 14th and 15th centuries: the Stewarts of Appin, of Atholl and of Balquhidder. The Appin Stewarts descend from Sir John Stewart of Bonkyl, son of Alexander, the fourth High Steward. Duncan, 2nd of Appin, was appointed chamberlain of the Isles by James IV. Duncan Mor, 8th of Appin, took the field under Montrose in 1645 at the battles of Inverlochy, Aldearn and Kilsyth. Consequently, he was outlawed and his lands were forfeited, although they were later restored after the restoration of Charles II to the throne. The Stewarts of Appin came out in 1715 for the 'Old Pretender', and fought at the Battle of Sheriffmuir. The chief was attainted for treason and fled into exile.

The Stewarts of Atholl descend from a son of Alexander Stewart, the notorious Wolf of Badenoch. James Stewart built a strong castle at Garth and settled there towards the end of the 14th century. In 1437 Queen Joanna, widow of James I, married the Black Knight of Lorne who was descended from the fourth High Steward. Her son by this marriage, Sir John Stewart of Balveny, was granted the earldom of Atholl by his half-brother, James II. John, the 5th Earl, died with no male issue. His daughter had married William Murray, 2nd Earl of Tullibardine, who was created Earl of Atholl in his own right in 1627. While Murray opposed the Stuarts in both 1689 and 1715, his heir, the Marquess of Tullibardine was a Jacobite and the Stewarts flocked to the banner of Bonnie Prince Charlie in 1745. General David Stewart of Garth, an Athollman, was an officer in the 42nd Regiment (the Black Watch) whose book, *Sketches of the Highlanders and Highland Regiments*, did much to popularize his homeland in Victorian England.

It is generally accepted that the Earls of Galloway now head the principal house of this great name.

Sutherland

CREST
A cat-a-mountain sejant
rampant Proper

MOTTO
Sans peur
(Without fear)

PLANT BADGE
Cotton-sedge plant

This is a territorial name from the county of Sutherland in the north east. Sutherland was the 'Sudrland', or 'Southland', of the Norsemen who had by the 10th century conquered all of the islands of Scotland and large tracts of the mainland as far south as Inverness. The original family were probably of Flemish origin, descended from Freskin, whose grandson, Hugh, was granted land in Moray around 1130 by David I. Hugh acquired estates in Sutherland and was referred to as Lord of Sutherland. His son, William, became Earl of Sutherland around 1235. Hugh's brother, also William, remained in Moray. His family took the surname Murray, and he is the ancestor of the many powerful families who bear this name, including the Dukes of Atholl.

Kenneth, 4th Earl of Sutherland, was killed fighting against the English in 1333 at the Battle of Halidon Hill. William, the 5th Earl, was married first to Princess Margaret, daughter of Robert the Bruce and sister of David II; their son was heir to the throne but died of plague in 1361. The royal connection was continued by Robert, the 6th Earl, who married the niece of Robert III in 1389, and later built the original Dunrobin castle.

John, the 8th Earl, was declared unfit to manage his own affairs in 1494 at the insistence of his son-in-law, Adam Gordon, a younger son of the Earl of Huntly. He brought a further charge of idiocy against the earl's heir, and rounded things off with a charge of illegit-imacy against Alexander Sutherland, son of the 8th Earl. Gordon's wife ultimately succeeded to the Sutherland lands and titles.

The death of the 17th Earl, leaving an only daughter, Elizabeth, led to a legal battle over the succession to the title. Her right as a woman to succeed was challenged by the nearest male heirs, George Sutherland of Forse and Sir Robert Gordon of Gordonstoun, a descendant of the second marriage of the 12th Earl. The House of Lords heard the case in 1771, and decided in Elizabeth's favour, confirming her as Countess of Sutherland in her own right. She married the Marquess of Stafford, of the prominent Leveson-Gower family, who was later created 1st Duke of Sutherland in 1833.

The 2nd Duke transformed Dunrobin from a traditional Scottish castle into a vast French chateau-style palace through the work of the architect Sir Charles Barry. Badly damaged by fire in 1915, it was later restored and partly remodelled by Sir Robert Lorimer.

On the death of the 5th Duke, the chiefship of the clan and the earldom of Sutherland devolved upon his niece, Elizabeth, the present Countess of Sutherland. The dukedom, however, was inherited by the Earl of Ellesmere, a descendant of a younger son of the 1st Duke. There is accordingly now a separate earldom and dukedom of Sutherland.

Urquhart

CREST
Issuant from a crest coronet Or,
a naked woman from the waist
upwards Proper, brandishing in
her dexter hand a sword Azure,
hilted and pommelled Gules,
and holding in her sinister hand
a palm sapling Vert

MOTTO
Meane weil speak weil and doe weil

The name Urquhart is derived from a place name, Airchart, which is first recorded in an early life of the great Celtic saint, Columba. The meaning of the word itself has been variously translated from the Gaelic, including 'woodside', or 'by a rowan wood' or 'fort on a knoll'.

William de Urchard is said to have defended the Moote of Cromarty against supporters of the English Crown in the time of William Wallace. The Urquharts were hereditary sheriffs of Cromarty from the reign of David II and in the early 16th century, Thomas Urquhart of Cromarty is said to have sired 25 sons, seven of whom were killed at the Battle of Pinkie in 1547.

Thomas's grandson, John Urquhart, commonly known as the Tutor of Cromarty, was guardian of his famous grand-nephew, Sir Thomas Urquhart of Cromartie. Sir Thomas was a student at Kings College in Aberdeen at the age of 11. By the age of 30 he had become a scholar, writer of note and a soldier. His translation of the French poet, Rabelais, is still considered to be a masterpiece. Literary undertakings did not prevent his joining the army of Charles I, and he fought at the Battle of Worcester in 1651, where he was taken prisoner. When released, he returned to the Continent, where he died in 1660, allegedly from laughter while celebrating the Restoration.

Colonel James Urquhart rose for the 'Old Pretender' in 1715, and was severely wounded at the Battle of Sheriffmuir. In the last years of his life, he was the principal Jacobite agent in Scotland. Sheriffmuir was also the last battle for another Urquhart, Captian

John Urquhart of Craigston who was know as 'the Pirate'. He had amassed a great fortune by means which he chose not to disclose, preferring instead to encourage romatic myths to explain its origin. Craigston Castle is still in family hands.

With the death of Colonel James in 1741 the chiefship passed to his cousin, William Urquhart of Meldrum, a cautious Jacobite who avoided the disaster at Culloden. His cousin, Adam Urquhart of Blyth, was more open in his loyalties and was a member of Bonnie Prince Charlie's court-in-exile at Rome. The last of this line, Major Beauchamp Urquhart, was killed in the Sudan at the Battle of Atbara in 1898.

In 1959, Wilkins Urquhart, a descendant of the Urquharts of Braelangswell, whose family had emigrated to America in the 18th century, established his right to be chief of Clan Urquhart. The chiefly seat is now established at the ancient Urquhart stronghold of Castle Craig on the southern coast of the Cromarty Firth; this was gifted to the 25th chief by Major Iain Shaw of Tordarroch as a sign of amity between two great Highland clans

Wallace

CREST
Issuant from a crest coronet of four
(three visible) strawberry leaves Or,
a dexter arm vambraced, the hand
brandishing a sword all Proper

MOTTO
Pro libertate
(For liberty)

There are two principal theories for the origin of this name, both of which indicate an ancient British origin. The Waleis were originally Britons from Wales who held land in Shropshire and who may have come north with David I in the early 12th century. More plausibly, it is believed that they were Britons who settled in the ancient kingdom of Strathclyde, having come north in the 10th century.

The name is certainly found in records by the 12th century in Ayrshire and Renfrewshire. Richard Walensis of Riccarton held land near Kilmarnock as a vassal of the High Steward of Scotland sometime before 1160. His grandson, Adam Walays, had two sons, the eldest of whom succeeded to the family estates in Ayrshire. Malcolm, Adam's younger son, received Elderslie and Auchinbothie in Renfrewshire. Malcolm was the father of the great Scottish patriot, Sir William Wallace of Elderslie.

Malcolm of Elderslie was one of very few Scottish nobles who bravely refused to submit to Edward I of England in 1296. He and his eldest son, Andrew, were both executed. His wife fled with her younger son, William, to the protection of relatives near Dundee. By 1297 he had gathered enough popular support to conduct a guerilla campaign against the English. His greatest victory came later that year at Stirling Bridge, where superior tactics carried the day against overwhelming English odds. He was knighted and granted the title 'Guardian of Scotland'. However, few of the major Scottish nobles supported Wallace because of his relatively low social status and he was defeated at a set-piece battle at Falkirk in 1298, when the

English superiority of numbers finally prevailed. Wallace escaped, but gave up the guardianship and faded into obscurity. In 1305, he was betrayed and taken to London, where he was executed with great brutality.

The Wallaces of Craigie descended from the uncle of the great patriot. In 1669 Hugh Wallace of Craigie was created a Baronet of Nova Scotia. Sir Thomas Wallace was the 5th Baronet, and when his son predeceased him, the estates passed to his daughter, Frances. In 1760 she married John Dunlop of Dunlop, the friend of the poet Robert Burns.

The representation of the chiefly line then passed to the Wallaces of Cairnhill, who had lived in Jamaica for several generations. Through marriage to an heiress, they inherited estates in Ayrshire at Busbie and Clancaird. In 1888, Captain Henry Wallace of Busbie and Clancaird established himself as chief of the name. Robert Wallace of that Ilk received both the French and Belgian Croix De Guerre during the First World War. His son, Malcolm, served in the Second World War, Korea, and Borneo, becoming chief on his father's death. He has since been succeeded by his brother.

Wemyss

CREST
A swan Proper

MOTTO
Je pense
(I think)

This name is derived from the Gaelic 'uaimh', meaning 'cave', and is believed to be taken from the caves and cliffs of the Firth of Forth in that part of Fife where the family made its home. Wemyss in Fife has been the seat of the chiefs since the 12th century. They are one of the few Lowland families directly descended from the Celtic nobility through the Macduff earls of Fife.

In 1296, Sir Michael swore fealty to Edward I of England, but he changed his allegiance to Robert the Bruce, and Wemyss Castle was sacked by the English. Sir David de Wemyss was killed at Flodden in 1513. His grandson, Sir John, fought under the Earl of Arran at the Battle of Pinkie in 1547. He was a great supporter of Mary, Queen of Scots, and fought for her at Langside in 1568. It was at the newly enlarged Wemyss Castle that the queen first met her future husband, Henry, Lord Darnley. Sir John's great-grandson, John Wemyss, was born in 1586 He was the second-born but eldest-surviving son of Sir John Wemyss of that Ilk, by his second wife, Mary Stewart. John was knighted in 1618 and created a Baronet of Nova Scotia in 1625, with a charter to the barony of New Wemyss in that province of Canada. Created a baron in 1628, he was later advanced to the title of Earl of Wemyss, the patent being presented to him personally by Charles I at Dunfermline.

The 4th Earl, born in 1699, married Janet, heiress of Colonel Francis Charteris of Amisfield. In the Jacobite rising of 1745, his eldest son, David, Lord Elcho, joined Prince Charles in Edinburgh. Appointed colonel of a troop of royal Horse Guards, he accompanied

the prince into England, and was with him until his defeat at the Battle of Culloden the following year. Elcho then escaped to France, and took part in the state entry of Prince Charles into Paris the following year. He was convicted of treason in his absence, and his estates were forfeited to the Crown. He continued to reside in France, and died childless in Paris in 1787.

Consequent upon the attainder, the Jacobite earl was succeeded by his second son, Francis, who changed his name to Charteris, the family name of his maternal grandmother. It is from Francis that the present Earl of Wemyss and March, whose seat is the magnificent Adam mansion of Gosford, is descended.

The estates in Fife and the chiefship of the name of Wemyss devolved upon the Earl's third son, the Honourable James Wemyss. He was MP for Sutherland, and married Lady Elizabeth Sutherland in 1757. His great-grandson married Millicent, the granddaughter of William IV, who, on the death of her husband in 1864, successfully took over the running of the estate for 30 years. Her son, Michael, married Lady Victoria Cavendish-Bentinck, the last surviving goddaughter of Queen Victoria.

APPENDIX I: Scottish monarchs to the Union of the Parliaments, 1707

Kenneth I (Macalpin)	843–860
Donald I	860–863
Constantine I	863–877
Aodh	877–878
Eocha	878–889
Donald II	889–900
Constantine II	900–943
Malcolm I	943–954
Indulph	954–962
Dubh	962–967
Culiean	967–971
Kenneth II	971–995
Constantine III	995–997
Kenneth III	997–1005
Malcolm II	1005–1034
Duncan I	1034–1040
Macbeth	1040–1057
Lulech	1057 (*slain*)
Malcolm III (Canmore)	1057–1093
Donald Bane	1093 (*deposed*)
Duncan II	1094 (*slain*)
Donald Bane (*restored*)	1094–1097
Edgar	1097–1107

Alexander I	1107–1124
David I	1124–1153
Malcolm IV (The Maiden)	1153–1165
William I (The Lion)	1165–1214
Alexander II	1214–1249
Alexander III	1249–1286
Margaret (Maid of Norway)	1286–1290
[First Interregnum	1290–1292]
John Balliol	1292–1296
[Second Interregnum	1296–1306]
Robert I (the Bruce)	1306–1329
David II	1329–1371
Robert II (Stewart)	1371–1390
Robert III	1390–1406
James I	1406–1437
James II	1437–1460
James III	1460–1488
James IV	1488–1513
James V	1513–1542
Mary, Queen of Scots	1542–1567
James VI	1567–1625
Charles I	1625–1649
[The Commonwealth & Protectorate	1651–1660]
Charles I	1660–1685

[*crowned at Scone 1651, exiled and restored 1660*]

James VII	1685–1688
Mary II (with William II)	1689–1694
William II	1689–1702
Anne	1702–1714

APPENDIX 2: Glossary of heraldic terms

addorsed   back to back.

affronty (affrontée)   facing the observer.

antique crown   a crown composed of five or more sharp points mounted on a circlet. This charge is also known as an eastern crown.

argent   silver or white.

armed   (i) describes the horns, tusks, teeth or talons of a beast, monster or bird of prey when of a different tincture from the body; (ii) wearing armour.

attires   the antlers of a stag.

attired   having antlers. This term can also refer to the garments of a man or woman.

azure   blue.

banded   tied with a band or ribbon.

beaked   describes the beaks of birds or monsters when of a different tincture from the body.

belled   having a bell or bells attached.

bend   one of the ordinaries; a broad band extending from dexter chief to sinister base.

bend sinister   a bend which runs from sinister chief to dexter base.

bendwise   descriptive of charges when shown at the same angle as a bend.

blazon (blason)   (i) the written description of armorial bearings; (ii) to describe a coat of arms using correct heraldic terminology.

bordure   one of the sub-ordinaries; a border round the edge of a shield, generally used as a difference or mark of cadency.

cabossed (caboshed)   describes an animal's head when depicted affronty and cut off behind the ears leaving no part of the neck showing.

cadency   the system whereby a coat of arms is differenced to distinguish the cadets of a family from its head and from one another.

canton   one of the sub-ordinaries; a square division of the shield, smaller than a quarter, in one of the upper corners of the shield, usually in dexter chief, often charged and used as an augmentation. In Scottish heraldry, a canton voided is used as a mark of cadency for an adopted child.

cap of maintenance   a chapeau.

cat-a-mountain   a wild cat.

chapeau   a velvet cap lined with fur, indicative of feudo-baronial rank.

charge   any device or figure placed upon a shield.

chief   one of the ordinaries; a broad horizontal band occupying at most, the top third of the shield.

colours   the principal heraldic colours are gules (red), azure (blue), sable (black), and vert (green). Other colours, less commonly used, are purpure (purple), bleu celeste (sky blue) and murrey (mulberry).

compartment   a grassy mound or other solid base, often elaborately blazoned, on which the supporters stand.

coronet   a lesser crown consisting of a cap of maintenance within a circlet of gold. Varying patterns of coronet have been assigned to the five ranks of the peerage. The circlet of a Lord of Parliament or baron's coronet has six (four visible) silver balls, all placed closely together; an earl's coronet has eight (five visible) balls on long spikes, alternating with eight (four visible) strawberry leaves; a marquess's four (two visible) balls on short spikes, alternating with four (three visible) strawberry leaves; a duke's coronet has eight (five visible) strawberry leaves. This form of coronet is also known as a 'coronet of rank' and should not be confused with the 'crest coronet'. Coronets of rank are sometimes represented as the circlet only, omitting the cap and the ermine edging.

couchant   lying down with head raised.

couped   cut off. This describes any charge that is cut off cleanly with a straight line. When used of an ordinary it means that its ends do not reach the edge of the shield.

crescent   (i) a half moon depicted with horns pointing upwards; (ii) the cadency mark used to distinguish the arms of a second son.

crest   a three-dimensional device set upon a wreath, chapeau or coronet and mounted upon a helmet. Crests are now displayed above the shield as an integral part of the full achievement.

crest coronet   a coronet of four strawberry leaves, three visible, depicted as part of a crest in place of, or in addition to, the wreath. This form of coronet is sometimes known as a 'ducal coronet'. In Scotland, a clan chief is entitled to petition the Lord Lyon for the grant of a crest coronet to replace the wreath in his coat of arms. Other forms of crest coronet include the antique crown, the mural crown and the naval crown.

cross   one of the ordinaries and perhaps the most widely used of all heraldic devices, having more variants than any other.

cubit   describes a hand and arm cut off at the elbow.

cutlass   a form of curved sword similar to a scimitar (a corruption of curtle-axe).

dancetty (dancettée)   describes a zig-zag line of partition or edge to an ordinary; similar to 'indented' but with fewer and wider indentations.

demi   half. This term invariably relates to human or animal charges when depicted from the waist upwards.

dexter   the right hand side of the shield as held by the bearer, but the left hand side from the viewpoint of the observer.

difference   an addition or alteration to a coat of arms usually marking a distinction between arms of closely related persons.

displayed   with wings outstretched.

dormant   in a sleeping posture.

doubled   describes the inner lining of mantling, mantles and chapeaux.

dovetailed   describes a line of partition or the edge of an ordinary in the shape of a series of dovetail joints.

ducal coronet   a gold coronet of four strawberry leaves (three visible) set on a rim the jewels of which are shown but not coloured.

embattled   describes a line of partition or the upper edge of an ordinary which is indented to resemble the battlements of a tower or castle.

embowed   bent or curved.

engrailed   describes a line of partition or the edge of an ordinary which is composed of semi   circular indents with the points turned outwards.

environed   encircled by.

erased   torn off, leaving a jagged edge.

erect   upright.

ermine   white fur with black tails.

estoile   a star of six wavy rays.

fenestrated   describes windows when of a different tincture from the rest of the building.

fess   one of the ordinaries; a broad horizontal band extending across the centre of the shield.

fess point   the centre of the shield.

fessways   describes any charge placed or borne in fess, i.e. in a horizontal line across the shield.

field   the background or surface of the shield on which charges are placed.

fitchy (fitchée)   describes a cross the lower limb of which is pointed. If a cross is blazoned 'fitchy at the foot', it is depicted normally but has a point added to the lower limb.

flaunches   a pair of concave indentations, one on each side of the shield. The flaunch is classified by most authorities as one of the sub-ordinaries.

fleur de lis   (i) a stylised lily; (ii) the cadency mark used to distinguish the arms of a sixth son.

fructed (fructuated)   bearing fruit.

gorged   collared.

gules   red

gryphon (griffin)   a winged monster with the foreparts of an eagle, including a pair of sharply pointed ears, and the hindparts of a lion. A male gryphon has no wings and has spikes or rays emerging from the body.

guardant   describes a beast or monster with its head turned to face the observer.

gyron   the lower half of a canton or quarter when divided diagonally from the dexter chief to the fess point. This charge is classified by some authorities as one of the sub-ordinaries.

gyronny   describes a field which is divided by three to six lines all passing through the fess point.

hart   a stag.

helmet   defensive armour for the head. In heraldry the helmet bears the crest and its form differs according to rank. The sovereign and princes of the blood have a barred helmet of gold which is always placed affronty. A peer's is silver and faces the dexter. It has a gold grille of five bars and is garnished with gold. The helmet of knights and baronets is of steel. It is placed affronty and has the visor raised. Where this helmet is incongruous, a steel tilting helm garnished with gold may be used. In Scotland, the rank of feudal baron has been assigned the great tilting helm garnished with gold. Esquires and gentlemen bear a steel barrel helm, that of an esquire garnished with gold. The helmet can also be used as a charge.

hilted   describes the handle and guard of a sword or dagger when of a different tincture from the blade.

imperial crown   literally, a crown attributed to an empire but commonly used to describe an arched or closed crown as opposed to an open crown or coronet.

indented   describes a line of partition or the edge of an ordinary which is composed of small indentations and resembles the blade of a saw.

inescutcheon   one of the sub-ordinaries; a small shield borne as a charge on a larger shield.

invected   similar to engrailed but having the points turned inwards.

issuant   issuing or emerging from.

jessed   describes a falcon which has leather straps or thongs attached to its legs.

label   a horizontal bar with a number of dependent points. A mark of cadency. When used as a permanent difference, it is invariably charged and classified by most authorities as one of the sub-ordinaries.

langued   tongued.

livery colours   the principal metal and tincture of the shield. In Scottish heraldry, the wreath is usually described as 'of the liveries'.

maned   describes a beast with a mane of a different tincture from the body.

mantling   a cloth cape, suspended from the top of the helmet and hanging down the wearer's back. It was originally intended to absorb the heat of the sun and in early examples is usually depicted as a plain or scalloped cloth. Over the course of centuries it became much developed by artists to give a decorative surround to the shield, helm and crest.

masoned   describes lines of pointing when of a different tincture from the building on which they appear.

membered   describes the legs and beak of a bird or the genitalia of a lion or other beast when of a different tincture from the body.

moor   a black man.

motto   a word or short phrase placed in a scroll either below the shield or, as is usual in Scotland, above the crest. It often reflects the sentiments of the armiger or may be of a punning nature relating to his name or arms. The motto of a clansman will often respond to that of his chief.

mullet   (i) a five-pointed star; from the french 'molette'- spur rowel; (ii) the cadency mark used to distinguish the arms of a third son.

naiant   swimming; describes a fish when shown in a horizontal position.

nebuly   describes a line of partition or the edge of an ordinary which is deeply waved to represent clouds.

nowed   tied in a knot.

or   gold.

ordinary   a major heraldic charge. Opinions differ as to the number of these charges but most authorities include the bend, bend sinister, chevron, chief, cross, fess, pale, pall, pile and saltire. Specific dimensions are often given for each of the ordinaries. However, as an ordinary may be placed between other charges or be itself charged, these dimensions will inevitably vary.

orle   one of the sub-ordinaries; a narrow border running parallel to the edge of the shield but not adjacent to it.

pale   one of the ordinaries, a broad vertical band placed in the middle of the shield.

partition, line of   a line which divides the surface of a shield or charge into a variety of geometrical shapes. The direction of a line of partition is indicated by relation to its corresponding ordinary. For example, if a shield is divided horizontally across the middle it is said to be parted 'per fess'. Similarly, the shield can be parted per bend, per bend sinister, per chevron, per pale and per saltire. The term 'quarterly' is used to describe a field which is divided per pale and per fess. A shield which is divided into three parts is said to be 'tierced' and when divided into a number of gyrons or triangular pieces radiating from a centre point, it is blazoned 'gyronny'. Lines of partition may be straight or ornamented.

passant   walking.

pheon   an arrowhead with the barbs engrailed on the inner edge.

pile   one of the ordinaries; a triangular charge issuing from the chief and tapering towards the base.

pommel   the rounded knob at the end of a dagger or sword hilt.

port   the door or gate of a castle.

portcullis   the protective grille over the gateway of a town or castle. It is usually depicted as a lattice of four horizontal bars and five vertical bars terminating in points at the bottom and with chains attached to the top corners.

proper   depicted in natural colours.

quarter   (i) to divide the shield into four or more compartments; (ii) a sub-ordinary occupying one quarter of the shield.

quarterly   a term used to signify that the shield is quartered.

raguly   describes a line of partition or the edge of an ordinary which is ragged or notched resembling the trunk or limb of a tree which has been lopped of its branches (see **partition**).

rampant   describes a beast or monster standing on one hind leg.

reguardant   describes a beast, bird or monster when looking back over its shoulder.

rowel (revel)   the spiked, revolving disk at the end of a spur; usually depicted as a pierced mullet.

sable   black.

salamander   a fabulous reptile, depicted as a lizard-like creature surrounded by flames.

salient   springing.

saltire   one of the ordinaries; depicted in the form of a diagonal cross. Also known as a St Andrew's cross.

savage   a long-haired, bearded man often depicted as being wreathed about the head and loins with foliage.

scimitar   a form of curved sword.

segreant   describes a gryphon when in the rampant position.

sejant   sitting.

sgian   see **skene.**

shakefork   a sub-ordinary in the form of a pall the arms of which do not reach the edge of the shield.

sinister   the left hand side of the shield as held by the bearer, but the right hand side from the viewpoint of the observer.

skene (sgian)   a Highland knife often depicted in heraldry as a short sword or dagger.

slipped   describes flowers and leaves when depicted with the stalk attached.

splendour, in his   describes the sun when depicted as a disc, sometimes with a human face, environed by rays which may be alternately straight and wavy.

standard   a long, narrow, tapering flag, granted by the Lord Lyon only to those who have a following, such as clan chiefs. As a 'headquarters' flag, its principal use is to mark the gathering point or headquarters of the clan, family or following and does not necessarily denote the presence of the standard's owner as his personal banner does. The standards of peers and barons have their ends split and rounded; for others the end is unsplit and rounded. At the hoist, the standard usually shows the owner's arms, though some are still granted with the former practice of having the national saltire in the hoist. The remainder of the flag is horizontally divided into two tracts of the livery colours for chiefs of clans or families, three tracts for very major branch-chieftains and four for others. Upon this background are usually displayed the owner's crest and heraldic badges, separated by transverse bands bearing the owner's motto or slogan. The whole flag is fringed with alternating pieces of the livery colours.

statant   standing.

sub-ordinary   one of a group of major charges which are subordinate to the ordinaries. Opinions vary as to which charges should be classed as sub-ordinaries. However, most authorities include the bordure, canton, flaunch, inescutcheon, lable, orle, quarter, shakefork and tressure. The billet, fret, fusil, gyron, loz-enge, mascle, roundle and rustre are also classified as sub-ordinaries by some authorities.

surmounted   describes a charge with another placed upon it.

targe (target)   a small circular shield.

thunderbolt   a heraldic charge conventionally depicted as a winged and twisted bar, inflamed at each end and having four forked and barbed darts in saltire issuing from its centre.

tierced   divided into three.

tinctures   the metals, colours and furs used in heraldry.

tines (tynes)   the branches of a stag's antlers.

torse   see **wreath.**

tracts   two or more horizontal strips of metal and colour which constitute the field of a heraldic standard. The number of tracts is dictated by the rank of the armiger: two for chiefs of clans or families, three for very major branch chieftains and four for others.

transfixed   pierced through.

tressure   one of the sub-ordinaries; a diminutive of the orle. Tressures are usually borne double and are often decorated with fleurs de lis or other figures.

trippant   describes a stag or deer when depicted as passant.

triumphal crown   a wreath or garland of laurel.

unguled   describes the hooves of an animal when of a different tincture from the body.

unicorn   an imaginary animal resembling a horse with cloven hooves, the beard of a goat, the tail of a lion and a long twisted horn growing out of its forehead.

vambraced   describes an arm clad in armour.

vert   green.

vested   habited or clothed.

volant   flying.

wavy   describes a line of partition or the edge of an ordinary which undulates like waves.

wreath   a twisted length of cloth originally intended to cover the join between crest and helmet. It is conventionally depicted as being composed of six alternate twists of the owner's livery colours. The wreath is often replaced by some form of crest coronet or chapeau. A garland of flowers, leaves or other stylised foliage is also described as a wreath.

wreathed   encircled with a wreath.

APPENDIX 3: Associated clans and families

Septs are a contentious issue and one which is difficult to resolve with any degree of historical accuracy. There are also endless variations of Scottish surnames and the list below is neither comprehensive nor definitive but is intended solely as a guide to the possible connections a name may have to a recognised clan or family featured in this book.

Name	Associated Clan	Name	Associated Clan
Abbot	Macnab	Bean	Macbain
Abbotson	Macnab	Beath	Macdonald,
Addison	Gordon		Maclean
Adie	Gordon	Beattie	Macbain
Airlie	Ogilvy	Begg	Macdonald
Airth	Graham	Berry	Forbes
Aitcheson	Gordon	Beton	Macleod
Aitken	Gordon	Binnie	Macbain
Alexander	Macalister,	Black	Lamont,
	Macdonald		Macgregor,
Alistair	Macalister		Maclean
Allan	Macdonald,	Blake	Lamont
	Macfarlane	Bonar	Graham
Allanson	Macdonald,	Bontein	Graham
	Macfarlane	Bontine	Graham
Allison	Macalister	Bowers	Macgregor
Arrol	Hay	Bowie	Macdonald
Arthur	Macarthur	Bowmaker	Macgregor
Askey	Macleod	Bowman	Farquharson
Austin	Keith	Boyes	Forbes
Ayson	Mackintosh	Brebner	Farquharson
Bain	Macbain,	Brewer	Drummond,
	Mackay		Macgregor
Balloch	Macdonald	Brieve	Morrison
Barrie	Farquharson,	Brown	Lamont,
	Gordon		Macmillan
Barron	Rose	Bryce	Macfarlane
Bartholomew	Macfarlane,	Bryde	Brodie
	Leslie	Buntain	Graham

Name	Associated Clan	Name	Associated Clan
Bunten	Graham	Comrie	Macgregor
Buntine	Graham	Conacher	Macdougall
Burdon	Lamont	Connall	Macdonald
Burk	Macdonald	Connell	Macdonald
Burnes	Campbell	Conochie	Campbell
Burns	Campbell	Constable	Hay
Caddell	Campbell	Cook	Stewart
Caird	Sinclair,	Corbet	Ross
	Macgregor	Cormack	Buchanan
Cariston	Skene	Coull	Macdonald
Carlyle	Bruce	Coulson	Macdonald
Carr	Kerr	Cousland	Buchanan
Carrick	Kennedy	Coutts	Farquharson
Carson	Macpherson	Cowan	Colquhoun,
Cassels	Kennedy		Macdougall
Cattanach	Macpherson	Cowie	Fraser
Caw	Macfarlane	Crerar	Mackintosh
Cessford	Kerr	Crombie	Macdonald
Charles	Mackenzie	Crookshanks	Stewart
Christie	Farquharson	Cruickshanks	Stewart
Clanachan	Maclean	Crum	Macdonald
Clark	Cameron,	Cullen	Gordon
	Macpherson	Cumin	Cumming
Clarke	Cameron,	Dallas	Mackintosh
	Macpherson	Daniels	Macdonald
Clarkson	Cameron,	Davie	Davidson
	Macpherson	Davis	Davidson
Clement	Lamont	Davison	Davidson
Clerk	Cameron,	Dawson	Davidson
	Macpherson	Day	Davidson
Cluny	Macpherson	Dean	Davidson
Clyne	Sinclair	Denoon	Campbell
Cobb	Lindsay	Denune	Campbell
Collier	Robertson	Deuchar	Lindsay
Colman	Buchanan	Dickson	Keith
Colson	Macdonald	Dingwall	Munro, Ross
Colyear	Robertson	Dinnes	Innes
Combie	Macthomas	Dis	Skene
Comine	Cumming	Dixon	Keith

301

Name	Associated Clan	Name	Associated Clan
Dobbie	Robertson	Fergus	Fergusson
Dobson	Robertson	Ferries	Fergusson
Dochart	Macgregor	Ferson	Macpherson
Docharty	Macgregor	Fife	Macduff
Doig	Drummond	Findlater	Ogilvy
Doles	Mackintosh	Findlay	Farquharson
Donachie	Robertson	Findlayson	Farquharson
Donaldson	Macdonald	Finlay	Farquharson
Donillson	Macdonald	Finlayson	Farquharson
Donleavy	Buchanan	Fisher	Campbell
Donlevy	Buchanan	Foulis	Munro
Donnellson	Macdonnell	France	Stewart
Dove	Buchanan	Francis	Stewart
Dow	Buchanan, Davidson	Frew	Fraser
		Frissell	Fraser
Dowe	Buchanan	Frizell	Fraser
Downie	Lindsay	Fyfe	Macduff
Drysdale	Douglas	Gallie	Gunn
Duff	Macduff	Galt	Macdonald
Duffie	Macfie	Garrow	Stewart
Duffus	Sutherland	Garvie	Maclean
Duffy	Macfie	Gaunson	Gunn
Duilach	Stewart	Geddes	Gordon
Duncanson	Robertson	Georgeson	Gunn
Dunnachie	Robertson	Gibb	Buchanan
Duthie	Ross	Gifford	Hay
Dyce	Skene	Gilbert	Buchanan
Eadie	Gordon	Gilbertson	Buchanan
Eaton	Home	Gilbride	Macdonald
Edie	Gordon	Gilchrist	Maclachlan, Ogilvy
Elder	Mackintosh		
Ennis	Innes	Gilfillan	Macnab
Enrick	Gunn	Gill	Macdonald
Esson	Mackintosh	Gillanders	Ross
Ewing	Maclachlan	Gillespie	Macpherson
Fair	Ross	Gillies	Macpherson
Fairbairn	Armstrong	Gillon	Maclean
Federith	Sutherland	Gilroy	Grant, Macgillivray
Fee	Macfie		

Name	Associated Clan	Name	Associated Clan
Glennie	Mackintosh	Higginson	Mackintosh
Gorrie	Macdonald	Hobson	Robertson
Goudie	Macpherson	Hossack	Mackintosh
Gow	Macpherson	Howe	Graham
Gowan	Macdonald	Howie	Graham
Gowrie	Macdonald	Howison	Macdonald
Greenlaw	Home	Hudson	Macdonald
Gregorson	Macgregor	Hughson	Macdonald
Gregory	Macgregor	Huntly	Gordon
Greig	Macgregor	Hutchenson	Macdonald
Greusach	Farquharson	Hutcheson	Macdonald
Grewar	Macgregor, Drummond	Hutchinson	Macdonald
		Hutchison	Macdonald
Grier	Macgregor	Inches	Robertson
Griesck	Macfarlane	Ingram	Colquhoun
Grigor	Macgregor	Innie	Innes
Gruamach	Macfarlane	Isles	Macdonald
Gruer	Macgregor, Drummond	Jameson	Gunn, Stewart
		Jamieson	Gunn, Stewart
Haddon	Graham	Jeffrey	Macdonald
Haggart	Ross	Kay	Davidson
Hallyard	Skene	Kean	Gunn, Macdonald
Hardie	Farquharson, Mackintosh	Keene	Gunn, Macdonald
Hardy	Farquharson, Mackintosh	Kellie	Macdonald
		Kendrick	Macnaghten
Harold	Macleod	Kenneth	Mackenzie
Harper	Buchanan	Kennethson	Mackenzie
Harperson	Buchanan	Kerracher	Farquharson
Harvey	Keith	Kilgour	Macduff
Hastings	Campbell	King	Colquhoun
Hawes	Campbell	Kinnell	Macdonald
Haws	Campbell	Kinnieson	Macfarlane
Hawson	Campbell	Knox	Macfarlane
Hawthorn	Macdonald	Lachie	Maclachlan
Hendrie	Macnaghten	Laidlaw	Scott
Hendry	Macnaghten	Lair	Maclaren
Hewitson	Macdonald	Lamb	Lamont
Hewitt	Macdonald		

Name	Associated Clan	Name	Associated Clan
Lambie	Lamont	Macaldonich	Buchanan
Lammond	Lamont	Macalduie	Lamont
Lamondson	Lamont	Macallan	Macdonald,
Landers	Lamont		Macfarlane
Lang	Leslie	Macalonie	Cameron
Lansdale	Home	Macandeoir	Buchanan,
Lauchlan	Maclachlan		Macnab
Lawrence	Maclaren	Macandrew	Mackintosh
Lawrie	Maclaren	Macangus	Macinnes
Lawson	Maclaren	Macara	Macgregor,
Lean	Maclean		Macrae
Leckie	Macgregor	Macaree	Macgregor
Lecky	Macgregor	Macaskill	Macleod
Lees	Macpherson	Macaslan	Buchanan
Leitch	Macdonald	Macauselan	Buchanan
Lemond	Lamont	Macauslan	Buchanan
Lennie	Buchanan	Macausland	Buchanan
Lenny	Buchanan	Macauslane	Buchanan
Lewis	Macleod	Macay	Shaw
Limond	Lamont	Macbaxter	Macmillan
Limont	Lamont	Macbean	Macbain
Linklater	Sinclair	Macbeath	Macbain,
Lobban	Maclennan		Macdonald,
Lockerbie	Douglas		Maclean
Lombard	Stewart	Macbeolain	Mackenzie
Lonie	Cameron	Macbeth	Macbain,
Lorne	Stewart,		Macdonald,
	Campbell		Maclean
Loudoun	Campbell	Macbheath	Macbain,
Low	Maclaren		Macdonald,
Lowson	Maclaren		Maclean
Lucas	Lamont	Macbride	Macdonald
Luke	Lamont	Macbrieve	Morrison
Lyall	Sinclair	Macburie	Macdonald
MacA'challies	Macdonald	Maccaa	Macfarlane
Macachounich	Colquhoun	Maccabe	Macleod
Macadam	Macgregor	Maccaig	Farquharson,
Macadie	Ferguson		Macleod
Macaindra	Macfarlane	Maccaishe	Macdonald

Name	Associated Clan	Name	Associated Clan
Maccall	Macdonald	Macconachie	Macgregor, Robertson
Maccalman	Buchanan		
Maccalmont	Buchanan	Macconchy	Mackintosh
Maccamie	Stewart	Maccondy	Macfarlane
Maccammon	Buchanan	Macconnach	Mackenzie
Maccammond	Buchanan	Macconnechy	Campbell, Robertson
Maccanish	Macinnes		
Maccansh	Macinnes	Macconnell	Macdonald
Maccartney	Farquharson, Mackintosh	Macconochie	Campbell, Robertson
Maccartair	Campbell	Maccooish	Macdonald
Maccarter	Campbell	Maccook	Macdonald
Maccash	Macdonald	Maccorkill	Gunn
Maccaskill	Macleod	Maccorkindale	Macleod
Maccasland	Buchanan	Maccorkle	Gunn
Maccaul	Macdonald	Maccormack	Buchanan
Maccause	Macfarlane	Maccormick	Maclean of Lochbuie
Maccaw	Macfarlane		
Maccay	Mackay	Maccorrie	Macquarrie
Macceallaich	Macdonald	Maccorry	Macquarrie
Macchlerich	Cameron	Maccosram	Macdonald
Macchlery	Cameron	Maccoull	Macdougall
Macchoiter	Macgregor	Maccowan	Colquhoun, Macdougall
Macchruiter	Buchanan		
Maccloy	Stewart	Maccrae	Macrae
Macclure	Macleod	Maccrain	Macdonald
Maccluskie	Macdonald	Maccraken	Maclean
Macclymont	Lamont	Maccraw	Macrae
Maccodrum	Macdonald	Maccreath	Macrae
Maccoll	Macdonald	Maccrie	Mackay
Maccolman	Buchanan	Maccrimmor	Macleod
Maccomas	Macthomas, Gunn	Maccrindle	Macdonald
		Maccririe	Macdonald
Maccombe	Macthomas	Maccrouther	Macgregor, Drummond
Maccombich	Stewart (of Appin)		
		Maccruithein	Macdonald
Maccombie	Macthomas	Maccuag	Macdonald
Maccomie	Macthomas	Maccuaig	Farquharson, Macleod
Macconacher	Macdougall		

Name	Associated Clan
Maccubbin	Buchanan
Maccuish	Macdonald
Maccune	Macewan
Maccunn	Macpherson
Maccurrach	Macpherson
Maccutchen	Macdonald
Maccutcheon	Macdonald
Macdade	Davidson
Macdaid	Davidson
Macdaniell	Macdonald
Macdavid	Davidson
Macdermid	Campbell
Macdiarmid	Campbell
Macdonachie	Robertson
Macdonleavy	Buchanan
Macdrain	Macdonald
Macduffie	Macfie
Macdulothe	Macdougall
Maceachan	Macdonald of Clanranald
Maceachern	Macdonald
Maceachin	Macdonald of Clanranald
Maceachran	Macdonald
Macearachar	Farquharson
Macelfrish	Macdonald
Macelheran	Macdonald
Maceoin	Macfarlane
Maceol	Macnaghten
Macerracher	Macfarlane
Macfadzean	Maclaine of Lochbuie
Macfall	Macpherson
Macfarquhar	Farquharson
Macfater	Maclaren
Macfeat	Maclaren
Macfergus	Ferguson
Macgaw	Macfarlane
Macgeachie	Macdonald of Clanranald
Macgeachin	Macdonald of Clanranald
Macgeoch	Macfarlane
Macghee	Mackay
Macghie	Mackay
Macgilbert	Buchanan
Macgilchrist	Maclachlan, Ogilvy
Macgill	Macdonald
Macgilledon	Lamont
Macgillegowie	Lamont
Macgillivantic	Macdonald
Macgillivour	Macgillivray
Macgillonie	Cameron
Macgilp	Macdonald
Macgilroy	Grant, Macgillivray
Macgilvernock	Graham
Macgilvra	Macgillivray, Maclaine of Lochbuie
Macgilvray	Macgillivray
Macglashan	Mackintosh, Stewart
Macglasrich	Maciver, Campbell
Macgorrie	Macdonald
Macgorry	Macdonald
Macgoun	Macdonald, Macpherson
Macgowan	Macdonald, Macpherson
Macgown	Macdonald, Macpherson
Macgrath	Macrae
Macgreusich	Buchanan, Macfarlane
Macgrewar	Macgregor,

Name	Associated Clan	Name	Associated Clan
	Drummond	Macilvrae	Macgillivray
Macgrime	Graham	Macilvride	Macdonald
Macgrory	Maclaren	Macilwhom	Lamont
Macgrowther	Macgregor,	Macilwraith	Macdonald
	Drummond	Macilzegowie	Lamont
Macgruder	Macgregor,	Macimmey	Fraser
	Drummond	Macinally	Buchanan
Macgruer	Fraser	Macindeor	Menzies
Macgruther	Macgregor,	Macindoe	Buchanan
	Drummond	Macinroy	Robertson
Macguaran	Macquarrie	Macinstalker	Macfarlane
Macguffie	Mcfie	Maciock	Macfarlane
Macgugan	Macneil	Macissac	Campbell,
Macguire	Macquarrie		Macdonald
Machaffie	Macfie	Maciver	Maciver,
Machardie	Farquharson,		Campbell
	Mackintosh	Macivor	Maciver,
Machardy	Farquharson,		Campbell
	Mackintosh	Macjames	Macfarlane
Macharold	Macleod	Mackail	Cameron
Machendrie	Macnaghten	Mackames	Gunn
Machendry	Macnaghten,	Mackaskill	Macleod
	Macdonald	Mackeachan	Macdonald
Machowell	Macdougall	Mackeamish	Gunn
Machugh	Macdonald	Mackean	Gunn,
Machutchen	Macdonald		Macdonald
Machutcheon	Macdonald	Mackechnie	Macdonald of
Macian	Gunn,		Clanranald
	Macdonald	Mackee	Mackay
Macildowie	Cameron	Mackeggie	Mackintosh
Macilduy	Macgregor,	Mackeith	Macpherson
	Maclean	Mackellachie	Macdonald
Macilreach	Macdonald	Mackellaig	Macdonald
Macilleriach	Macdonald	Mackellaigh	Macdonald
Macilriach	Macdonald	Mackellar	Campbell
Macilrevie	Macdonald	Mackelloch	Macdonald
Macilvain	Macbean	Mackelvie	Campbell
Macilvora	Maclaine of	Mackendrick	Macnaghten
	Lochbuie	Mackenrick	Macnaghten

Name	Associated Clan	Name	Associated Clan
Mackeochan	Macdonald of Clanranald	Maclamond	Lamont
		Maclardie	Macdonald
Mackerchar	Farquharson	Maclardy	Macdonald
Mackerlich	Mackenzie	Maclarty	Macdonald
Mackerracher	Farquharson	Maclaverty	Macdonald
Mackerras	Ferguson	Maclaws	Campbell
Mackersey	Ferguson	Maclea	Stewart (of Appin)
Mackessock	Campbell, Macdonald of Clanranald	Macleay	Stewart (of Appin)
Mackichan	Macdonald of Clanranald, Macdougall	Maclehose	Campbell
		Macleish	Macpherson
		Macleister	Macgregor
Mackieson	Mackintosh	Maclergain	Maclean
Mackiggan	Macdonald	Maclerie	Cameron, Mackintosh, Macpherson
Mackilligan	Mackintosh		
Mackillop	Macdonald		
Mackim	Fraser	Macleverty	Macdonald
Mackimmie	Fraser	Maclewis	Macleod
Mackindlay	Farquharson	Maclintock	Macdougall
Mackinlay	Buchanan, Macfarlane, Stewart (of Appin)	Maclise	Macpherson
Farquharson,		Macliver	Macgregor
		Maclucas	Lamont, Macdougall
Mackinley	Buchanan	Maclugash	Macdougall
Mackinnell	Macdonald	Maclulich	Macdougall, Munro, Ross
Mackinney	Mackinnon		
Mackinning	Mackinnon	Maclure	Macleod
Mackinven	Mackinnon	Maclymont	Lamont
Mackirdy	Stewart	Macmanus	Colquhoun, Gunn
Mackissock	Campbell, Macdonald of Clanranald		
		Macmartin	Cameron
		Macmaster	Buchanan, Macinnes
Macknight	Macnaughton		
Maclae	Stewart (of Appin)	Macmath	Matheson
		Macmaurice	Buchanan
Maclagan	Robertson	Macmenzies	Menzies
Maclaghlan	Maclachlan	Macmichael	Stewart (of Appin)
Maclairish	Macdonald		

Name	Associated Clan	Name	Associated Clan
Macminn	Menzies	Macoran	Campbell
Macmonies	Menzies	MacO'Shannaig	Macdonald
Macmorran	Mackinnon	Macoull	Macdougall
Macmunn	Stewart	Macourlic	Cameron
Macmurchie	Buchanan, Mackenzie	Macowen	Campbell
		Macowl	Macdougall
Macmurchy	Buchanan, Mackenzie	Macpatrick	Lamont, Maclaren
Macmurdo	Macpherson	Macpetrie	Macgregor
Macmurdoch	Macpherson	Macphadden	Maclaine of Lochbuie
Macmurray	Murray		
Macmurrich	Macdonald of Clanranald, Macpherson	Macphater	Maclaren
		Macphedran	Campbell
		Macphedron	Macaulay
Macmutrie	Stewart	Macpheidiran	Macaulay
Macnair	Macfarlane, Macnaghten	Macphillip	Macdonald
		Macphorich	Lamont
Macnamell	Macdougall	Macphun	Matheson, Campbell
Macnayer	Macnaghten		
Macnee	Macgregor	Macquaire	Macquarrie
Macneilage	Macneil	Macquartie	Macquarrie
Macneiledge	Macneil	Macquey	Mackay
Macneilly	Macneil	Macquhirr	Macquarrie
Macneish	Macgregor	Macquire	Macquarrie
Macneur	Macfarlane	Macquistan	Macdonald
Macney	Macgregor	Macquisten	Macdonald
Macnider	Macfarlane	Macquoid	Mackay
Macnie	Macgregor	Macra	Macrae
Macnish	Macgregor	Macrach	Macrae
Macniter	Macfarlane	Macraild	Macleod
Macniven	Cumming, Mackintosh, Macnaghten	Macraith	Macrae, Macdonald
		Macrankin	Maclean
Macnuir	Macnaghten	Macrath	Macrae
Macnuyer	Buchanan, Macnaghten	Macritchie	Mackintosh
		Macrob	Gunn, Macfarlane
Macomie	Macthomas		
Macomish	Macthomas	Macrobb	Macfarlane
Maconie	Cameron	Macrobbie	Robertson,

Name	Associated Clan	Name	Associated Clan
	Drummond	Macvicar	Macnaghten
Macrobert	Robertson, Drummond	Macvinish	Mackenzie
Macrobie	Robertson, Drummond	Macvurich	Macdonald of Clanranald, Macpherson
Macrorie	Macdonald	Macvurie	Macdonald of Clanranald
Macrory	Macdonald		
Macruer	Macdonald	Macwalrick	Cameron
Macrurie	Macdonald	Macwalter	Macfarlane
Macrury	Macdonald	Macwattie	Buchanan
Macshannachan	Macdonald	Macwhannell	Macdonald
Macshimes	Fraser (of Lovat)	Macwhirr	Macquarrie
		Macwhirter	Buchanan
Macsimon	Fraser (of Lovat)	Macwilliam	Gunn, Macfarlane
Macsorley	Cameron, Macdonald	Malcolmson	Maccallum
		Malloch	Macgregor
Macsporran	Macdonald	Mann	Gunn
Macswan	Macdonald	Manson	Gunn
Macsween	Macdonald	Mark	Macdonald
Macswen	Macdonald	Marnoch	Innes
Macsymon	Fraser	Marshall	Keith
Mactaggart	Ross	Martin	Cameron, Macdonald
Mactary	Innes		
Mactause	Campbell	Mason	Sinclair
Mactavish	Campbell	Massey	Matheson
Mactear	Ross, Macintyre	Masterson	Buchanan
Mactier	Ross	Mathie	Matheson
Mactire	Ross	Mavor	Gordon
Maculric	Cameron	May	Macdonald
Macure	Campbell	Means	Menzies
Macvail	Cameron, Mackay	Meikleham	Lamont
		Mein	Menzies
Macvanish	Mackenzie	Meine	Menzies
Macvarish	Macdonald of Clanranald	Mennie	Menzies
		Meyners	Menzies
Macveagh	Maclean	Michie	Forbes
Macvean	Macbean	Miller	Macfarlane
Macvey	Maclean	Milne	Gordon, Ogilvy

Name	Associated Clan	Name	Associated Clan
Milroy	Macgillivray	O'Shannachan	Macdonald
Minn	Menzies	O'Shannaig	Macdonald
Minnus	Menzies	Park	Macdonald
Mitchell	Innes	Parlane	Macfarlane
Monach	Macfarlane	Paton	Macdonald,
Monzie	Menzies		Maclean
Moodie	Stewart	Patrick	Lamont
Moray	Murray	Paul	Cameron,
Morgan	Mackay		Mackintosh
Morren	Mackinnon	Pearson	Macpherson
Morris	Buchanan	Peterkin	Macgregor
Morton	Douglas	Petrie	Macgregor
Munn	Stewart, Lamont	Philipson	Macdonald
Murchie	Buchanan,	Pinkerton	Campbell
	Menzies	Piper	Murray
Murchison	Buchanan,	Pitullich	Macdonald
	Menzies	Pollard	Mackay
Murdoch	Macdonald,	Polson	Mackay
	Macpherson	Porter	Macnaughton
Murdoson	Macdonald,	Pratt	Grant
	Macpherson	Purcell	Macdonald
Murphy	Macdonald	Raith	Macrae
Neal	Macneil	Randolf	Bruce
Neil	Macneil	Reidfurd	Innes
Neill	Macneil	Reoch	Farquharson,
Neilson	Macneil		Macdonald
Nelson	Gunn, Macneil	Revie	Macdonald
Neish	Macgregor	Riach	Farquharson,
Nish	Macgregor		Macdonald
Niven	Cumming,	Richardson	Ogilvie,
	Mackintosh		Buchanan
Nixon	Armstrong	Risk	Buchanan
Noble	Mackintosh	Ritchie	Mackintosh
Norie	Macdonald	Robb	Macfarlane
Norman	Sutherland	Roberts	Robertson
O'Drain	Macdonald	Robinson	Gunn,
Oliver	Fraser		Robertson
O'May	Sutherland	Robison	Gunn,
O'Shaig	Macdonald		Robertson

Name	Associated Clan	Name	Associated Clan
Robson	Gunn, Robertson	Spittel	Buchanan
Rome	Johnstone	Sporran	Macdonald
Ronald	Macdonald, Gunn	Stalker	Macfarlane
		Stark	Robertson
Ronaldson	Macdonald, Gunn	Stenhouse	Bruce
		Stewart	Stewart
Rorison	Macdonald	Storie	Ogilvy
Roy	Robertson	Stringer	Macgregor
Rusk	Buchanan	Summers	Lindsay
Ruskin	Buchanan	Suttie	Grant
Russell	Russell, Cumming	Swan	Gunn
		Swanson	Gunn
Sanderson	Macdonald	Syme	Fraser
Sandison	Gunn	Symon	Fraser
Saunders	Macalister	Taggart	Ross
Scobie	Mackay	Tarrill	Mackintosh
Shannon	Macdonald	Tawesson	Campbell
Sharp	Stewart	Tawse	Farquharson
Sherry	Mackinnon	Thain	Innes, Mackintosh
Sim	Fraser (of Lovat)		
		Todd	Gordon
Sime	Fraser (of Lovat)	Tolmie	Macleod
		Tonnochy	Robertson
Simon	Fraser (of Lovat)	Torry	Campbell
		Tosh	Mackintosh
Simpson	Fraser (of Lovat)	Toward	Lamont
		Towart	Lamont
Simson	Fraser (of Lovat)	Train	Ross
		Turner	Lamont
Skinner	Macgregor	Tyre	Macintyre
Small	Murray	Ure	Campbell
Smart	Mackenzie	Vass	Munro, Ross
Smith	Macpherson, Mackintosh	Wallis	Wallace
		Walters	Forbes
Sorely	Cameron, Macdonald	Wass	Munro, Ross
		Watt	Buchanan
Spence	Macduff	Weaver	Macfarlane
Spittal	Buchanan	Webster	Macfarlane
		Whannell	Macdonald

Name	Associated Clan	Name	Associated Clan
Wharrie	Macquarrie	Williamson	Gunn, Mackay
Wheelan	Macdonald	Wilson	Gunn, Innes
White	Macgregor, Lamont	Wright	Macintyre
		Wylie	Gunn, Macfarlane
Whyte	Macgregor, Lamont		
		Yuill	Buchanan
Wilkie	Macdonald	Yuille	Buchanan
Wilkinson	Macdonald	Yule	Buchanan
Will	Gunn		

APPENDIX 4: The chiefly retinue

The following posts commonly made up the household and personal following of a chief prior to 1745. The actual number maintained was dependant on the importance of the chief.

Ard Ghillean an-tighe (gentlemen of the household): aides or courtiers. The number of these varied according to the importance of the chief.

An Seanachaidh (the sennachie, or genealogist of the chief's house): at table, the Sennachie sat among the chief families, sharing precedence with the doctors of medicine. It was his duty to keep the clan register, its records, genealogies and family history; to pronounce the addresses of ceremony at clan assemblies; to deliver the chief's inauguration, birthday and funeral genealogical orations; and as inaugurator, to invest him on succession.

Am Bard (the bard): the bard was often synonymous with the sennachie and was generally a hereditary position; if not, he was inferior in status to the sennachie.

An Clarsair (the harper): this was generally a hereditary office.

Am Marischal-tighe (the seneschal): In every great household there were two seneschals, the principal of whom was well versed in the genealogies and precedences of all the clans. At table, he assigned to each guest his place by touching the appointed seat with his white wand of office.

Am Bladier (the spokesman): Otherwise known as the pursuivant, the spokesman carried the chief's messages (which were ,in primitive days, conveyed orally rather than in writing). He made the chief's proclamations.

Am Fear Sporain (the purse-bearer): the treasurer.

Am Fear Brataich (the standard-bearer or bannerman): A hereditary office.

Am Piobaire (the piper): A hereditary office.

An Gille-mor (the sword- or armour-bearer): Also called the *Gall-oglach*, it was this person's duty to carry the *clogaid*, or helmet, and the *claidheamh-da-laimh*, or two-handed sword of the chief. As armour was not continuously worn, he had to carry it when on the march.

An Gille-coise (the henchman): this retainer performed the function of a personal bodyguard and was in continual attendance upon the chief. He stood fully armed behind the chair of his master at mealtimes, and if the peace of the occasion were doubtful, the henchman had his pistols loaded.

An Luchd-tighe (the bodyguard): these were all young gentlemen, chosen from the finest youths of the clan, and each had one or more attendants of his own. The members of the bodyguard were all well trained in the use of the sword, the target and the bow, and were adept in wrestling, swimming, leaping and dancing; those of the coastal and the island clans were also versed in the sounding and navigation duties of seamanship, and the management of the *bior-linns*, or galleys. The *Luchd-tighe* always attended the chief when he went abroad, and when his residence was on an island in a lake, they had barracks and a guard-house on the mainland for keeping open the access to the chief's castle.

Am Fear Fardaiche (the quartermaster): the quartermaster's duties were to provide lodgings for all attendants, both at home and abroad. He held no lands in consideration of his services but received a duty off the hides of all the cattle killed at the principal festivals or in a *creach*, or foray.

An Cupair, or Gille-copain (the cup-bearer): there were several cup-bearers, according to the importance of the chief. The duty of the principal one was to taste the contents of the cup before it was carried round the board. The office of principal cup-bearer was hereditary and its occupant held land granted in charter from the chief.

An Gocaman (the warder): a guard who kept watch from the top of the chief's castle.

Am Forsair **(the forester):** for this service, the postholder held a croft and grazing in the forest, and was entitled to claim the hunting dress and weapons of the chief when he returned home from hunting. This right, like many ancient perquisites of a similar kind, was only a scale of value, and was compounded by a fee in meal or money.

An Gille-cas-fhliuch: a servant whose duty it was to carry the chief over the fords when the chief was travelling on foot.

An Gille-couston: the leader of the chief's horse.

An Gille-comhsreang: a guide who at dangerous precipices led the chief's horse by a long rein.

An Gille-trusairneis: the baggage-man who had charge of the sumpter, or pack horses.

An Leinc-chneas: a confidant or privy counsellor.

An Gille-sguain **(the train bearer):** it is recorded that when the Lords of the Isles were in power, among their train was a person designated *Fear sguabadh dealt*, whose duty it was to brush away the dew on the grass before his master.

An Gille-chlarsair **(the harper's attendant):** he carried the harp of the harper.

An Gille-Phiobaire **(the piper's servant):** he carried the pipes, presented them to the piper when he was about to play, and received them again when the piper had concluded his performance. This attendant was only, however, attached to pipers of the first rank.

An Gille-Ruith: a running footman

An Cleasaiche: a fool or jester.

APPENDIX 5: Ceremonial for the inauguration of a clan chief

The clan will assemble at the appointed place which should, if possible, be the clan 'Chymmes' or 'sacred place'. A stone from the Chymmes may be brought instead and placed under or at the side of the chief's chair. The chair should be carved with the chief's arms or have the shield affixed to it. The chair will be placed in a prominent position, like a throne, facing the body of clansmen.

The chief's councillors or *derbhfine*, along with the officers of his household not taking part in the procession, and other prominent persons or guests, should be seated in rows on either side of the chair, creating a form of aisle. Seats will also be required for the members of the procession accompanying the new chief. Exactly how the seats are arranged will depend upon the location of the ceremony, but if it is outdoors they should be used to create as dramatic an effect as possible, yet still be practical. A table for regalia will also be necessary.

The procession will be marshalled by *An Marischal-tighe* (the senneschal) according to the Laws of Arms on the orders of *An Seanachaidh* (the sennachie). When all is ready, a trumpet or horn may be sounded to mark the beginning of the ceremony. The procession will be proceeded by the chief's pipers, usually three in number. They will be followed by *An Seanachaidh*, suitably robed, carrying the extract matriculation from the Lyon Court. This function may actually be performed by one of the officers of the Lyon Court. If the chief is entitled to a coronet or chapeau, it may be carried behind the sennachie on a velvet cushion. Next come the officers of the chief's household, either in single file or two abreast. They are led by *An Marischal-tighe* (there may be more than one), followed by *Am Bladier* (the spokesman), *An Fear Sporain* (the purse-bearer carrying the chief's seal in an embroidered bag), *An Leinc-chneas* (the most senior councillor or councillors), and *An Ceann-cath* (the war commander or senior cadet). After a small gap, escorted by two files of *An Luchd-tighe* (the bodyguard), follows *An Gille-mor* (the armour-bearer) bearing a suitable ancestral sword. He is followed by the chief himself, behind whom is *An Fear Brataich* (the standard-bearer) carrying the heraldic banner. If the chief is wearing a robe of estate, his train will be carried by *An Gille-sguain* (the train-bearer). The procession concludes with *An Gille-coise* (the henchman or bodyguard). The various elements of the procession will proceed to their allotted places and lay any regalia on a suitable table, possibly draped with tartan. The bannerman and henchman take their places on either side to the rear of the chief's chair.

When the chief has taken his position, the chaplain or other clergyman may invoke a blessing on the proceedings and lead the assembly in prayer. The chaplain may deliver a brief homily on the significance and solemnity of the ceremony.

At this point, *Am Bladier* (the spokesman) may himself deliver, or call upon *Am Bard* (the bard) to deliver a panegyric on the history and glorious deeds of the clan and its chiefs. This may be done to the accompaniment of appropriate music, perhaps on the harp. Thereafter, the inauguration itself begins. *An Marischal-tighe* calls upon the sennachie to show the sovereign's confirmation of the chief's rights. *An Seanachaidh*, as inaugurator, now addresses the assembly:

'I here present to you (the chief's full style and title), the undoubted chief of this clan, inheritor thereof by the laws of God and man who is willing to accept the chiefship.'

The assembly answers, 'God bless our chief and us for his/her cause.'

An Seanachaidh will then announce:

'There is here produced the judgement/diploma of the Lord Lyon, King of Arms, Her Majesty's supreme officer of honour, confirming unto (the style and title of the chief) the ensigns armorial of X of X (or avouching the addition to the genealogy in the public register of all genealogies and birthbrieves in Scotland as now the stem, representer and chief of Clan McX).'

Am Bladier then reads the text of the document. At the conclusion of the reading, *An Seanachaidh* will cry, 'God bless the chief and the clan.' He then takes up the ancestral sword and presents it to the

chief, who receives it sitting on his chair, accepting it either physi-
cally or symbolically by touching the hilt. There is no ceremony of
crowning, and the chief will already be wearing his bonnet.

The chief then demands delivery of any symbolic ancestral insignia
or relics which may exist, by which act he takes upon himself representation of his ancestors and the obligations of chiefship.

An Seanachaidh, falling on one knee, hails the chief by declaiming
his full styles and titles together with his genealogy. The chaplain
then requires the chief to take an oath:

'Do you promise to be a loving father/mother to the Clan McX?'

The chief signifies his assent using whatever form of words is traditional to each clan. The oath may have additional elements to it,
and the chief may take it standing on or touching a stone from the
Chymmes. The chief then swears a general oath in these terms:

'I swear and hold up my hand to maintain, defend and support
thee as I wish the Lord in my need to help me. Amen.'

Am Marishal-tighe now places the chief's bonnet on a cushion at
the chief's feet and each chieftain or other nobles of the clan will
swear allegiance by kneeling upon one knee and touching the bonnet, repeating the words:

'So mote God help me as I shall support thee.'

When the last of these has returned to his or her place, at a suitable signal from *An Seanachaidh*, the whole assembly will cry, 'Hail
to the chief' three times.

The clan song or another suitable hymn may then be sung, whilst
the procession takes up its respective insignia and is marshalled in
the same order as before to march out. When the singing stops, the
pipers strike up the clan march and the procession moves off, bringing the ceremony to a close.